Sucesión Presidencial

Published in cooperation with
the University of California Consortium
on Mexico and the United States (UC MEXUS)

Sucesión Presidencial

The 1988 Mexican Presidential Election

EDITED BY

Edgar W. Butler and Jorge A. Bustamante

Westview Press

BOULDER • SAN FRANCISCO • OXFORD

This Westview softcover edition is printed on acid-free paper and bound in library-quality, coated covers that carry the highest rating of the National Association of State Textbook Administrators, in consultation with the Association of American Publishers and the Book Manufacturers' Institute.

Published in 1991 in the United States of America by Westview Press, Inc., 5500 Central Avenue, Boulder, Colorado 80301, and in the United Kingdom by Westview Press, 36 Lonsdale Road, Summertown, Oxford OX2 7EW

A CIP catalog record for this book is available from the Library of Congress.
ISBN 0-8133-7886-9

Printed and bound in the United States of America

The paper used in this publication meets the requirements of the American National Standard for Permanence of Paper for Printed Library Materials Z39.48-1984.

10   9   8   7   6   5   4   3   2   1

This book is dedicated to the memory of
Manuel J. Clouthier
for his fundamental role
in the democratization process in Mexico.

Contents

FOREWORD

The United States and Mexico are bound together by a shared border, an intertwined history and, in many ways, their relationship is mutually beneficial: Mexico is the United States' third largest trading partner; two-thirds of Mexico's trade normally is with the United States; and Mexico's labor force has contributed significantly to the success of California's agriculture.

But the two countries are not always at ease with one another. They are divided by economic conditions, lack of mutual understanding, distinct cultures, and differing views of mutual problems. Attempts to resolve real differences too often are obstructed by misperceptions and stereotypes. The bilateral relationship is influenced, too, by global challenges which can expand or delimit expectations. Environmental crises, the debt of developing nations, instability in Central America, rapid change in Eastern Europe, and the quickening economic pace of the Pacific Rim are examples of world-wide issues to which Mexico and the United States both must respond.

Within this changing milieu, the 1988 Mexican presidential election took place, an election that clearly held the potential for significant alterations in the Mexican political system and, thus, in the Mexican response to the United States-Mexico bilateral relationship and to international events. Expectations of change and fears of destructive conflict ran high in Mexico and in the United States both before and after the election. The electoral process and its outcomes emerged as critical issues in each country's intellectual, academic, media, and political circles.

The academic examination of such issues has been the basis of the work of the University of California Consortium on Mexico and the United States (UC MEXUS) since its establishment in 1980. The more than three hundred faculty members of the University of California who work in Mexican studies, United States-Mexico relations, Chicano studies, and scientific problems of interest to both countries are joined by a multitude of collaborating scholars, scientists, and institutions of Mexico.

Researchers are often reluctant, though, to commit themselves to predictions of their work's value to society. At the same time, politicians and public administrators are criticized frequently for operating from unilateral perspectives and without benefit of scholarly research. Both groups are wary of the media, with its power to influence public opinion about researchers' topics and politicians' programs. Finally, researchers, politicians, and the media all have difficulty tolerating the others' interference in their work. This lack of collaboration, in both Mexico and the United States, contributes to misunderstanding which in turn becomes the basis for one country's policy toward the other.

In 1987 UC MEXUS established the Critical Issues Program in United States-Mexico Relations, bringing together scholars, public officials, and the media from both countries to discuss issues most central to the bilateral relationship and, more importantly, to devise from their perspectives, expertise, and experience plans for cooperative action to address the pressing social, economic, and environmental problems that the United States and Mexico share. The Critical Issues Program is supported by a three-year grant from the John D. and Catherine T. MacArthur Foundation's Program in International Peace and Cooperation.

This volume, the first of the Critical Issues series, explores the implications of the 1988 Mexican presidential election for Mexico, for the United States, and for the bilateral relationship. The explosive changes in the Mexican electoral system, the reasons for these changes, and their implications for the exercise of government in Mexico, have significant bearing on the country's international relationships. These are changes to which the United States must be sensitive in the formulation and practice of its policies toward Mexico.

Mexico's 1988 presidential succession is one historical event in a series that marks a period of rapid evolution in concepts and practice of democracy around the world. This volume will be of assistance to current and future scholars of a period that may come to be known as the *world-wide democratic current*. It is our hope also that this examination of Mexico's internal political changes, and their potential international impacts, will serve to inform the development of policy, the portrayal of Mexico in the media of the United States, and public opinion in the two countries.

Arturo Gómez-Pompa*
Riverside, California

* Arturo Gómez-Pompa is director of the University of California Consortium on Mexico and the United States (UC MEXUS), a nine-campus organization headquartered at the University's Riverside campus. In addition, he is professor of botany at the University of California, Riverside.

ACKNOWLEDGEMENTS

The work reported in this volume was made possible by the "Critical Issues in United States-Mexico Relations" program of The University of California Consortium on Mexico and the United States (UC MEXUS). The Critical Issues program of UC MEXUS is sponsored by support from The John D. and Catherine T. MacArthur Foundation. We wish to express our great appreciation to UC MEXUS and the MacArthur Foundation for the funds necessary to carry out this research effort.

We want to express our great gratitude to the staff of UC MEXUS for the funding and the freedom they gave us in carrying out the project. Dr. Arturo Gómez-Pompa, Director of UC MEXUS, was instrumental in whatever success of our effort is reflected in this volume. He was ably assisted by the Assistant Director, Kathryn L. Roberts, whose dedication to our project was far beyond what anyone could expect. Her contributions were countless, but among many others included intellectual discussions, taking care of everyday nitty-gritty problems, editing the manuscript, and moral support. Richard Walsack, formerly of UC MEXUS, first broached the possibility of this venture to us and to UC MEXUS and we are grateful for that initial effort and for countless hours of discussion involving the Mexican political situation. Yvonne Pacheco Tevis translated some of the manuscripts from Spanish to English and was of great assistance in editing the entire manuscript. Leobardo Saravia Quiroz, *Director del Departmento de Publicaciones, El Colegio de la Frontera Norte*, very ably reviewed the Spanish language portion of the manuscript. Dora A. Velasco was always cheerful and helpful in solving the myriad of financial, travel, supply, and other problems; without her effort the project would not have been successfully completed.

Dr. James B. Pick and Glenda Jones of the University of California Mexico Database Project are co-authors of two of the chapters. But in addition, they contributed in other ways to the completion of this monograph. Dr. Pick generously reviewed some of the other chapters in the volume and made a number of insightful suggestions. Glenda Jones produced the ARC/INFO maps included in chapters 2 and 3 in addition to co-authoring those chapters. The entire manuscript was placed into Ventura by John Chow and Susan Lam. Their willingness to review and revise the multiple edits was far beyond the call of duty and we are extremely grateful for their substantial contribution. Ms. Marge Souder of the Sociology Department, University of California, Riverside, very ably took care of the budgetary requisites. Ms. Wanda Clark, in her usual manner, assisted us in many ways.

Much of the computer analysis reported in this volume was carried out at the University of California, Riverside, Academic Computer Center; Larry Sautter, Alex Ramirez, and Bill Vanore, as always, were extremely helpful and we are pleased to be able to acknowledge their contribution.

The project benefitted from innumerable scholars, members of the media, representatives of the PRI, PAN, and FDN, and others in Mexico and the United States who shared their thoughts, concerns, and vision with us. In particular we would like to thank Sergio Muñoz, Eugenio Elorduy, Rafael Segovia, Dolores Ponce, and Barnard Thompson whose offerings varied but were very much cherished.

Clearly, the numerous authors in this volume deserve the major credit for whatever contribution this volume makes to a better understanding of the 1988 Mexican presidential election and to the future of Mexico. Their willingness to share their analyses and insights is readily apparent in each of the chapters. While there is obvious disagreement on some issues among the authors of the various chapters, they all obviously share in common their love of Mexico and its people.

We wish to express our great indebtedness to all of the above persons, and to many others not specifically mentioned who contributed to our project. We acknowledge that in the final analysis we are responsible for the final edit of this volume and, consequently, if there are any errors of interpretation or conclusions attributed to the various contributions to this volume, we are the ones who should be held accountable.

Edgar W. Butler
Riverside, California

Jorge A. Bustamante
Tijuana, Baja California

1

Introduction

Edgar W. Butler[1]
Jorge A. Bustamante[2]

The 1988 Mexican Presidential Election

There was no question by anyone in Mexico during the few months prior to the 1988 Mexican presidential election that it was going to have a great impact upon Mexico and, of course, upon Mexico-United States relations. The importance of the 1988 Mexican presidential election to the United States was increasingly obvious. The election in Mexico was a critical one because increasingly it was being recognized in the United States that what happens in Mexico concerns the United States, especially its security. What transpires in Mexico, whether it is elections, control of the border, debts, or its cultural future impacts the United States (Langley, 1988: 279). There is an inevitable connection between Mexico and the United States that must be recognized if the future is to be different than the past.

Contrary to appearances, the endurance and continuity of the political system in Mexico have not resulted from a static electoral system. Rather, the stability of Mexico's political system is the consequence of a high propensity for change and reform in the electoral arena. Thus, adaptability and not rigidity has undergirded Mexico's electoral continuity (Molinar, 1986:106). As a result, the Mexican political system has moved from one period to the next without any important breakdown. The relative lack of repression in Mexico is largely a

---

1 Edgar W. Butler is a former chair and currently professor of sociology at the University of California, Riverside. He is co-director of the UCR Database Project which is computerizing population and economic development data on the Mexican states and *municipios* for statistical analysis and geographic base mapping. He has co-authored a series of articles on fertility, migration, and various other aspects of Mexico and is co-author of the *Atlas of Mexico* (Westview Press).

2 Jorge A. Bustamante is president of *El Colegio de la Frontera Norte* (COLEF), professor of sociology at *El Colegio de México*, and adjunct professor of sociology at the University of California, Riverside. He is an advisor at the highest levels of the Mexican government and his editorial writings about Mexico-United States relations have been published widely in the popular press of both countries. Among his research interests are economic crisis along Mexico's northern border and Mexico-United States migration.

result of the *Partido Revolucionario Institucional* (PRI) and the government being able to exercise state administrative controls over mass organizations. These mass organizations are part of the historical heritage from the Mexican revolution of 1910-1917; organized labor and peasant movements constitute the regime's principal mass base. They are major components of support for the PRI and historically have provided the level of political legitimacy that has existed in Mexico. However, the state has placed broad limitations on these organizations which have severely restricted their actions and have reduced opportunities for opposition political parties to mobilize mass groups. In addition, because of controls on the mass organizations and their members, the use of negotiation, compromise, elite rotation, cooptation of opposition leaders, and selective repression, many argue that the government and the PRI have "engaged in massive fraud to deny opposition parties electoral victories when they have posed a threat to the PRI's dominance" (Middlebrook, 1986:81).

The Mexican regime *is at once elite dominated and mass based* (Middlebrook, 1986: 75). Further, "the Mexican system is strongly presidential; major political initiatives remain under the firm control of the federal executive" (Middlebrook, 1986:76). Notwithstanding the past, an expected result of the 1988 Mexican presidential election was that great change would take place in the Mexican political system, including dilution of presidential power. Up until 1988, the dominant position of the PRI had insulated the elite from major electoral defeat.

Despite the number of political parties in Mexico, Molinar (1986) argues that the electoral system is different from the total political system which is highly manipulable. Thus, elections *per se* do not decide who will govern Mexico. He further suggests that if in future elections the government corrects mistakes made in previous elections, the long tradition of continuity by change in Mexico will remain intact. Many would argue that up through the 1988 Mexican presidential election, liberalization still had not occurred, manipulation was still commonplace, and that democratization of the political system was still a dream to be realized.

The Mexican Political System[3]

Mexico is a democratic, representative federal republic. The Mexican political system allows for free participation of different political parties ranging from the right to the left, including the Communist Party. In 1988, over 50 city mayors, more than 100 federal representatives, and at least 150 local or state

---

3 For an excellent, more extensive discussion, see Cornelius and Craig, 1988.

representatives belonged to opposition parties. Eight parties were officially registered for the 1988 Mexican presidential election.

The Mexican political system is commonly considered as "presidentially centered." That is, the president of Mexico plays *the* central role in Mexico. "The principle of executive dominance over the legislative and judicial branches of government is firmly established in the Mexican system" (Cornelius and Craig, 1988). The president and state governors are elected for a six year term, although states have different dates upon which the election takes place (see Table 10-4). In the past, the president has been the dominant factor in the choice of governors.

Every three years, 32 members of the Senate's 64 members, and new federal and state representatives are elected. Within each state there are *municipios*[4] governed by a council which is elected every three years. Typically, the PRI-government nexus controls the selection of council members (Cornelius and Craig, 1988:206). City mayors are elected for a three year term. Reelection of the president and governors since the revolution of 1910 has been prohibited. Further, there is no immediate reelection to the same Legislative Branch; however, a person may skip a session and then be eligible to run and serve again.

Mexico guarantees representation of minority parties in the national Chamber of Deputies even if they do not win by direct majority. At least 30% of the seats in the Chamber of Deputies are reserved for minority parties with more than 1.5% of the popular vote. In the various states, 25% of the seats in the state legislatures also are filled by minority party representatives.

Legal Framework of Mexico's Electoral System

Mexico is a federal system consisting of 31 states and the Federal District-- which includes Mexico City -- often referred to as México. In addition to the president, there is a Chamber of Senators and Chamber of Deputies. There are 64 members in the Chamber of Senators, two from each state and two from the Federal District. Allocation to the Chamber of Deputies changed as a result of "reforms" introduced in 1987. Of the 500 deputies, one each is allocated to 300 electoral districts. The remaining 200 deputies are seated according to the principle of proportional representation. Of these 200, 150 must be members of minority parties. The 150 guaranteed minority seats were established to ensure that minority parties are represented in the Federal Congress. In elections for the Chamber of Deputies, a voter simultaneously casts two different ballots -- one for direct election of a candidate and a second to indicate

---

4 *Municipios* are similar to counties in the United States; there is a highly variable number in each of the states. The Federal District is divided into somewhat similar units called *delegaciones*.

party choice for proportional representation. The first ballot contains the names of candidates, party names, and party logos, while the second ballot lists only party names and icons. The number of votes received on the second ballot determines the distribution of seats in the proportional share of the Chamber of Deputies.

Each state also has an electoral system that guarantees the participation of minority parties in the Chamber of Deputies. There are no state senators in the state electoral system. Governors of the 31 states are elected by citizens in each state. The chief of the Federal District is appointed by the president of Mexico and is generally considered a presidential cabinet member.

In each polling place there are supposed to be electoral officers, presumably selected at random, and approved by each political party. In addition, each registered party and each candidate for office may have a representative present at each polling station (*casilla*) as a "poll watcher." This procedure is intended to minimize voting irregularities.

All those present may examine the ballot boxes to determine that they are initially empty. At the end of election day, electoral officers, candidates, and party representatives are present for the vote count. On finishing the count, ballot boxes are sealed and a poster is displayed outside the voting place so everyone may know the turnout and results. Then, electoral officers, and anyone else who wishes to accompany them, take the ballot boxes to the District Electoral Committee. The Committee carries out a new count and verification is accomplished by all contending parties on Sunday after the election. Even so, there are constant complaints about irregularities.

Subsequently, the Federal Electoral Commission, which is made up of representatives from all registered parties, issues Certificates of Majority and publishes the election results. An electoral college convenes on August 15th to certify the results for presidential elections. The Electoral College consists of 100 elected deputies, of whom 60 are from the party that won the majority and 40 from opposition parties. Since 1987, a Federal Electoral Court hears complaints about any possible irregularities that may have occurred. Some complaints could be taken to the Supreme Court.

Political Reforms

Mexico modified its electoral code seven times between 1918 and 1946, with many of these changes being insignificant. Since 1946 the government has issued four different electoral laws and significantly reformed them six times. According to Molinar (1986:108), those introduced before 1963 restricted the possibility of opposition; those introduced after that year aimed at stimulating the formation of permanent opposition parties.

One critic of the electoral reforms that brought opposition parties into the Chamber of Deputies in the 1970s argued that this coopted their leaders by giving them titles and government salaries (Migdail, 1987:116).

One goal of political reform in 1977 was to increase the rate of voter participation; however, voter absenteeism of 49.3% in the 1979 election for the federal Chamber of Deputies was actually greater than in previous elections (Middlebrook, 1986:96). The 1977 reform made it possible for a party to qualify for electoral participation by polling 1.5% or enrolling at least 65,000 members. In the 1982 presidential election, the national voter registration list included 94.9% of all eligible citizens, and 74.8% of all registered voters participated in the election; these were the highest rates since 1946. Middlebrook (1986: 97) suggests two factors that reversed the long-term trend of growing voter absenteeism. First, the government worked effectively to bring out the vote. Second, the eight other political parties and six alternative presidential candidates (two of the parties, the Popular Socialist Party [PPS] and Authentic Party of the Mexican Revolution [PARM] supported the PRI candidate) stimulated interest in the election.

The liberalization process that began with the 1977 political reform altered Mexico's national political map in ways that were not easily reversible (Middlebrook, 1986:99). In 1982, the government recognized a series of local-level (*municipio*) elections in which the opposition parties won in major cities in the Pacific North, North, and Center regions. This included the five state capitals of Chihuahua, Durango, Guanajuato, San Luis Potosí, and Hermosillo (Sonora), and the major border city of Ciudad Juárez in the state of Chihuahua. All but one of these elections were won by the National Action Party (PAN). In Ensenada, Baja California, the PST[5] won the election. Middlebrook (1986: 98) argues that the decreased absenteeism in the 1982 elections "suggests that much of the previously high abstention rate reflected a generalized disinterest in the electoral process rather than a form of protest against the established regime."

Previous elections, especially in 1979 and 1982, demonstrated that support for opposition parties varies considerably by region. In these latter two years, the PAN's electoral strength was concentrated in the Pacific North, North, and Central regions. Support for the PCM in 1970 and for the PSUM in 1982 also came from the Pacific North and Central regions. Vote for the PDM and the PRT was concentrated in the Central states. Generally it appears that opposi-

---

5 Political party acronyms are defined in the next section of this chapter.

tion parties consist of heterogenous populations in the principal urban areas (Middlebrook, 1986:95).

Perhaps as a result of the voting in these elections, approaching the 1985 elections, the government did not want to negotiate with the PAN and it took a course of frontal collision with that party (Molinar, 1986:113). Antisystem opposition was expected to increase in 1985 because of three reasons: (1) The Electoral Commission chose an electoral formula that transferred more earned representation from larger to smaller opposition parties; (2) the Commission added another multi-seat electoral district to the detriment of the larger opposition parties; and (3) the PMT which had always opposed the electoral law earned a place on the ballot for the first time and stood a very good chance of winning a permanent place in the system (Molinar, 1986:112).

In 1986 political reform resulted in the lower house of Congress being expanded from 400 to 500 seats with a 350 limit on seats for the PRI. A multiparty tribunal, dominated by the PRI, was created to settle election disputes.

Political Parties

The Federal Constitution of Mexico established the nation as a democratic, representative federal republic. The Federal Constitution of Mexico also established the rights and responsibilities of political parties. The Mexican political system allows different political parties, and, during the 1988 presidential election, the parties ranged from the right-wing conservative to the left-wing socialist. At the time of the July, 1988, presidential election, there were eight political parties in Mexico.

Generally the Mexican political system is described as being a corporatist system in which various interest groups, most of whom are sanctioned by the government, are related systematically to the structure. The relationship between the government and the PRI is so close that it is difficult to separate them. While the PRI has dominated Mexico, Cornelius and Craig (1988) argue that the opposition parties perform a stabilizing function in the Mexican system.

The PRI (Institutional Revolutionary Party). The PRI had its precursors in the Mexican revolution of 1910; thus it grew out of a coalition formed almost 60 years ago that became the forerunner of the current PRI. The party has been reorganized several times and the official party was formed in 1946. In the beginning the PRI, and its forerunners, advocated social justice and opposed the Catholic Church, big business, large landowners, and all foreign intervention (Migdail, 1987). The PRI's wide umbrella historically has embraced those on the right as well as those on the left. The party has been able to coopt dissidents, bringing them into the fold.

Three major sectors make up the PRI: (1) The peasants, (2) labor, and (3) the middle-class, or what has been called the "popular" sector. Organizations representing these sectors form a vast interlocked political and economic network which helps control the country and contain criticism within the bounds of the party framework. However, a number of powerful organized interest groups -- foreign and domestic entrepreneurs, the military, the Catholic Church -- are not formally represented in the PRI (Cornelius and Craig, 1988).

Most observers of Mexico argue that the PRI is more than a political party. For example, Migdail (1987) declares that the PRI is "at once a (1) political, economic, and social system; (2) a governing coalition of almost all of the major institutions in Mexico; and (3) a power equilibrium among local, regional, and national competing groups, all of which are intent on sharing in the spoils of the Mexican economy."

The president of Mexico is the product of a coalition system and serves as moderator of various interest groups and organizations. Historically this has meant that the president must be able to coopt, promote compromise, and to bring dissidents into the fold to ensure party unity. One of the major tasks of the president is to pick his successor, who will be able to continue to control the coalition that makes up the PRI. In 1988, the consultation process within the PRI resulted in the selection of Carlos Salinas de Gortari as its presidential candidate.

The program of the PRI presidential candidate Salinas emphasizes opening Mexico to external investment, selling off non-profitable state enterprises, streamlining the federal bureaucracy by eliminating jobs and paperwork, and reducing subsidies. For the first time, the continuation of the PRI dominance of Mexican society was seriously challenged in the 1988 Mexican presidential election.

The PAN (National Action Party). The PAN was established in 1946 (1939 according to Migdail, 1987). The PAN is generally described as the conservative party representing the Mexican "right" with middle-class roots. The 1988 PAN candidate for president was Manuel J. Clouthier, a "white-haired, bearded businessman, known for off-color conversation in private and fiery oratory on the stump" (Williams and Miller, 1988). The PAN and Clouthier platform included eliminating communal farms known as *ejidos* by handing out individual titles to the land, reducing the size of government, reversing government policy to encourage more foreign investment, e.g., in general engendering a weaker state. Clouthier said that his election would induce Mexican businessmen to bring back to Mexico billions of dollars they stashed in foreign banks. Prior to the 1988 election, the PAN was considered as the leading party challenger to the PRI. The PAN has shown some indications of taking up increasingly radical positions. For example, the PAN threatened to embark upon a campaign of civil disobedience if fraud occurred during the 1988 election (Williams and Miller, 1988).

The FDN (National Democratic Front). Shortly after the PMS primary election, Cuauhtémoc Cárdenas Solórzano, son of President Lázaro Cárdenas and the former PRI governor of Michoacán, announced his presidential candidacy. Cárdenas, until his presidential candidacy, was head of the "Democratic Current" in the PRI party. He had proposed a radical reorganization of the PRI's internal procedures which were rejected. He then became a member of the Authentic Party of the Mexican Revolution (PARM) which named him as its presidential candidate. Subsequently, several different political parties formed an alliance for the 1988 presidential election (see PARM, PPS, and PFCRN below) -- the FDN. The presidential candidate of the FDN, then, became Cuauhtémoc Cárdenas. A major theme of the FDN is that of developing internal markets rather than depending upon foreign investment and foreign markets and eliminating the foreign debt by fiat. Also, the FDN focused on the necessity for the government to expand the *ejido* system, spend more money on public education and the universities, develop state-run industries, the need to continue governmental ownership in the oil and other industries, and to develop new jobs for the ever-expanding labor force. Cárdenas also would stop providing incentives to what he calls the "speculative economy" that has grown up around the stock market and the partly denationalized banks (Reding, 1988:334). The overall emphasis would be on a mixed economy with appropriate state intervention. Payment of the foreign debt would come only after economic growth had taken place in Mexico.

After the 1988 Mexican presidential selection, the FDN dissolved and several of the parties formed the Party of the Democratic Revolution (PRD). The PRD's goal was to unite former *Priístas* from the Democratic Current, with liberals, nationalists, and socialists. The emergence of the FDN in 1988, part of which now has coalesced into the PRD, clearly has changed the political climate in Mexico.

The PPS (Popular Socialist Party). The PPS was first organized in 1948 by left wing dissidents from the PRI. However, except for 1952 and 1988, the PPS has supported the PRI candidate for president (Reding, 1988). The PPS joined the FDN electoral coalition in 1988 by supporting Cárdenas.

The PDM (Mexican Democratic Party). The PDM was established in 1978; its presidential candidate in 1988 was Gumersindo Magaña.

The PMS (Mexican Socialist Party). The PMS originated in 1978; however, in 1988 the United Mexican Socialist Party (PSUM) and the Mexican Workers' Party (PMT) merged to form the current PMS. The Mexican Communist Party also has been amalgamated into the PMS. Its 1988 Mexican presidential candidate was Heberto Castillo Martínez whose selection was open to all Mexican citizens regardless of party membership. The PMS was formed with the notion of it becoming the party around which the left could consolidate its opposition to the PRI; however, the emergence of the FDN coalition preempted the PMS.

Then Castillo, former leader of the PMT and political prisoner, defeated three other candidates for the new party's presidential nomination (Reding, 1988).

The PFCRN (Party of the Cardenista Front for National Reconstruction). The PFCRN was formerly known as the PST (Workers' Socialist Party), established in 1978. The party essentially is an offshoot of the PRI's left wing (Reding, 1988). The PFCRN was part of the coalition that supported Cárdenas as its 1988 presidential candidate.

The PRT (Workers' Revolutionary Party). The PRT began in 1981 and obtained 1.5% of the votes in 1985. The PRT's candidate for president in 1988 was Rosario Ibarra de Piedra, a well-known human rights activist who holds strong anti-government attitudes.

The PARM (Authentic Party of the Mexican Revolution). The PARM, established in 1952, traditionally was viewed as being almost an arm of the PRI and subordinated to the federal government. However, in 1988 it joined the serious opposition by supporting Cárdenas for president and forming part of the FDN coalition.

Conclusions. Even though the 1988 presidential election resulted in substantial reduction in vote for the PRI, it remains the largest, most stable party in Mexico. It continues to dominate the country via its corporatism and control of the government. It continues to be able to coopt those in opposition by political appointments, economic resources, control of mass organizations, and by influencing the mass media. The question remains whether or not the events of July, 1988 will substantially realign the political forces in Mexico.

The Remainder of This Book

This book was generated out of presentations made at the *Sucesión Presidencial: Bi-National Reflections* conference held in Los Angeles, California on October 7, 1988, and by several subsequently invited authors. The conference was sponsored by the University of California Consortium on Mexico and the United States (UC MEXUS). Funding for the conference and completion of this manuscript was provided by The John D. and Catherine T. MacArthur Foundation. The main goal of the conference was to examine presidential succession in Mexico and its potential impact upon United States-Mexico relations.

All chapters except the first and last were written during the latter part of 1988. The first and last chapters were written later when all of the remaining chapters were in hand. Thus, these two chapters had the benefit of the knowledge and expertise of the other authors and the opportunity to consider events that took place during the first half of 1989.

The overall goals of this book are as follows:

1. To analyze the outcomes of the 1988 Mexican presidential election.

2. To determine what socioeconomic and other factors were related to the election outcome.

3. To evaluate the election process in Mexico, especially in regards to possible irregularities.

4. To make available to persons in Mexico and the United States the results of various evaluations and empirical analyses of the election process.

5. To make available scholarly interpretations of the election to correct any distortions the media may have generated in the United States about the Mexican electoral process and election outcome.

6. To make observations about future elections in Mexico, including the location and thrust of the opposition.

7. To determine what the election results may portend for democratization in Mexico and for future alternative political scenarios.

8. To speculate about what the election results imply for future Mexico-United States relations.

Each subsequent chapter in this book explores one or more of these goals. Thus, this volume presents a wide perspective on the Mexican presidential election of 1988. Included in the volume are chapters by Mexican and United States academics, representatives of the major political parties in Mexico, as well as other observers. It should be specifically noted that virtually all of the chapters in this volume were written soon after the election; thus, some of the events various authors may have expected to happen may have, or may not have, since occurred. The authors deserve full credit for being willing to project the future in what obviously is a changing Mexico.

The book contains both essays and empirical analyses concerned with the 1988 Mexican presidential election. Thus, there is a blending of empirical work and commentary. In any country, and for any election, there always is a substantial amount of rhetoric. In contrast, in this volume systematic analysis is carried out by various authors. Some of the chapters utilize "official" election results from 1988 and earlier elections. While there has been criticism of the use of official election results from Mexican elections, they are "social facts" and thus are utilized by some of the authors; of course, others in the volume are highly critical of such statistics. The conclusion one reaches very quickly about Mexican elections is that there is substantial disagreement on a variety of topics, including the use of official election results.

The chapters raise a number of questions about elections in Mexico and about future alternative political scenarios. Some of these questions are dealt with in detail while others are raised for future researchers to answer. Some of them will only be answered by events in Mexico yet to be determined. All prognostications about Mexico's future must deal with the debt, population expansion, urbanization, and education, all of which have been included under the rubric of modernization.

References

Baer, M. Delal. 1988. "The Mexican Presidential Elections: Pre-election Analysis." Washington, D.C.: Center for Strategic & International Studies, Report No.1, March 24.

Cornelius, Wayne A. and Ann L. Craig. 1988. *Politics in Mexico: An Introduction and Overview*. San Diego: Center for U.S.-Mexican Studies, Reprint Series 1, University of California.

Langley, Lester D. 1988. *MexAmerica: Two Countries, One Future*. New York: Crown Publishers.

López Moreno, Javier. 1987. *Elecciones de ayer y de mañana*. Mexico: Costa-Amic Editores.

Middlebrook, Kevin J. 1986. "Political Liberalization in an Authoritarian Regime: The Case of Mexico," in *Elections and Democratization in Latin America, 1980-1985*, Paul W. Drake and Eduardo Silva (eds.). San Diego: Center for U.S.-Mexican Studies, University of California.

Migdail, Carl J. 1987. "Mexico's Failing Political System," *Journal of Interamerican Studies and World Affairs*, 29 (Fall):107-123.

Molinar Horcasitas, Juan. 1986. "The Mexican Electoral System: Continuity by Change," in *Elections and Democratization in Latin America, 1980-1985*, Paul W. Drake and Eduardo Silva (eds.). San Diego: Center for U.S.-Mexican Studies, University of California.

Reding, Andrew. 1988. "The Democratic Current: A New Era in Mexican Politics," *World Policy Journal*, V (Spring):323-366.

Williams, Dan and Marjorie Miller. 1988. "Rightist Prescription for Mexico," *Los Angeles Times*, June 14.

2

An Examination of the Official Results of the 1988 Mexican Presidential Election

By Edgar W. Butler[1]
James B. Pick[2]
Glenda Jones[3]

Introduction

Mexico is a major nation of the Americas, with an estimated population in 1987 of 81.9 million (Population Reference Bureau, 1987), and it is a key economic and strategic neighbor of the United States. The Mexico-United States border is two thousand miles long and stretches from Brownsville, Texas, to San Ysidro, California. Mexico's "impact upon our politics, our economy, and our culture reaches deep into the heartland of America" (Langley, 1988: 265). While it is clear that Mexico is to some degree dependent upon the United States, it is clear also that what happens in Mexico concerns the United

1 Edgar W. Butler is a former chair and currently professor of sociology at the University of California, Riverside. He is co-director of the UCR Database Project which is computerizing population and economic development data on the Mexican states and *municipios* for the statistical analysis and geographic base mapping. He has co-authored a series of articles on fertility, migration, and various other aspects of Mexico and is co-author of the *Atlas of Mexico* (Westview Press).

2 James B. Pick is a lecturer in the Graduate School of Management and director of its Computing Facility at the University of California, Riverside. He has been involved in research projects on Mexican demography, including studies of fertility, migration, and population geography. He also does research on the management of information systems. He is a co-author of the *Atlas of Mexico* (Westview).

3 Glenda Jones is a Ph.D. candidate in the Department of Sociology, University of California, Riverside. Her research focus has been on fertility in Mexico and in the United States borderlands and on information systems as they apply to socio-demographic factors.

States, whether it is control of the border, debts, our international economic difficulties, our security, trade, tourism, supply of essential labor, or export of natural resources. The reality is that the two countries have a linked past and a linked future. What happens in Mexico has implications for all of the United States. Thus, many people perceived that the 1988 presidential election in Mexico would influence Mexico-United States relations because the possibilities for economic and social change in Mexico were enormous.

Prior to the Mexican presidential election of 1988, there was widespread discontent with the political process in Mexico, stemming from the preceding six years of economic stagnation and an extremely high inflation rate. Nevertheless, it was generally expected that the candidate of the ruling *Partido Revolucionario Institucional* (PRI), Carlos Salinas de Gortari, would be elected president. However, with the *Partido Acción Nacional* (PAN) on the right, and the emergence of the *Frente Democrático Nacional* (FDN) on the center-left, virtually everyone knowledgeable about Mexico expected more formidable opposition to the dominant party in the 1988 presidential election than in previous years.

Prior to the election, the center-left candidate, Cuauhtémoc Cárdenas, was making an impressive showing in rallies and demonstrations. There were reports of massive support for him in some rural areas, and polls indicated that he was running a strong second to Salinas in Mexico City. Another candidate with a strong presence was the right-center PAN candidate, Manuel Clouthier. His strength appeared to lie in the north -- especially in the state of Sonora, in some cities, and in Yucatán. The deepening economic crisis and serious disagreement within the PRI leadership about conduct of the election and liberalization of the political process suggested that the presidential election of 1988 would be different from previous elections.

Official election results of July 1988 illustrated that Mexico indeed, in some respects, was undergoing radical shifts insofar as electoral politics were concerned. The 1988 election subsequently has been reported as setting the stage for the development of a pluralistic party structure in Mexico (see Reyna and Butler, forthcoming). Of course, these conclusions may be premature; however, it is clear that a new course of electoral politics has been established in Mexico, one which holds vast implications for the country's future, its internal stability, and its relationship with the United States and other nations (Reyna and Butler, forthcoming).

Quantitative studies of election outcomes also have been carried out for several border states and cities. These studies focused on irregularities (Aziz, 1987), surveys of party preferences of youth in Mexico City and six border cities (Hernández, 1987), and political parties and political attitudes in Chihuahua

(Guillén, 1987). Each of these studies suggested hypotheses that are examined in the body of this paper.

There are several caveats that need to be kept in mind in this chapter. First, the data analysis is from a *macro* and *ecological* or spatial perspective. Second, the analysis is based upon official election results and as such reflects only information from that source. Ames (1970: 154) points out that most potential errors of official election results do not affect the overall statistical analysis or obviate the conclusions of the analysis if the errors are either random and/or systematic from all states, other than generally attenuating relationships. The one exception that could affect relationships is if voting data errors are not either random or systematic but related to some unknown variables (also see Köppen, 1985). Part of our analysis also covers presidential elections from 1934 through 1988 (and other elections not reported here) for a fifty-four year period. Thus, it is obvious that the existence of historical patterns bears upon 1988 official election results and their credibility. That is, the extensive time frame in our analyses allows a perspective on official election results that a one-election analysis does not.

Third, a macro analysis, of course, does not take into account what one opposition party official said to us: "You had to live the election to know what it means." One implication of this comment is that we do not know of the irregularities that took place in the election. However, whether or not irregularities took place, official election results are "real" and are part of the political reality of contemporary Mexico. And, as indicated above, a longitudinal perspective incorporating previous elections allows certain statements to be made about the 1988 election in a larger time context, in a frame of reference that covers over fifty years.

Our discussion is based upon a much larger number of political analyses that have been carried out but are too extensive to report completely here. These numerous analyses will be reported in another volume (Butler et al., forthcoming). The remainder of this chapter discusses the methodology utilized, results of voter participation, and general analytic results with an emphasis on demographic and social dimensions related to voter participation and to the PRI, the PAN, and the FDN votes. In addition, a more detailed examination is accomplished of the five states lost by the PRI and won by the FDN. Finally, research results are summarized, several predictions about the future are made, and several implications for Mexico-United States relations are explored.

There have been several qualitative studies of recent Mexican elections (López Moreno, 1987; Fernández and Rodríguez, 1986; Alvarado, 1987; Cornelius and Craig, 1984; Cornelius, 1986), but they did not systematically interrelate electoral results with other variables. However, there is an emerging series of studies that does systematically examine election outcomes in Mexico. One based on the 1982 Chamber of Deputies election (Klesner, 1987), indicated that there are substantial differences in electoral outcomes in Mexico based upon religion, rural-urban location, and other factors. A number of other systematic research efforts have emphasized variables collectively labeled as modernization and industrialization (Ames, 1970; Walton and Sween, 1971; Estévez and Ramírez, 1985; Oranday, 1985).

Methodology

The statistical analyses and graphics presented in this chapter focus on the states of Mexico, primarily on the 1988 presidential election.[4] However, some longitudinal data are incorporated into the discussion and analysis to present a perspective on the 1988 election. Substantial parts of this research effort focus on associated demographic and socioeconomic determinants of election outcomes as reflected in official electoral results for the Mexican states (treating the Federal District as a state). Reliance was made upon the Mexico Database Project for information to interrelate with election results (Pick et al., 1989; Butler et al., 1988). The Mexico Database project contains information from a variety of sources including censuses and government agencies. All data were key-entered into the Mexico Database system for analysis by the ARC/INFO geographic information database system (ESRI, 1988), and major statistical packages.

Dependent electoral variables analyzed are official election results derived from several different sources (*Proceso. . .*, 1988; *El Día*, 1988). Many independent variables included in our evaluation have been used by previous investigators under the rubric of "modernization theory" (see in particular Estévez and Ramírez, 1985; Klesner, 1987; Lehr, 1985). Statistics reported in this chapter are primarily descriptive and exploratory rather than multivariate or exhaustive. Analyses underway incorporate more sophisticated statistical techniques (Butler, et al., forthcoming), utilize more extensive qualitative information, and explore some implications of the election upon United States-Mexico relations (Reyna and Butler, forthcoming).

Longitudinal Analysis: 1934-1982

Middlebrook (1986: 93) has pointed out that historically most support for opposition parties has come from areas in which the PRI's strength was already in decline. Our analysis of presidential elections, beginning in 1934 and concluding in 1988, illustrates that he essentially was correct since opposition vote

---

4 Because the universe of 32 states was used in this analysis, tests of statistical significance do not apply since all relationships reported are real. In the various tables, statistical tests were used as a general guide to determine "strong" relationships.

states could have been identified as early as 1940. Thus, while the magnitude of the relationship between the PRI and opposition vote varied during this time period, the opposition states or areas remained remarkably similar for almost 50 years. That is, while there has been variation in the percentage of opposition vote as shown in Figure 2-1, the opposition vote has consistently been from the same states. While parties may have changed their names and/or orientations, and areas may have changed in demographic and other social characteristics, states that voted for the opposition in 1940 remained relatively stable in their opposition between 1940 and 1988 (see Table 2-1). Opposition states became especially solidified by the 1952 presidential election and have remained so since. We believe that subsequent analysis by electoral districts (N = 300) will show similar consistencies.

Evidence from our longitudinal analysis suggests that the 1934 presidential election was an anomaly. For example, the Pearsonian zero-order correlations presented below, for the sample of 32 Mexican states, establish the relationship between the PRI's 1988 percent vote and the percent PRI votes for presidential elections from 1934 to 1982. When comparing areas in Mexico which voted for the PRI in 1988 and 1934, there was a negative relationship in 1934 ($r = -16$). However, beginning in 1940 and continuing in subsequent presidential elections there was a strong positive relationship, which in some years was stronger than in others. Variation in the strength of these relationships can be attributed to circumstances of particular elections, including the extent of party competition (1940 and 1952), the personalities involved (1946 and 1952), and structural electoral reforms (1982).

Election Year	Correlation between Earlier and the 1988 PRI Results
1934	-16
1940	36
1946	52
1952	67
1958	28
1964	47
1970	55
1976	41
1982	69

In the 1988 presidential election, five states were won by the FDN--Baja California, the Federal District, México, Michoacán, and Morelos. Figure 2-2 and Table 2-2 illustrate the opposition vote in these states from the 1934 through 1988 presidential elections. Baja California, the Federal District, and México have long been strongholds of opposition vote. These states, almost without exception in presidential races, have had an opposition vote above the national average. In Michoacán, opposition was especially strong in the contested 1946 and 1952 elections, then dropped to less than average, but was strong again in 1988. Opposition in Morelos also was strong in the 1946 and 1952 elections, dropping to below average in the interim years, but increasing substantially in the 1988 election.

In any case, opposition to the major party has been consistent by state but not necessarily in strength. Apparently some states have latent opposition that appears only under specific circumstances. Whenever these circumstances arise, this latent opposition is brought into operation in the form of votes for opposition candidates.

Voter Participation: 1988

Of particular importance in any election is the extent of voter participation or turnout (see Oranday, 1985; Ames, 1970; González, 1985). In the past, the main causes for voters' non-voting in Mexico probably have been: (a) the inevitability of the PRI victory and (b) the inability, for whatever reasons, of the opposition (left or right) to develop a large enough base to challenge the ruling party (Langley, 1988: 255). Non-voting in past Mexican elections has been interpreted by some experts as a "protest" vote, while Ames (1970: 163) interpreted lack of turnout to political parties not being salient to Mexican voters. From this perspective, there is a maximum turnout to be expected *regardless* of the number of political parties contesting the election. Thus, new parties only draw votes from already existing parties and have little appeal to non-voters.

Political reform measures instituted in 1977 had the goal of increasing the rate of voter participation; however, the turnout of 50.7% in the 1979 election for the Federal Chamber of Deputies was actually a decrease from previous elections (Middlebrook, 1986: 96). However, in the 1982 presidential election, the national voter registration list included 94.9% of all eligible citizens and 74.8% of all registered voters participated in the election; these were the highest rates since 1946 (Middlebrook, 1986: 96). Middlebrook (1986: 97) suggests two factors that reversed the long-term trend of decreasing voter participation. First, the government worked effectively to bring out the vote (or perhaps the vote was artificially increased). Second, there were eight other political parties and six alternative presidential candidates (two of the parties, the PPS[5] and the PARM, supporting the PRI candidate) that succeeded in stimulating interest in the elections. Middlebrook (1986: 98) concluded that decreased abstention in the 1982 election "suggests that much of the previously high abstention rate reflected a generalized disinterest in the electoral process rather than a form of protest against the established regime."

In the 1988 presidential election, the voter participation rate was just over 50% (¿Qué Pasó?, 1988: 31). However, as Table 2-3 and Map 2-1 illustrate, there was wide variation among states in turn-out rates. The range was from a high of 58.2% in Querétaro to a low of 37.9% in Coahuila. Voter participation in states won by the FDN ranged from a near high (Federal District - 57.0%) to a near low (Michoacán - 40.2%). There is no discernable regional pattern in voter turnout except that states around the Federal District generally had higher voter participation rates than the rest of the country, and the border region generally had lower rates. There were insignificant relationships between levels of voter turnout and voting for the PAN, the PRI, or the FDN. Table 2-4 shows that voter turnout correlation ranged from .09 with the PRI vote, to -.08 and .01 with the FDN and the PAN, respectively. The conclusion, then, is that the extent of voter participation, or voter abstention, did not impact the presidential election of 1988.

While data are not presented here, there also was variation in voter participation levels within states by voting district. Some states had rather large internal variation while districts in other states were substantially similar in voter participation, e.g., the Federal District. These data may reflect the "real" turnout and/or may have been impacted by the degree of monitoring by the PRI and opposition parties.

Electoral Results: 1988

As in past elections, the 1988 presidential election demonstrated that support for the PRI and opposition parties varies considerably by state, municipio, urban-rural areas, and districts (Lehr, 1985; Ames, 1970). As shown in Table 2-4, in the 1988 Mexican presidential election at the state level, the PRI vote had a substantial negative correlation with both the FDN and the PAN vote. The PAN and the FDN vote also had a significant negative correlation with each

---

5 See chapter 1 for a description of the PPS and the PARM political parties.

other. As noted previously, the relationship of the vote for all parties with voter participation was small and statistically insignificant.

Our analyses of the demographic and social characteristics associated with votes for various parties generally revealed some consistencies with past elections, and some surprises.

The PRI

The distribution of the PRI vote is illustrated on Map 2-2. Data for each state were shown in Table 2-1. Significant zero-order correlations of social and demographic characteristics with the PRI vote are shown in Table 2-5. The two major factors associated with the PRI vote are dimensions that one would expect to be negatively associated with each other -- urbanization and the agricultural labor force (for similar results, see Ames, 1970; Lehr, 1985). Urbanization, as measured by different levels of urban population, is consistently negatively associated with the PRI vote. On the other hand, the agricultural labor force, as measured by several different indicators, is consistently positively associated with the PRI vote (also see Lehr, 1985: 60). Other important dimensions associated with the PRI vote are education (the higher the level of education in a state, the lower the PRI vote), literacy (the higher the level of literacy in a state, the lower the PRI vote), any occupational category other than agriculture (the higher percentage of other occupational categories, the lower the PRI vote), lack of potable water (see Ames, 1970: 163), lack of electricity, no TVs, and using the kitchen as a bedroom (the higher these percentages are, the greater likelihood of voting for the PRI), and income (low level is positively associated with the PRI vote while medium and high level incomes are negatively associated with the PRI vote).

Several other results are of particular interest. First, the sex ratio is positively related to the PRI vote, which means that the greater the percentage of males in a state the higher the PRI vote. Also, there is a substantial positive association between non-Catholics and the PRI vote. Not shown in Table 2-3 are correlations illustrating that measures of most of these same variables for 1970 with 1988 election outcomes result in virtually the same conclusions as reported here. That is, these socioeconomic patterns and the vote are long-standing and are not the result of temporary social and/or economic forces.

Generally, the conclusion is that agricultural (rural) areas, low incomes, and a lack of housing amenities are positively associated with the PRI vote, whereas higher education, literacy, and middle and higher level incomes are negatively associated with the PRI vote.

The PAN

The distribution of the PAN vote is shown on Map 2-3. Data for each state were reported in Table 2-1. Demographic and social characteristics with significant positive and negative correlations were shown in Table 2-3; zero-order correlations of the PAN vote with demographic and social characteristics were reported in Table 2-3. In contrast to the PRI, the PAN vote is negatively associated with agricultural occupations and has positive correlations with education, literacy, medium and higher level incomes, all occupations other than agriculture, unemployment, and with several measures related to corporate structure, e.g., the number/capita and value (for similar results, see Ames, 1970; Lehr, 1985).

There also are some unusual or unexpected relationships, e.g., strong negative correlations with ever married and currently married, cumulative fertility for women over 45, and positive correlations with several dimensions implying family planning or birth control, e.g., contraceptive pill usage and pregnancies that did not result in births (wasted pregnancies). These latter associations are particularly interesting because the PAN vote is negatively associated with non-Catholics, which implies a positive relationship with Catholics. Another interpretation is that lower fertility and greater family planning represent proxies for higher education and income levels. Further, growth areas are more likely to be PAN oriented than non-growth areas. As with the demographic and social characteristics related to the PRI vote, when the 1988 PAN vote is examined in relationship to measures of these very same variables earlier in time, the conclusions reached are the same.

In summary, the PAN vote in the 1988 presidential election was positively associated with medium and higher level incomes, all occupational categories other than agriculture, education and literacy, several different family-related dimensions, and negatively with non-Catholic religion.

The FDN

While a number of demographic and social characteristics are associated with the PRI and the PAN vote, almost invariably in opposite directions, few dimensions are strongly correlated with the FDN vote! The geographic distribution of the FDN vote is illustrated in Map 2-4; data were presented in Table 2-1. Table 2-3 presented significant zero-order correlations between the FDN vote and various demographic and social variables.

Growth states, more dense areas, 1979-1980 outmigration, and lifetime outmigration, are positively associated with the FDN vote, while there is a strong negative relationship with native-to-state population. The impression from these analytic results is that the FDN vote is strongest in areas undergoing population change.

An analysis of the political parties making up the FDN (i.e., PPS, PMS, PFCRN, PARM, and Other has been carried out). However, we have not yet examined the results in detail. Nevertheless, even a cursory comparison of the various political party vote components, and of voter participation of the FDN vote with various demographic and social characteristics demonstrates that the FDN vote is *made up of various political parties and interest groups* and is associated with demographic and social characteristics in contrasting ways. For example, the overall relationship between voter turnout and the FDN vote is virtually nonexistent. However, this is because there are substantial *negative* and *positive* relationships for the various political party components that make up the FDN which result in *no difference* for the overall FDN vote and voter participation. The multiplicity of parties making up the FDN may also aid in the explanation of why so few demographic and social characteristics are linked to the FDN vote. Again, positive and negative relationships for each component party result in no relationship when they are combined. An alternative explanation (one that we reject), is that the FDN appealed equally to virtually all segments in Mexico, i.e., lower, middle, and high income levels, rural and urban, etc.

The PAN and the FDN Critiques of the 1988 Election

Both the PAN and the FDN carried out studies of the 1988 Mexican presidential election. Their methodologies, however, were strikingly different. The PAN conducted two population surveys in July and August of 1988, after the election (PAN, 1988). The FDN took another approach by applying several statistical analytic techniques to official election results (Barberán, et al., 1988).

The general conclusion reached by the PAN analysis at the national level is that the PRI vote was inflated by slightly over 15%, the PAN vote reduced by somewhere in the neighborhood of 13%, and the official national vote reported for the FDN was just slightly *over* what it should have been.

The FDN reported large variation in voting abstentions and in the vote, which it attributed to "the alteration of the real results" (Barberán et al., 1988: 30). The FDN examined 29,999 of the 54,642 total *casillas*[6] and the 300 electoral districts in Mexico. They described a *zone of competition* consisting of about two-thirds of the *casillas*; in this zone the PRI garnered fewer votes than the FDN. They also delineated a second zone, called the *zone of no competition*. The PRI won by an extremely large count in almost a fourth of these *casi-*

---

6 *Casillas* are much like voting precincts in the United States.

llas, and the PRI won 96% or more of the votes in eight percent of the *casillas* in this zone.

Official election results and the PAN and FDN analysis for the nation as a whole are presented below (percentages do not add up to 100% because of "other" political parties and/or rounding error).

Political Party	Official Vote	PAN[1] Surveys	FDN[2] Analysis
PRI	50.4%	34.9%	37.0%
PAN	17.1%	30.0%	22.0%
FDN	32.0%	31.0%	42.0%

[1]Mean of two survey samples (PAN, 1988).
[2]Average of several estimates (Barberán, et al., 1988).

By official results the PRI won the election handily over the two other parties, but only barely when the votes of the PAN and the FDN are combined. In addition, both the PAN surveys demonstrate that the PRI won the election, albeit by a much lower margin than that reported by official election results. That is, the PRI, according to the PAN, still won the election but by a reduced margin of approximately 15%. The PAN concludes that these votes were taken from its party since the PAN reports that the FDN actually received one percent less vote than that reported in the official results!

The FDN analysis, similar to the PAN examination, also suggests that the official PRI vote was inflated, but less than that suggested by the PAN. The FDN also concluded that the PAN vote was under-reported, but substantially less so than that estimated by the PAN. In contrast, the FDN analysis concludes that its own vote was substantially under-reported and that the "true" election results were such that the FDN actually won the election, i.e., with 42% of the vote compared to 32% for the PRI and 31% for the PAN.

Chapter 3 offers a more detailed critique of the PAN and the FDN methodologies. Further discussion of contrasting results in that chapter may assist one in making an independent decision regarding the validity of the official 1988 Mexican presidential election results.

Conclusions

Several general conclusions can be drawn from our macro-analysis of the 1988 election and of historical trends. First, there is substantial consistency in opposition voting by state over a fifty year time period in Mexico (also see Estévez and Ramírez, 1985). That is, while the percentage of opposition vote varies, opposition states are substantially consistent over time. Fluctuations can be explained by the degree of contested election, candidate personalities, and/or structural conditions related to a specific election, e.g., electoral reform. In many instances, the election results of 1988 had their precursors as far back in time as 1940. Opposition regions in 1988, then, did not develop overnight--most of them had a long history of opposition which was noticeable long before the 1988 election.

Second, given the long history of opposition trends, the role the economic crisis of the past several years has played in the 1988 election has to be re-evaluated. That is, while the economic crisis may have been an important factor, it was more important in some states than others. Areas where it perhaps was most important also are the same states that historically have been the bastions of opposition to the PRI. Thus, apparently there was an interaction effect of the economic crisis and other factors in developing opposition in certain ecological areas.

Third, a number of experts have concluded that a multiple, pluralistic party structure and society may be expected in Mexico in the future (for alternative scenarios, see Reyna and Butler, forthcoming; Baer, 1990). Generally those who adhere to this future view assume that the PRI, the FDN, and the PAN all will continue as major contending parties. However, several other alternative possibilities exist. The FDN may fragment into its original parties in the future since its component parties may withdraw from the FDN. In the 1988 election the FDN was made up of several different parties that were differentially strong in varying states. For the FDN to develop into a continuing major party, sub-party differences will have to be resolved so that participants are comfortable within the structure. Another distinct possibility is that many of the FDN supporters will be reintegrated and/or incorporated into the PRI. In the past, the PRI has been quite successful in bringing dissidents into the fold (Molinar, 1986: 108). That is, if there are defections from the PRI and/or the FDN, the net direction of flow may be from the FDN rather than to the FDN as current wisdom implies.

Fourth, in the unlikely circumstances that the FDN should coalesce into a long-term viable political party, subsequent elections in Mexico will primarily be a struggle between the FDN and the PRI and not between the PAN and the PRI, or the PAN and the FDN. This conclusion is based upon the fact that the PAN was not able to mobilize any greater popular support in half of the states during the 1988 presidential election than it did during previous elections. Its relative growth strength was variable; eight states remained static (plus or minus 1%), eight states actually reduced their support for the PAN, while sixteen states had some increase in the PAN vote.

In addition to these general conclusions, our analyses interrelating 1988 Mexican presidential election results with a number of demographic and social characteristics lead to the following conclusions:

(1) Areas of major growth are negatively associated with the PRI vote.

(2) The PRI vote is generally negatively associated with higher levels of economic development.

(3) The PRI vote is generally positively associated with rural areas and agricultural occupations.

(4) The FDN vote generally is positively correlated with population growth and change indicators, but there is a peculiarity in that the FDN vote is negatively correlated with measures of corporate activity and some economic indicators. There are few other strong relationships of the FDN vote with demographic and social characteristics.

(5) The PAN vote is strongly positively associated with urbanization and projected population growth. Further, the PAN vote is substantially positively associated with indicators of economic strength, especially those reflecting non-agricultural occupations, corporate activity, and medium and high level incomes. Also, the PAN vote is positively associated with higher levels of education and literacy.

(6) The strong positive relationship of the PAN vote with urbanization, income, and education and literacy would appear to bode well for the future of the PAN since it is anticipated that in the future Mexico will have an increasingly urbanized, educated, literate population. Yet this contrasts with official election results.

Several points of interest regarding the 1988 election have not been resolved. For example, at least some pundits have suggested that the 1988 presidential election resulted in increased political interest and participation in Mexico. While there may or may not have been an increased interest, official voting records clearly show that in fact almost half of the potential voters did not vote, or if they did, their votes were not counted (¿Qué Pasó? 1988). Another possibility, of course, is that the actual vote was even less than that reported; that is, some persons may not have voted even though their votes were counted.

Further, some have implied that the 1988 election is evidence of a more democratic, pluralistic society emerging in Mexico. At least for the 1988 election this clearly appears to be the case. However, others have noted that within the PRI, the process of selecting the presidential candidate was virtually the same in 1988 as in previous years. It thus remains to be seen whether within the PRI the process of selecting the presidential candidate (and perhaps other candidates) will change in the future.   Of course, a similar question can be asked of the PAN and the FDN! That is, do these parties also select candidates democratically?   Officials in the PAN argue that they follow the democratic process in selecting their presidential candidate.   Then, after candidates have been selected by political parties and voting takes place, will all political parties accept defeat as well as victory, and negotiate in the legislature so that the government can effectively function?   Clearly, there are several conceivable scenarios of future political development in Mexico (see Reyna and Butler, forthcoming).

Several important questions emerge from our general analytic results and from the past electoral experience of Mexico. First, will the PRI incorporate substantial segments of the FDN, resulting in an alteration of the PRI, perhaps to a somewhat more democratic and pluralistic party? A corollary of this point is whether or not Mexico develops an unquestionably honest electoral process. Second, will the FDN be able to continue as a major opposition party? Carlos Monsiváis has suggested that the FDN already has outlived its usefulness. Third, can the PAN continue to be a major opposition party when it continues to appeal to a maximum of 20-25% of the electorate, even though it appears that conditions for its growth are favorable, e.g., increasing urbanization and literacy?   Fourth, will minor parties be able to develop into major parties, or will they be either incorporated into the PRI or fall to the wayside?

If all of these questions are answered in keeping with the past electoral and political behavior in Mexico, it can be anticipated that the PRI will remain the dominant party with perhaps some liberalization.   It may be that a new era has dawned in Mexico as some have predicted; in the meantime, past experience is probably the best predictor of the future.

Binational Policy Implications

What happens in Mexico impacts relations with the United States. Thus, implications of the 1988 Mexican presidential election on Mexico-United States bilateral relations are numerous. While the opposition may have been predicted, the extent of its success was not anticipated. As a result, the Mexico that the United States must deal with now is not the Mexico of the past.   In other words, enormous changes are taking place in Mexico as a result of the 1988 presidential election.

What impacts the changes of 1988 will have upon the Mexican political system still have not been made clear. What is certain is that the Mexican political system will not become a carbon copy of the United States system since Mexico has different intellectual, political, and social traditions.   While it is possible that Mexico could remain much the same as the past, it appears for the moment that presidential power in Mexico has been reduced; how much it has been reduced remains to be seen.   While the United States must continue to negotiate with the president of Mexico, internally the president must now keep under control various sectors within his own party, contend with two opposition parties who will have influence in the legislature, and mold public opinion.   The national concerns of Mexico may run counter to those of the United States. This perhaps may best be shown in the concern over drugs.   Many Mexicans see drugs as a United States problem, while in the United States there is a substantial governmental and public view that if the presumed flow of drugs from Mexico could be controlled, the drug problem in the United States would be solved.   Further, there are substantially different points of view regarding debt payment.   Mexico wants and needs some form of debt relief, while the United States may not be predisposed to grant it.   Related to the debt, the Mexican government undoubtedly will have to come to grips with the counter-currents that exist over the attraction of external investment to Mexico and how much control to exert over external investments.   These are only several of many issues in Mexico-United States binational relations that will be influenced over the next few years by the outcome of the 1988 Mexican presidential election.

Acknowledgements

This chapter benefitted from the critiques of Kathryn Roberts and José Luis Reyna.   Also, discussions with Richard Walsack and Arturo Gómez-Pompa were instrumental in its completion.

Table 2-1
Mexican Presidential Election Results: 1934-1982

State	1934	1940	1946	1952	1958
AGUASCALIENTES	95.96	93.89	70.36	67.92	89.25
BAJA CALIFORNIA	97.18	93.92	63.26	61.74	60.67
BAJA CALIFORNIA SUR	99.59	-	91.68	82.25	93.42
CAMPECHE	0.00	98.06	75.08	86.98	87.73
COAHUILA	93.54	95.06	81.36	80.79	94.88
COLIMA	94.77	95.33	66.83	80.10	89.66
CHIAPAS	0.00	98.05	87.26	90.53	98.00
CHIHUAHUA	99.82	97.09	75.66	63.86	64.60
DISTRITO FEDERAL	97.32	71.99	57.01	51.39	78.87
DURANGO	99.66	96.75	65.37	65.02	84.73
GUANAJUATO	98.71	95.94	63.96	64.12	89.49
GUERRERO	99.98	95.43	85.06	82.48	98.19
HIDALGO	99.99	99.46	90.35	88.69	98.09
JALISCO	99.09	98.71	78.89	64.70	88.95
MEXICO	99.78	94.86	84.05	81.06	98.92
MICHOACAN	98.83	92.90	67.33	55.37	87.20
MORELOS	99.76	98.13	57.31	68.46	95.83
NAYARIT	99.99	96.98	85.27	97.33	98.68
NUEVO LEON	84.45	89.32	70.40	80.83	90.33
OAXACA	99.95	99.36	90.20	79.76	95.62
PUEBLA	99.26	98.83	81.85	80.87	95.24
QUERETARO	-	95.72	91.42	95.25	79.88
QUINTANA ROO	99.46	98.75	84.30	82.00	89.50
SAN LUIS POTOSI	99.92	98.18	80.15	88.90	94.33
SINALOA	97.65	89.51	89.89	68.27	98.09
SONORA	99.91	92.42	81.49	81.09	97.28
TABASCO	0.00	99.83	95.58	79.33	98.85
TAMAULIPAS	97.15	88.09	72.41	69.53	94.78
TLAXCALA	99.61	95.64	81.09	81.22	98.39
VERACRUZ	99.06	94.80	90.54	91.53	97.63
YUCATAN	99.39	88.08	75.94	81.48	77.38
ZACATECAS	93.82	94.32	67.63	71.78	91.73
Nacional	98.19	93.89	77.91	74.32	90.56

Table 2-1 (Continued)
Mexican Presidential Election Results: 1934-1982

State	1964	1970	1976	1982
AGUASCALIENTES	91.23	87.38	93.81	75.60
BAJA CALIFORNIA	81.39	74.35	92.42	56.35
BAJA CALIFORNIA SUR	96.83	68.09	94.23	74.11
CAMPECHE	95.94	98.07	99.62	90.04
COAHUILA	93.40	91.20	99.76	68.07
COLIMA	87.33	90.74	97.29	90.48
CHIAPAS	98.89	98.91	99.55	92.07
CHIHUAHUA	78.72	81.10	89.34	65.50
DISTRITO FEDERAL	74.86	69.25	80.38	52.09
DURANGO	90.00	86.73	98.79	75.94
GUANAJUATO	79.60	80.82	97.99	67.29
GUERRERO	96.95	95.68	98.74	84.17
HIDALGO	98.36	97.16	96.48	84.49
JALISCO	87.02	82.76	93.85	59.79
MEXICO	91.72	84.66	90.57	59.09
MICHOACAN	86.00	86.77	97.77	78.19
MORELOS	94.21	90.29	92.21	76.75
NAYARIT	91.62	96.49	97.06	80.61
NUEVO LEON	84.26	84.18	90.45	72.66
OAXACA	96.64	96.57	99.73	84.53
PUEBLA	93.65	85.50	95.46	83.93
QUERETARO	96.58	98.21	97.65	92.18
QUINTANA ROO	91.29	90.74	97.07	78.29
SAN LUIS POTOSI	91.57	90.23	97.76	84.14
SINALOA	98.07	94.57	97.93	79.23
SONORA	98.36	93.50	99.55	76.14
TABASCO	99.33	98.85	99.57	92.57
TAMAULIPAS	96.51	91.62	96.08	77.64
TLAXCALA	98.43	94.31	99.98	82.13
VERACRUZ	96.80	92.67	98.50	83.01
YUCATAN	85.38	85.27	92.59	80.27
ZACATECAS	79.48	90.75	98.57	86.16
Nacional	88.62	85.80	93.60	71.00

DEFINITION: Percent of official vote for the PRI candidate.
SOURCE: *Fundación Javier Barros Sierra AC* (1987).

Table 2-2
Non-PRI Presidential Vote: 1934 - 1988

YEAR	BAJA CALIFORNIA %	FEDERAL DISTRICT %	MEXICO %	MICHOACAN %	MORELOS %	NATIONAL AVERAGE %
1934	2.82	2.68	0.22	1.17	0.24	1.81
1940	6.08	28.01	5.14	0.10	1.87	6.10
1946	36.74	42.99	15.95	32.67	42.69	22.09
1952	38.26	48.61	18.94	44.63	31.54	25.67
1958	39.33	20.13	1.08	0.00	4.17	9.44
1964	18.61	15.27	8.28	0.00	5.79	10.95
1970	25.65	30.77	15.34	13.23	9.71	14.20
1976	7.58	19.62	19.43	2.23	7.79	6.40
1982	43.57	47.59	40.87	21.79	23.23	29.00
1988	63.34	72.75	70.21	76.79	66.26	49.64

Table 2-3
Mexican Presidential Vote, 1988

State	PRI %	FDN* %	PAN %	Other %	Voter Participation %
AGUASCALIENTES	50.21	18.67	28.42	2.70	50.43
BAJA CALIFORNIA	36.66	37.19	24.39	1.77	50.64
BAJA CALIFORNIA SUR	54.02	25.87	19.00	1.10	56.96
CAMPECHE	70.88	16.30	12.37	0.46	50.49
COAHUILA	54.27	29.95	15.34	0.43	37.89
COLIMA	47.83	35.74	47.80	1.63	44.63
CHIAPAS	89.91	6.45	3.39	0.24	55.36
CHIHUAHUA	54.58	6.77	38.19	0.46	40.31
DISTRITO FEDERAL	27.25	49.22	22.01	1.52	57.00
DURANGO	63.63	18.82	16.99	0.56	52.24
GUANAJUATO	44.03	22.01	29.93	4.03	46.18
GUERRERO	60.53	35.80	2.44	1.23	42.54
HIDALGO	64.72	28.26	5.84	1.19	51.94
JALISCO	42.57	23.87	30.76	2.80	47.49
MEXICO	29.79	51.58	16.33	2.30	55.64
MICHOACAN	23.21	64.16	10.28	2.35	40.18
MORELOS	33.74	57.65	7.44	1.17	47.67
NAYARIT	56.56	36.80	5.72	0.91	50.63
NUEVO LEON	72.08	3.83	23.70	0.39	46.65
OAXACA	63.81	30.25	4.63	1.30	46.03
PUEBLA	71.55	17.69	9.87	0.89	64.39
QUERETARO	63.34	15.81	19.43	1.42	58.15
QUINTANA ROO	65.70	24.14	9.69	0.47	50.12
SAN LUIS POTOSI	68.25	8.81	21.15	1.79	43.81
SINALOA	50.81	16.75	32.07	0.37	56.01
SONORA	68.59	9.98	20.85	0.59	45.64
TABASCO	74.30	19.94	5.25	0.51	42.24
TAMAULIPAS	59.33	30.15	9.91	0.61	41.98
TLAXCALA	60.21	31.00	5.88	2.92	55.44
VERACRUZ	62.59	31.05	5.21	1.16	49.78
YUCATAN	67.08	1.61	31.19	0.12	51.10
ZACATECAS	66.17	22.31	10.77	0.76	48.72
State Mean	56.82	25.89	16.04	1.25	49.32
National Average	50.4	32.0	17.1	0.5	50.3

*FRENTE DEMOCRATICO NACIONAL.
SOURCE: *Proceso Electoral Federal*, July 7, 1988.

Table 2-4
Pearsonian Correlations among
Political Parties and Voter Participation,
1988 Mexican Presidential Election

Political Party	FDN	PAN	Voter Participation
PRI	-78	-29	09
FDN	-	-38	-08
PAN	-	-	-01

Table 2-5
Significant Pearsonian Correlations between
Political Parties and Demographic and Social Characteristics:
1988 Mexican Presidential Election[1]

Characteristics	PRI	PAN	FDN
Labor Force			
Agricultural	53	-65	
Construction	-42	50	
Administration and Managerial	-36	46	
Service	-49	47	
Other	-35	51	
Unemployment	-38	51	
Urbanization			
2,500+	-51	53	
5,000+	-53	58	
Population Size	-44		36
Population Density	-38		31
Population Projection to 1985	-44	43	
Sex Ratio	52		
Non Catholics	48	-32	
Education			
Primary (15-29)	-30		
Primary (30+)	-35	46	
Secondary (14+)	-44	30	
High Education (17+)	-45	37	
Literacy	-35	53	
Income			
Low	38	-30	
Medium	-33	36	
High	-35	38	

Table 2-5 (Continued)
Significant Pearsonian Correlations between
Political Parties and Demographic and Social Characteristics:
1988 Mexican Presidential Election[1]

Characteristics	PRI	PAN	FDN
Amenities			
Kitchen/Bedroom	38		
Potable Water	-58	48	
Electricity	-43	60	
Television	-39	77	
Phones	-34	43	
Vehicles	-41	35	
Gas Consumption	-21	40	
Family Planning			
Childern Desired	38	-24	
Wasted Pregnancies	-36	30	
Ever Married		-67	
Currently Married		-65	
Cummunitive Fertility (45+)		-33	
Pill Usage		30	
Migration			
Outmigration '79-80	-30		42
Lifetime Outmigration			38
Native Population		-29	
Tourism		31	
Indigenous Language	37	-34	
Corporations			
Vale/Capita		29	
Number/Capita		60	

[1]Note that only significant correlations are shown.

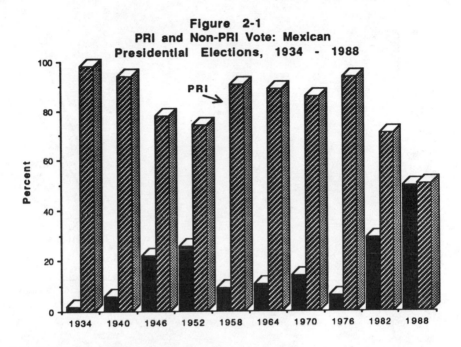

Figure 2-1
PRI and Non-PRI Vote: Mexican
Presidential Elections, 1934 - 1988

SOURCE: Fundación Javier Barros Sierra AC (1987)

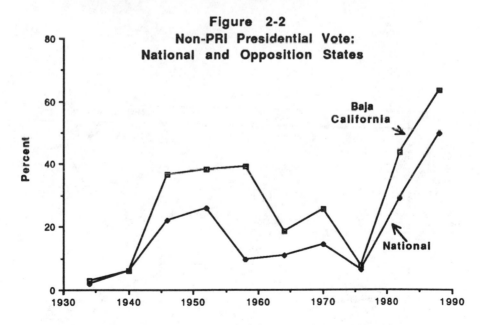

Figure 2-2
Non-PRI Presidential Vote:
National and Opposition States

Figure 2-2 (cont.)

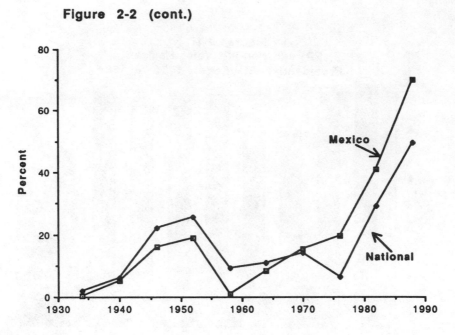

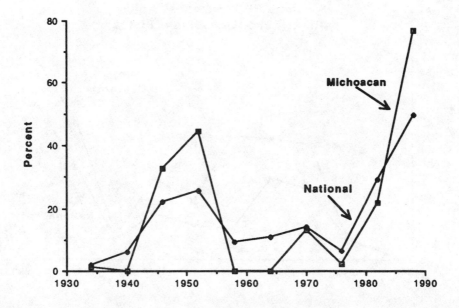

Figure 2-2 (cont.)

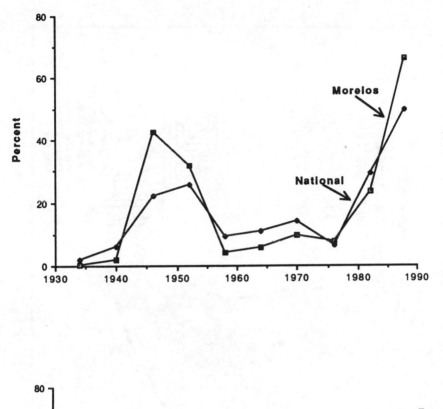

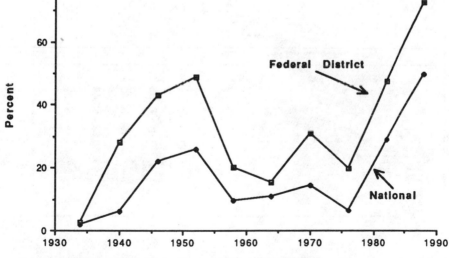

SOURCE: Fundación Javier Barros Sierra AC (1987)

38

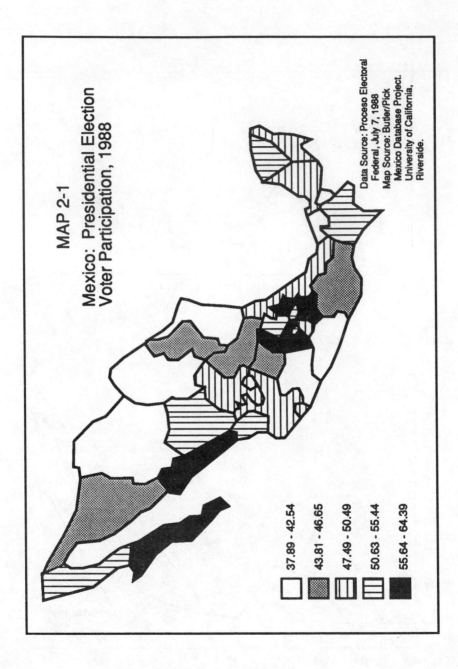

MAP 2-1

Mexico: Presidential Election
Voter Participation, 1988

37.89 - 42.54
43.81 - 46.65
47.49 - 50.49
50.63 - 55.44
55.64 - 64.39

Data Source: Proceso Electoral
Federal, July 7, 1988
Map Source: Butler/Pick
Mexico Database Project.
University of California,
Riverside.

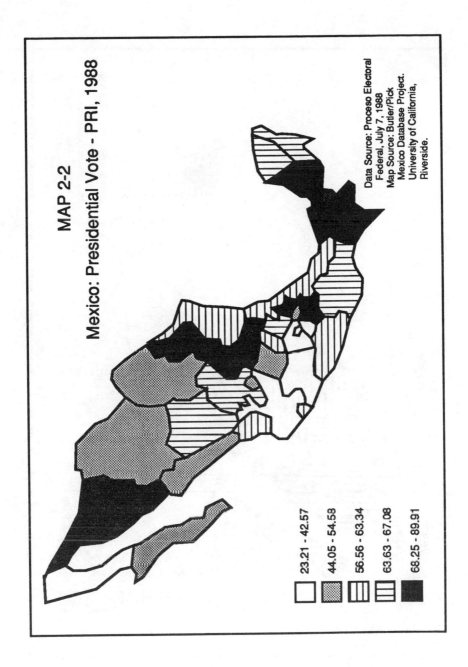

MAP 2-2

Mexico: Presidential Vote - PRI, 1988

23.21 - 42.57

44.05 - 54.58

56.56 - 63.34

63.63 - 67.08

68.25 - 89.91

Data Source: Proceso Electoral
Federal, July 7, 1988
Map Source: Butler/Pick
Mexico Database Project.
University of California,
Riverside.

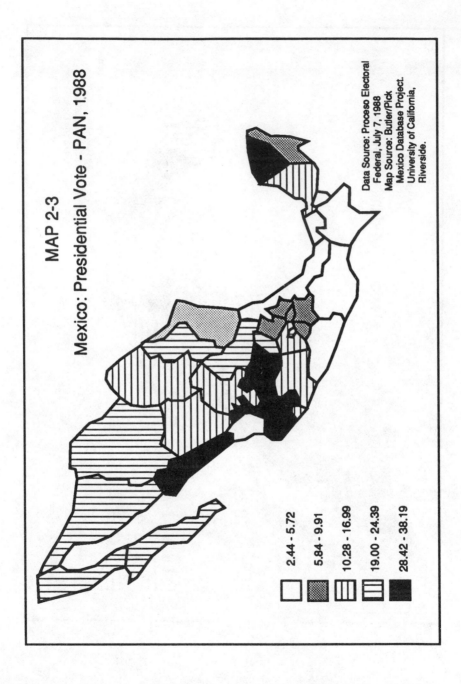

MAP 2-3

Mexico: Presidential Vote - PAN, 1988

Data Source: Proceso Electoral
Federal, July 7, 1988
Map Source: Butler/Pick
Mexico Database Project.
University of California,
Riverside.

2.44 - 5.72

5.84 - 9.91

10.28 - 16.99

19.00 - 24.39

28.42 - 38.19

MAP 2-4

Mexico: Presidential Vote - FDN, 1988

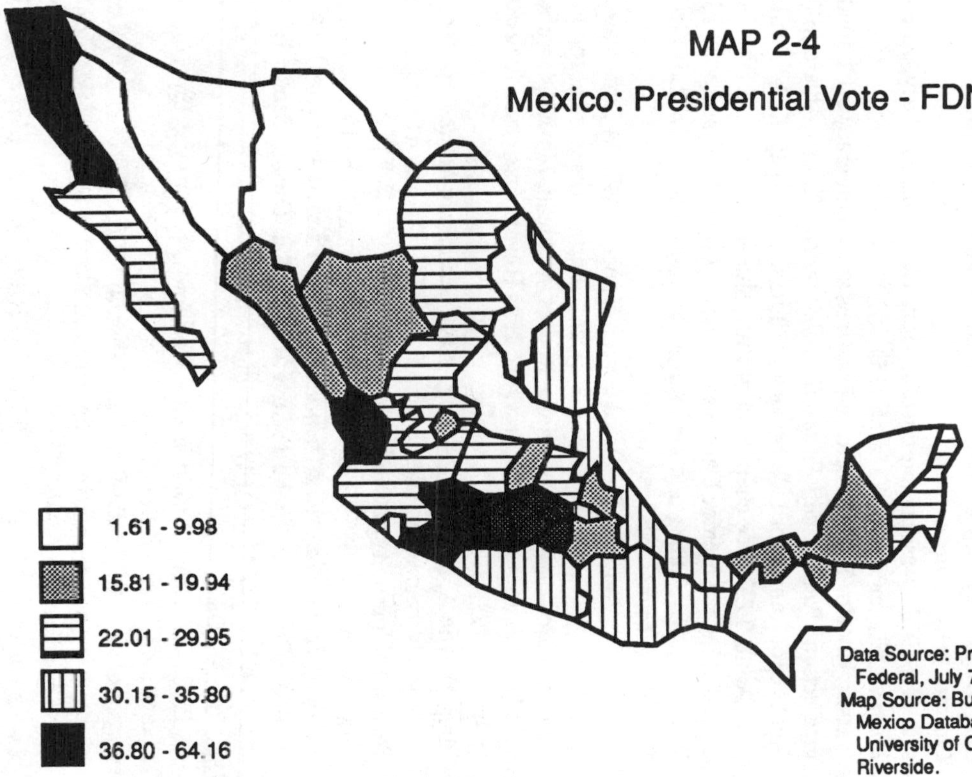

1.61 - 9.98
15.81 - 19.94
22.01 - 29.95
30.15 - 35.80
36.80 - 64.16

Data Source: Proceso Electoral
Federal, July 7, 1988
Map Source: Butler/Pick
Mexico Database Project.
University of California,
Riverside.

References

Alvarado, Arturo (ed.). 1987. *Electoral Patterns and Perspectives in Mexico.* San Diego: Center for U.S. - Mexican Studies, Monograph Series 22, University of California.

Ames, Barry. 1970. "Bases of Support for Mexico's Dominant Party," *American Political Science Review*, (March):153-167.

Aziz Nassif, Alberto. 1987. "Electoral Practices and Democracy in Chihuahua," in *Electoral Patterns and Perspectives in Mexico*, Arturo Alvarado (ed.). San Diego: Center for U.S.-Mexican Studies, University of California.

Baer, M. Delal. 1990. See chapter 11 of this volume.

Barberán, José, Cuauhtémoc Cárdenas, Adriana López Monjardín, and Jorge Zavala. 1988. *Radiografía del fraude.* Mexico: Colección: Los Grandes Problemas Nacionales.

Butler, Edgar W., James B. Pick, and Glenda Jones. 1988. "A Systematic Approach to a Database System on Mexico." Paper presented at the Pacific Coast Council on Latin American Studies, Mexicali, Mexico, October 22.

Butler, Edgar W., James B. Pick, and José Luis Reyna, *Presidential Succession in Mexico: 1934-1988*, forthcoming.

Cornelius, Wayne A. and Ann L. Craig. 1984. *Politics in Mexico: An Introduction and Overview.* San Diego: Center for U.S. - Mexican Studies, Reprint Series, 1, University of California.

Cornelius, Wayne A. 1986. "Political Liberalization and the 1985 Elections in Mexico," in *Elections and Democratization in Latin America, 1980-1985*, Paul W. Drake and Eduardo Silva (eds.). San Diego: Center for U.S.-Mexican Studies, University of California.

El Día, July 7, 1988.

ESRI. 1988. *ARC/INFO Version 4.0.* Redlands, California: Environmental Science Research Institute.

Estévez, Federico and Mario Ramírez Rancaño. 1985. "Leña de árbol caído: el cambio socioeconómico y la dirección del voto," *Estudios Políticos*, January-March, pp. 41-52.

Fernández Christlieb, Paulina and Octavio Rodríguez Araujo. 1986. *Elecciones y partidos en México.* Mexico: Ediciones El Caballito.

González Casanova, Pablo. 1985. "Palabras Preliminares," in *Las elecciones en México*, P. González Casanova (coord.). Mexico: Instituto de Investigaciones Sociales de la UNAM, Siglo XXI.

Guillén López, Tonatiuh. 1987. "Political Parties and Political Attitudes in Chihuahua," in *Electoral Patterns and Perspectives in Mexico*, Arturo Alvarado (ed). San Diego: Center for U.S. - Mexican Studies, University of California.

Hernández Hernández, Alberto. 1987. "Political Attitudes among Border Youth," in *Electoral Patterns and Perspectives in Mexico*, Arturo Alvarado (ed.). San Diego: Center for U.S. - Mexican Studies, University of California.

Klesner, Joseph L. 1987. "Changing Patterns of Electoral Participation and Official Party Support in Mexico." in *Mexican Politics in Transition*, Judith Gentleman (ed.). Boulder, Colorado: Westview Press.

Köppen, Elke. 1985. "Sobre la dificultad de estudiar las estadísticas electorales de 1982," in *Las elecciones en México: evolución y perspectivas*. Mexico: Siglo XXI, pp. 211-213.

Langley, Lester D. 1988. *MexAmerica: Two Countries, One Future*. New York: Crown Publishers.

Lehr, Volker G. 1985. "Modernización y movilización electoral: 1964-1976. Un estudio ecológico," *Estudios Políticos*, (January-March), pp. 54-61.

López, Arturo (Coordinator). 1988. *Geografía de las elecciones presidenciales de México, 1988*. Mexico: Fundación Arturo Rosenblueth.

López Moreno, Javier. 1987. *Elecciones de ayer y de mañana*. Mexico: Costa-Amic Editores, S.A.

Middlebrook, Kevin J. 1986. "Political Liberalization in an Authoritarian Regime: The Case of Mexico," in *Elections and Democratization in Latin America, 1980-1985*. Paul W. Drake and Eduardo Silva (eds.). San Diego: Center for U.S. - Mexican Studies, University of California.

Molinar Horcasitas, Juan. 1986. "The Mexican Electoral System: Continuity by Change," in *Elections and Democratization in Latin America, 1980-1985*, Paul W. Drake and Eduardo Silva (eds.). San Diego: Center for U.S.-Mexican Studies, University of California.

Oranday, Rogelio Ramos. 1985. "Oposición y abstencionismo en las elecciones presidenciales, 1964-1982," in *Las elecciones en México*, P. González Casanova (coord.). Mexico: Siglo XXI, pp. 163-194.

PAN. 1988. *Mitos y verdades de las elecciones presidenciales de 1988 y comentarios al proceso electoral federal de México de 1988*. Mexico: PAN.

Pick, James B., Edgar W. Butler, and Elizabeth Lanzer. 1989. *Atlas of Mexico*. Boulder, Colorado: Westview Press.

Ponce, Dolores G. and Antonio Alonso C. 1987. *Política interna: escenario tendencial*. Mexico: Centro de Estudios Prospectivos AC de la Fundación Javier Barros Sierra (Documento Preliminar).

Population Reference Bureau. 1987. *World Population Data Sheet*. Washington, D.C.: Population Reference Bureau.

44

Proceso Electoral Federal, July 7, 1988.

¿Qué Pasó? Elecciones 1988. 1988. Mexico: Editorial Diana.

Reyna, José Luis. 1987. "La estructura social mexicana: una aproximación global," unpublished paper.

Reyna, José Luis and Edgar W. Butler. Forthcoming, "The Political Transition in Mexico: Its Impact upon Mexico - U.S. Relations," in *Neighbors in Crisis*, Daniel G. Aldrich, Jr. and Lorenzo Meyer (eds.). Boulder, Colorado: Westview Press.

Rodríguez Araujo, Octavio. 1986. "Partidos políticos y elecciones en México, 1964 a 1985," in *Elecciones y partidos en México*, P. Fernández Christlieb and O. Rodríguez Araujo (eds.). Mexico: Ediciones El Caballito, pp. 145-213.

Walton, John and Joyce A. Sween. 1971. "Urbanization, Industrialization and Voting in Mexico: A Longitudinal Analysis of Official and Opposition Party Support," *Social Science Quarterly*, 52 (No.3): 721-745.

3

Political Change in the Mexico Borderlands[1]

By Edgar W. Butler[2]
James B. Pick[3]
Glenda Jones[4]

Introduction

As we have pointed out in chapter 2, prior to the Mexican presidential election of 1988 there was widespread discontent with the political process in Mexico. With the *Partido Acción Nacional* (PAN) on the "right" and the emergence of the *Frente Democrático Nacional* (FDN) on the center-left, virtually everyone knowledgeable about Mexico expected more formidable and real opposition to the dominant *Partido Revolucionario Institucional* (PRI) in the 1988 election than in any previous one. The increased intensity and success of the opposition in the 1988 election would set the stage for either the development

1 Without the contributions of Adalberto Aguirre, Eugenio Elorduy, José Luis Reyna, Rafael Segovia, Robert Singer, and Barnard Thompson this chapter could not have been completed. None of the above, however, is responsible for the analyses, interpretations, or conclusions of this chapter.

2 Edgar W. Butler is a former chair and currently professor of sociology at the University of California, Riverside. He is co-director of the UCR Database Project which is computerizing population and economic development data on the Mexican states and *municipios* for statistical analysis and geographic base mapping. He has co-authored a series of articles on fertility, migration, and various other aspects of Mexico and is co-author of the *Atlas of Mexico* (Westview Press).

3 James B. Pick is a lecturer in the Graduate School of Management and director of its Computing Facility at the University of California, Riverside. He has been involved in research projects on Mexican demography, including studies of fertility, migration, and population geography. He also does research on the management of information systems. He is a co-author of the *Atlas of Mexico* (Westview Press).

4 Glenda Jones is a Ph.D. candidate in the Department of Sociology, University of California, Riverside. Her research focus has been on fertility in Mexico and in the United States borderlands and on information systems as they apply to socio-demographic factors.

of a more pluralistic party structure and government in Mexico, or its opposite -- a more authoritarian regime (Reyna, 1987; Reyna and Butler, forthcoming; Baer, 1990). Of course, this conclusion may have been premature since there are other possible outcomes (Butler and Reyna, 1990). However, it is clear that a new course of electoral politics has been established in Mexico, one which holds vast implications for the country's future, its internal stability, and its relationship with the United States and other nations. The border states of Mexico, in particular, have been an area of political confrontation in the past. This chapter presents an analysis of official election results for the border region and each of the border states, evaluates the critiques of each state's official election results by the PAN and the FDN, and, finally, raises questions about the validity of the PAN and the FDN criteria for evaluating official election results.

Primary election data were derived from the following: (A) official election results obtained from several different sources (*Proceso...*, 1988; *El Día*, 1988; and *Proceso Electoral Federal* computer runs of July 13, 1988); (B) the July and August, 1988, post-election surveys carried out by the PAN (PAN, 1988); and (C) analyses of official election results accomplished by the FDN (Barberán, et al., 1988). Information from these sources was supplemented by data from the University of California, Riverside, Mexico Database Project. In addition, official voting district maps were consulted to determine boundaries of districts, their urban-rural composition, and other characteristics. This paper overcomes some deficiencies of past electoral studies in Mexico which either relied solely upon official election results or primarily upon a limited portion of the data offered by the opposition and/or by limited participant observation (R. Guadarrama, 1987: 53-54). Thus, data and viewpoints from all three major political parties in Mexico are incorporated into this chapter.

The Border Region

In the 1988 presidential election, all border states except Baja California had lower-than-national-average voter participation. Baja California had only a slightly higher than average turnout. As shown in Table 3-1, Baja California, with the highest voter turnout, had the lowest PRI vote among the border states. The vote by electoral districts for the six Mexican border states is shown on Maps 3-1 to 3-4. By a slight margin, Baja California gave a relative majority of its vote to the FDN and almost another quarter of its vote to the PAN. All of the other border states were above average in vote for the PRI. The FDN vote in Baja California approximated the national average for the FDN, but the additional large vote for the PAN ensured the FDN a relative majority in Baja California. The PAN received an average vote higher than the national average vote in four of the six border states: Baja California, Chihuahua, Nuevo León, and Sonora, with Coahuila being only slightly under the national average. Thus, only Tamaulipas in 1988 was not a substantially PAN-oriented state. In addition to Baja California, the FDN approximated the national average in Tamaulipas and Coahuila. At the district level in the borderlands, Salinas (PRI) won 29 districts, Cárdenas (FDN) carried three, and Clouthier (PAN) won only the Ciudad Juárez district. Subsequent sections of this chapter present a state-by-state comparison of official election results with the PAN post-election surveys and the FDN evaluation of official election results.

Baja California

As shown in Table 3-2, official election results for Baja California gave the PRI 36.7% of the vote, the PAN 24.4%, and the FDN 37.2%; thus, according to official election results, the FDN won the state by a small relative majority. In its analysis of Baja California, the FDN concluded that Baja California was one of the few states with accurate election results (Barberán, et al., 1988: 55). However, as shown in Table 3-2, if the PAN surveys are accepted as reflecting the actual vote, *the PRI won the state with a percentage of 34.2, the PAN had 32.5, and the FDN not only did not have a relative majority of the vote to win Baja California but in fact was the third-place party!* Thus, while the official vote was approximately two percent too high for the PRI, according to the PAN, the PRI still should have won the state because the FDN vote was over six percent higher than it should have been; the PAN argues that in both instances the overage for the PRI and FDN must have been taken from the PAN since the party's post-election surveys indicate PAN's vote was under-estimated by approximately eight percent.

If the PAN surveys are used as the criterion measure, official election results for the PRI in Baja California are substantially reflective of the actual vote cast. However, in that case, the PRI actually won the state by a relative majority. If the PAN surveys are taken as the criterion, the official PRI vote for Baja California was relatively accurate, whereas the PAN vote was under what it should have been, while the FDN vote was inflated by between seven to nine percent!

All in all, correspondence of the PAN surveys to the official PRI vote is rather remarkable given the charges of fraud and manipulation and possible sampling errors in the surveys. However, considering the closeness of the election and the discrepancy in votes between the PAN and the FDN, more detailed analysis of each district and *casilla*[5] in Baja California seems to be in order.

---

5 *Casillas* are much like precincts in the United States.

Coahuila

Official election results for Coahuila gave the PRI 54.3%, the PAN 15.3%, and the FDN 30.0%. The PAN survey results in Coahuila imply that the FDN official vote was reported accurately, while the PRI vote was about six or seven percent higher than it should have been, with the overage of PRI actually belonging to the PAN (see Table 3-2). In any case, the PRI won the state handily with a majority by official election results and with a relative majority by the PAN surveys. However, the FDN's analysis of the official vote in Coahuila implies that in fact the vote for the PRI in Coahuila was "threadbare" (Barberán, 1988: 50).

A closer examination, however, reveals that in fact the PAN surveys were carried out in only two of the four electoral districts in Coahuila -- Saltillo and Torreón. The official vote for these two districts parallels almost exactly survey results reported by the PAN. Thus, the PAN reports that the PRI should have received 46.9% of the vote, while the PRI vote actually recorded in the district was 46.4%; similarly, the PAN survey recorded 23.1% for its party while the official results were 23.6%. For the FDN vote, comparable figures were 29.3% for the PAN survey districts and 30.0% for the official election results. If these comparisons between the PAN surveys and official election results in the districts surveyed by the PAN are used as a guideline for the remainder of the state, then in fact official election results for Coahuila are reflective of the actual vote cast in that state.

Chihuahua[6]

Official election results for Chihuahua indicate that the PRI obtained 54.6% of the vote while the PAN and the FDN received 38.2% and 6.8%, respectively. At the state level, the PAN surveys indicate that the FDN vote was reported accurately but reduce the PRI vote from 54.6 % to 44.2 %. With this reduction and the increased vote of PAN from 38.2% to 49.0%, the PAN results indicate that it won the state instead of the PRI. This perhaps validates to some degree or another the opinion that "in Chihuahua, the PRI is the opposition" (see Aziz, 1987: 186). Also, these 1988 results generally parallel municipal and legislative votes in 1983 for the PRI but not for the PAN, and are more or less consistent with election results in 1985 for Federal Deputies.

A close inspection of the PAN surveys indicates that of the ten electoral districts in Chihuahua, only the four districts and/or cities of Chihuahua, Ciudad

_____

6 See Aziz (1987), Bath and Rodríguez (1988), and Guillén (1987) for an elaboration of earlier electoral results and political attitudes in Chihuahua.

Juárez, Camargo, and Delicias were surveyed. This is especially important since all of these areas historically have been strongholds of the PAN (see Martínez, 1987: 39; Guillén, 1987: 246), and the PAN won mayoralty races in these cities in 1983 (Bath and Rodríguez, 1988: 13). According to 1988 official election results, again these districts voted for the PAN candidate. However, it cannot be determined from the PAN report if all of the Camargo district, which includes Delicias, was surveyed, or if only the two cities were surveyed. In any case, a more valid comparison may be made between the PAN surveys and the official election results from the four districts in which the PAN carried out the surveys, rather than the entire state. In this comparison, the PRI officially received approximately three and one-half percent higher vote and the PAN about three percent less than reported by the PAN surveys. The FDN vote is quite close. The FDN's examination of official election statistics in Chihuahua demonstrated that the number of *casillas* with an extremely high percentage of PRI vote was very large.

Given the lack of knowledge about the extent of sampling in rural areas in the selected districts, we consider the official election results to be quite close to the actual vote cast. These results are not too far removed from recent polls conducted in Chihuahua City and Ciudad Juárez (see Guillén, 1987: 228).

Nuevo León[7]

A comparison of official election statistics for Nuevo León with the PAN survey results indicates great disparities. According to the PAN surveys, the PRI still won the state, but by a majority reduced from 72.1% to 51.7%. The PAN data suggests that the majority of this overage for the PRI was taken from the PAN vote, although the FDN vote also was somewhat under-reported.

However, as with several other border states, close inspection of the PAN surveys indicates that they did not interview in all electoral districts. In Nuevo León, the PAN surveys were conducted only in four of eleven electoral districts located in the greater Monterrey metropolitan zone, and in the Santa Catarina district. From the PAN report it is difficult to ascertain whether or not all areas in these districts were sampled. In addition, in the Santa Catarina district the PAN report indicates that surveys were carried out in Montemorelos, which contains only approximately 20% of the population of the Santa Catarina electoral district. Thus, two calculations were carried out for Nuevo León, one with

---

7 For a brief historical review, see G. Guadarrama (1987).

the four Monterrey districts and the Santa Catarina district which contains Montemorelos, and a second calculation excluding the Santa Catarina district.

Both of these calculations result in a higher percentage of official PRI vote than projected for these districts by the PAN surveys. This, in turn, means that the PAN vote was lower, as was the FDN vote. Excluding the Santa Catarina electoral district brought the two into closer alignment. However, the direction of the disparities remained consistent and fairly large. No definitive statement can be made about the lack of correspondence in these districts because of the unknown urban and rural sampling that took place in the state by the PAN. The FDN's analysis of the official election results in Nuevo León demonstrated that a large number of *casillas* had virtually 100 percent vote for the PRI.

Sonora[8]

As with Nuevo León, while the PRI won the state according to the PAN, it was by a relative majority rather than by an overwhelming majority; the PRI proportion vote was reduced from 68.6% to 42.4%. The PAN surveys increased their vote from 20.9% to 35.9% and the FDN vote from 10.6% to 19.7%.

According to the PAN report, however, their surveys were carried out in only three of seven electoral districts, primarily in the cities of Hermosillo, Guaymas, and Ciudad Obregón, all of which have been PAN centers in the past (R. Guadarrama, 1987). Results of the PAN surveys imply a substantial reduction in vote for the PRI and substantial increases in votes for the PAN and the FDN. However, the impact of possible selective sampling is important because of historical differentiation in the state (Pick, et al., 1989; G. Guadarrama, 1987: 84-85). Official results calculated for the surveyed districts are much closer to the official state results. Once again, the FDN is severely critical of official election results because of the large number of non-competitive *casillas*.

Tamaulipas[9]

Official election results for Tamaulipas gave the PRI a substantial majority; however, the PAN surveys again gave the PRI only a relative majority -- a reduction in vote from 59.2% to 41.6%. As in other states, the PAN reports that most of this overage was taken from the PAN rather than the FDN. As with Sonora, the discrepancies are large and in the direction of the PRI. The statewide com-

---

8 For a historical overview of elections in Sonora, see R. Guadarrama (1987).

9 For a review, see Salinas (1987).

parison, however, may not be valid since the PAN surveys were conducted in only three of the nine districts. However, the survey results for the three districts are almost exactly representative of the official state results.

Summary of the Comparison between Official Election Results and the PAN Surveys and the FDN Analysis

A summary of the PAN's surveys for the border states implies that the PRI won five of the six states, as did the official election results. However, the relative PRI vote in each state was less than the official results. While the PAN's surveys concede that the PRI did win five of the six border states, the identity of the non-PRI state is in contention, as is the winning party. Rather than the FDN winning Baja California, the PAN concludes that the PRI won Baja California and the PAN won Chihuahua! Thus, the overall conclusion that the PRI won five out of six states remains, but the PAN survey results have the PAN winning Chihuahua instead of the FDN winning Baja California.

While there were few percentage points difference between the PAN surveys and official results for the PRI in Baja California, it is quite intriguing that, while official results have the PRI losing the state to the FDN, the PAN results have the PRI winning the state and the FDN being the third-ranked party!

For four states, the FDN vote reported by the PAN substantially matched official results, but for Baja California official results were high enough over for that party to win the state, while in Sonora there was a substantial reduction in the official results according to the PAN surveys. The congruence between official results and the PAN surveys is closest in Baja California and Coahuila, with substantial similarities in Chihuahua. Results in Nuevo León are mixed. However, there is very little correspondence between official election results and the PAN surveys in Sonora and Tamaulipas.

The FDN was extremely critical of the official results in all states except Baja California. Of course, official results conclude that FDN won Baja California. But as noted above, the PAN surveys question this result.

A Critique of the PAN Surveys

Before the PAN survey results can be accepted, an evaluation of the sampling process must be made. The PAN surveys were carried out during July and August, 1988. The election, of course, took place in early July, 1988. The results of the two PAN surveys were substantially comparable. This is not unexpected, given sampling theory and the utilization of similar sampling frames. Nevertheless, given the problem of respondent recall, the similarity in results is truly remarkable. A more significant problem, however, is that the sample frames did not cover all 300 electoral districts. Most districts sampled were urban, and rural districts were neglected. This neglect is important because an overall analysis of official election results at the state level resulted in the conclusion that the PAN vote is primarily an urban vote, whereas the PRI vote is substantially higher in rural areas (see chapter 2). Finally, even in urban districts there are rural parts, and it cannot be determined from the PAN surveys whether or not rural sections of urban districts were sampled.

The impact of the sampling frame is illustrated by Coahuila, a state in which both the PAN and the FDN reported variation from official results. The PAN sampled only in the districts of Torreón and Saltillo. These urban districts are not necessarily representative of the other districts in Coahuila. Data presented in Table 3-2 for the Torreón and Saltillo districts contrasted official election information with the PAN survey results for these urban districts. In that analysis, official election results and the PAN surveys were almost exactly the same. Thus the comparison base in any evaluation of official election results must be carefully observed.

If survey results are compared to official election results in these specific districts, official election results and the PAN surveys are highly comparable, at least in some districts; in other districts there may be distinct and large differences. Unfortunately, both the similarities and differences may be due to the limitations of the survey sampling frames and/or the manipulation of the vote. Generally, until shown otherwise, we attribute the closeness of official election results and the surveys to legitimize official election results. On the other hand, where there are discrepancies we postpone a definitive decision until more is known of the actual sample frame design, and have more detailed information on each *casilla* in the districts.

A Critique of the FDN Statistical Analyses

The most puzzling analyses of official results are those carried out by the FDN. The analyses rely upon standard statistical notions and they have appeal because of their innovative nature. The FDN's analyses utilize official election results and make several assumptions about statistical distributions of voting results. At the state level it is difficult to ascertain actual vote percentages by party using the FDN analyses. Among the border states, the FDN reports that Baja California is the only one with accurate data.

One analysis carried out by the FDN assumed that digits (e.g., 0, 1, 2, . . . 9) in voting results for various *casillas* should be generally uniformly distributed within the numerical vote totals. In the FDN's zone of competition, the digits were substantially uniformly distributed. On the other hand, in the zone of noncompetition as defined by FDN, there was a substantial overage for the digit 0. The extent of the overage is shown by the appearance in vote tallies of each digit other than zero about 1,000 times, and the appearance of the digit zero about 1,500 times. Further, the zero typically occured in *casillas* (289 out of ca. 500) reporting 100% of the vote for the PRI (see Barberán et al., 1988:84).

Another approach by the FDN was to analyze the *casilla* vote in each state. The basic assumption was that there should be a normal distribution in the percentage of votes by *casilla* for each of the three main political parties. While the vote for each party would vary, each distribution should be a normal one. This was substantially the case only in Baja California among the border states. However, even in Baja California, as shown in Figure 3-1, both the PRI and FDN had elevated tails on the upper end of the distribution which results in a not quite normal distribution. As noted earlier, substantial variation exists in the other states. So the main question that remains to be answered is whether or not, in fact, the assumption of a normal distribution is a viable one for election results.

According to the FDN analysis, among the states with a "threadbare" vote for the PRI was the border state of Coahuila. Figure 3-2 illustrates the distribution of votes by *casilla* for Coahuila. The FDN argues that the vote in Coahuila was manipulated in favor of the PRI. This, so the argument goes, is shown by the lack of a normal distribution and the large number of *casillas* that voted virtually unanimously for the PRI. Obviously, the lack of a normal distribution is greater in Coahuila for the PRI than for the PAN and the FDN.

In Chihuahua, Nuevo León, Sonora, and Tamaulipas there is substantial departure in the normal distribution for the PRI, with some variation for the FDN, and somewhat less departure for the PAN. One possible explanation for these departures from a normal distribution may be the ability of the PRI to mobilize the rural vote, and in some cases to receive over 90% (Bath and Rodríguez, 1988: 11).

Conclusions

Undoubtedly one of the most important questions that can be asked regarding our analysis is to what extent it demonstrates fraud and/or manipulation of the vote during the 1988 Mexican presidential election. Unfortunately, before that question can be answered, another one must be asked. That is, are postelection surveys and/or analyses of the digits and/or normal distribution of votes by *casillas* viable criterion measures? In other words, can official election results be evaluated by these criterion measures? This is not an idle question; it gets to the heart of deciding whether or not fraud and/or manipulation occurred.

Currently we are not aware of any other research carrying out such an examination for elections in Mexico or elsewhere. This, then, results in a complete lack of knowledge regarding the assumptions made by the FDN in evaluating official election results. As a clearly secondary level of inquiry, several United States politicians and politically active persons were consulted regarding the question of fraud. All of them professed a lack of knowledge of actual election results in either Mexico or the United States in the context of these assumptions. None of them knew anything about the assumption of an equal distribution of digits, or of the expectation of a normal distribution of election results by district. The conclusion reached by these consulted individuals fell into the realm of guessing that it could be expected that a disproportionate number of precincts would have elevated higher percentages of votes for a particular candidate. This is the nature of the political game.

As a preliminary examination of this type, we examined precincts of a 1982 congressional election in southern California as a test case of the equal distribution of digits and of the normal distribution hypothesis. The results were different from the analysis carried out by the FDN in Mexico, but they did not support the FDN's assumptions. For example, in the California congressional district, there was not a uniform distribution of digits. The numbers with a greater proportion were not zeros as in Mexico but sixes, sevens, and eights; however, the magnitude of difference was similar to that in Mexico. Similarly, the analysis of the California congressional district, in a two-party rather than three-party system, resulted in a distribution somewhat like that shown for Coahuila but with a less marked tail at the upper end. So in general, the initial test of these assumptions in another political contest far removed from Mexico resulted in an indeterminate decision.

In conclusion, at this time we are unwilling to state categorically that fraud took place in the six border states of Mexico during the 1988 presidential election. If the PAN surveys are used as a criterion measure against which official election results are compared, at least in some districts the results are comparable. Interestingly, if these comparisons are valid, the FDN did not win with a relative majority in Baja California and the PRI did.

In any case we will now utilize the classic finishing line: This analysis clearly leaves us with more questions than answers, and more questions than we began with -- further research is clearly necessary (for a similar conclusion see R. Guadarrama, 1987: 63).

Table 3-1
Presidential Vote: Mexican Borderlands, 1988

State	PRI (%)	FDN (%)	PAN (%)	Voter Participation (%)
BAJA CALIFORNIA	36.7	37.2	24.4	50.6
COAHUILA	54.3	30.0	15.3	37.9
CHIHUAHUA	54.6	6.8	38.2	40.3
NUEVO LEON	72.1	3.8	23.7	46.7
SONORA	68.6	10.0	20.9	45.6
TAMAULIPAS	59.3	30.2	9.9	42.0
National	50.4	32.0	17.1	50.3

SOURCE: *Proceso Electoral Federal*, July 7, 1988.

Table 3-2
A Comparison of
Official Mexican Election Results with PAN Surveys,
1988 Presidential Election

State	Official Results (%)	PAN Surveys[1] (%)	PAN District Surveys[1] (%)
BAJA CALIFORNIA			
PRI	36.7	34.2	N/A
PAN	24.4	32.5	N/A
FDN	37.2	30.8	N/A
COAHUILA			
PRI	54.3	46.9	46.4
PAN	15.3	23.1	23.6
FDN	30.0	29.3	30.0
CHIHUAHUA			
PRI	54.6	44.2	47.9
PAN	38.2	49.0	45.7
FDN	6.8	6.0	6.4
NUEVO LEON[2]			
PRI	72.1	51.7	64.8/58.6
PAN	23.7	40.2	30.8/36.6
FDN	3.8	7.7	4.4/3.2
SONORA			
PRI	68.6	42.4	62.9
PAN	20.9	35.9	27.8
FDN	10.6	19.7	9.4
TAMAULIPAS			
PRI	59.2	41.6	59.6
PAN	9.9	24.3	11.1
FDN	30.2	33.9	29.4

[1]Mean values for the two PAN surveys.
[2]Two district figures are given (1) for the 4 Monterrey districts, and (2) for the 4 Monterrey districts minus the Santa Catarina district, as per text.

Figure 3-1
1988 Mexican Presidental Election
Voting Patterns by Casillas: Baja California

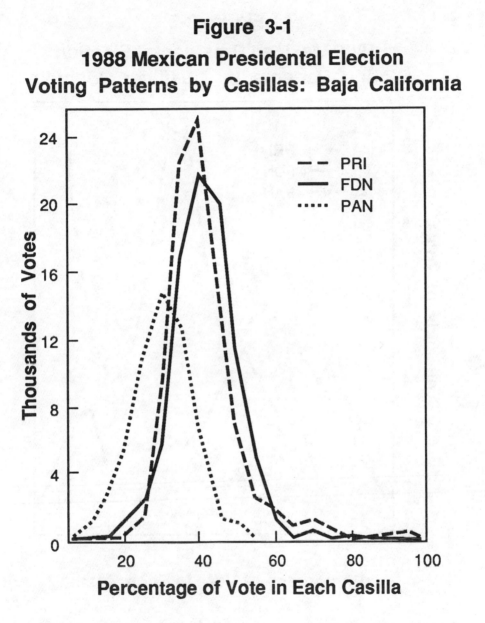

Source: Adapted from Barberán, et. al., 1988

Figure 3-2

1988 Mexican Presidental Election
Voting Patterns by Casillas: Coahuila

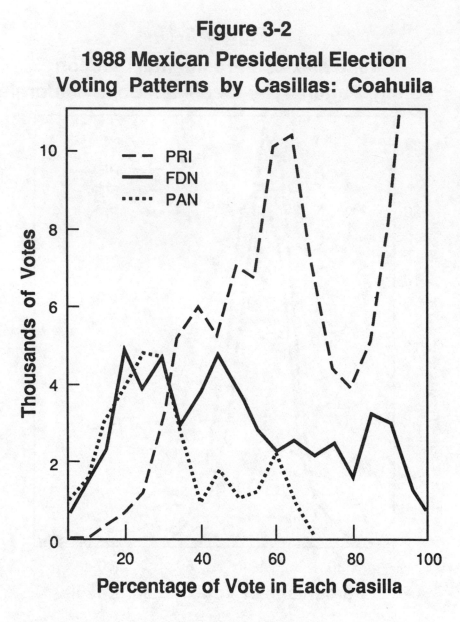

Source: Adapted from Barberán, et. al., 1988

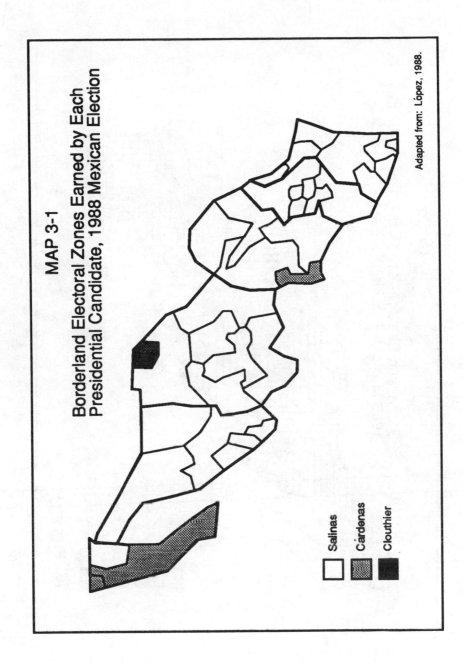

MAP 3-1

Borderland Electoral Zones Earned by Each
Presidential Candidate, 1988 Mexican Election

Salinas

Cárdenas

Clouthier

Adapted from: López, 1988.

60

MAP 3-2

Borderland Electoral Zones Won by Carlos Salinas,
1988 Mexican Presidential Election

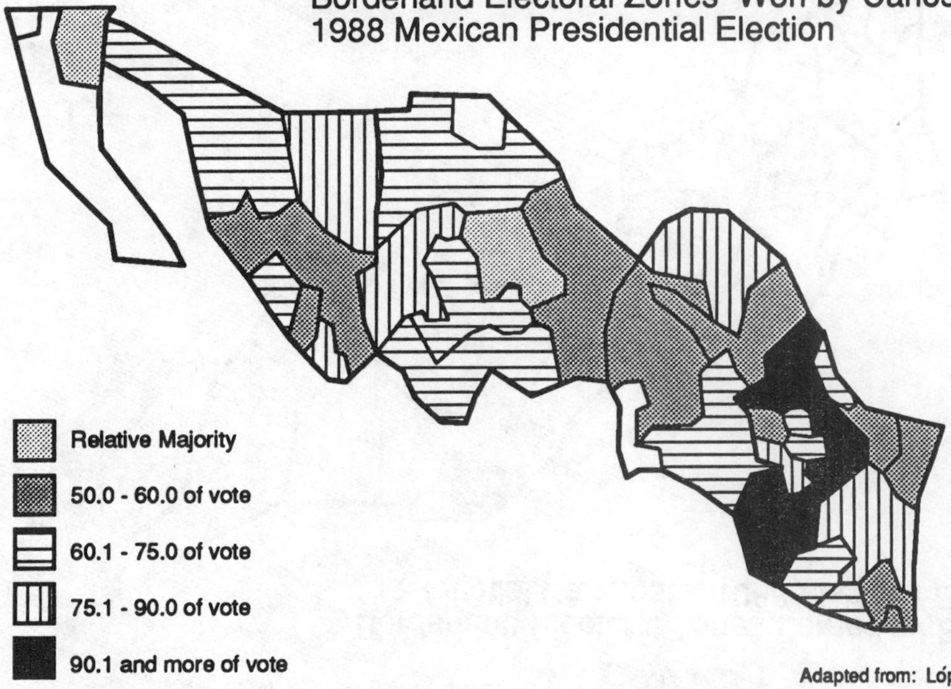

Relative Majority

50.0 - 60.0 of vote

60.1 - 75.0 of vote

75.1 - 90.0 of vote

90.1 and more of vote

Adapted from: López, 1988.

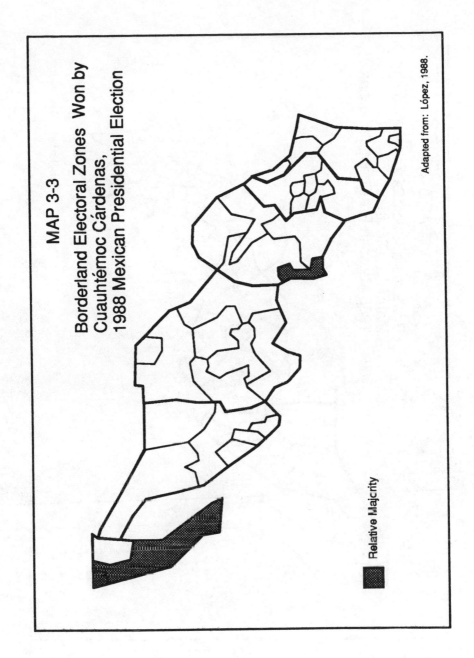

MAP 3-3

Borderland Electoral Zones Won by
Cuauhtémoc Cárdenas,
1988 Mexican Presidential Election

Relative Majority

Adapted from: López, 1988.

62

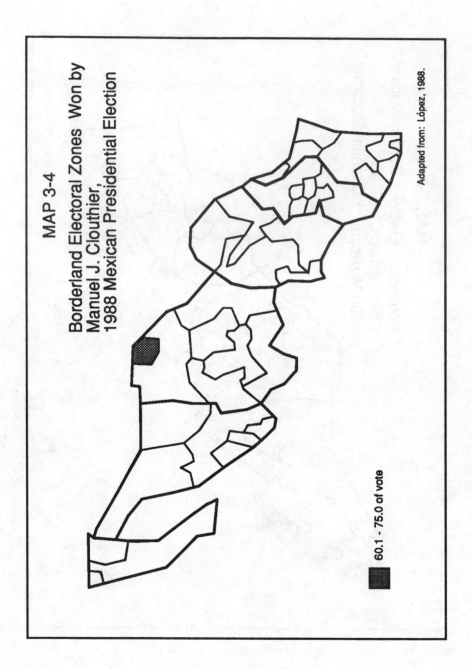

MAP 3-4

Borderland Electoral Zones Won by
Manuel J. Clouthier,
1988 Mexican Presidential Election

60.1 - 75.0 of vote

Adapted from: López, 1988.

References

Aziz Nassif, Alberto. 1987. "Electoral Practices and Democracy in Chihuahua, 1985," in *Electoral Patterns and Perspectives in Mexico*, Arturo Alvarado (ed.). San Diego: Center for U.S.-Mexican Studies, University of California.

Baer, M. Delal. 1990. See chapter 11 of this volume.

Barberán, José, Cuauhtémoc Cárdenas, Adriana López Monjardín, and Jorge Zavala. 1988. *Radiografía del fraude*. Mexico: Colección: Los Grandes Problemas Nacionales.

Bath, C. Richard and Victoria E. Rodríguez. 1988. "The *Partido Acción Nacional* in Chihuahua in the 1980s," paper presented at the Annual Meeting of the Association of Borderlands Scholars, Denver, Colorado.

Butler, Edgar W., and José Luis Reyna. 1990. See chapter 16 of this volume.

Butler, Edgar W., James B. Pick, and Glenda Jones. 1990. See chapter 2 of this volume.

Carreño Carlón, José. 1990. See chapter 12 of this volume.

El Día, July 7, 1988.

Gándara, José Antonio. 1990. See chapter 13 of this volume.

Guadarrama S., Graciela. 1987. "Businessmen in Electoral Contests in Sonora and Nuevo León, July 1985," in *Electoral Patterns and Perspectives in Mexico,* Arturo Alvarado (ed.). San Diego: Center for U.S.-Mexican Studics, University of California.

Guadarrama, Rocío. 1987. "Elections in Sonora," in *Electoral Patterns and Perspectives in Mexico*, Arturo Alvarado (ed.). San Diego: Center for U.S.-Mexican Studies, University of California.

Guillén López, Tonatiuh. 1987. "Political Parties and Political Attitudes in Chihuahua," in *Electoral Patterns and Perspectives in Mexico,* Arturo Alvarado (ed.). San Diego: Center for U.S.-Mexican Studies, University of California.

López, Arturo (Coordinator). 1988. *Geografía de las elecciones presidenciales de México, 1988.* Mexico: Fundación Arturo Rosenblueth.

Martínez Assad, Carlos. 1987. "State Elections in Mexico," in *Electoral Patterns and Perspectives in Mexico,* Arturo Alvarado (ed.). San Diego: Center for U.S.-Mexican Studies, University of California.

Oranday, Rogelio Ramos. 1985. "Oposición y abstencionismo en las elecciones presidenciales, 1964-1982," in *Las elecciones en México: evolución y perspectivas*. Mexico: Siglo XXI Editores, pp. 163-194.

64

PAN. 1988. *Mitos y verdades de las elecciones presidenciales de 1988 y comentarios al proceso electoral federal de México de 1988*. Mexico: PAN.

Pick, James B., Edgar W. Butler, and Elizabeth Lanzer. 1989. *Atlas of Mexico*. Boulder, Colorado: Westview Press.

Proceso Electoral Federal, July 7, 1988.

Proceso Electoral Federal, computer runs dated July 13, 1988.

¿Qué Pasó? Elecciones 1988. 1988. Mexico: Editorial Diana.

Reyna, José Luis. 1987. "La estructura social mexicana: una aproximación global," unpublished paper.

Reyna, José Luis and Edgar W. Butler. Forthcoming. "The Political Transition in Mexico: Its Impact upon Mexico - U.S. Relations," in *Neighbors in Crisis*, Daniel G. Aldrich, Jr. and Lorenzo Meyer (eds.). Boulder, Colorado: Westview Press.

Salinas Domínguez, Carlos F. 1987. "Tamaulipas: Mafias, Caciques, and Civic-Political Culture," in *Electoral Patterns and Perspectives in Mexico*, Arturo Alvarado (ed.). San Diego: Center for U.S.-Mexican Studies, University of California.

4

Modernization and Political Restoration

By Rafael Segovia[1]

It is difficult to determine at what point the change in Mexico's political development curve took place. To say 1968, or during the elections in Chihuahua of 1985, does not leave room for an explanation of the July 6, 1988, elections. The surprise generated by the election results, the consequences of the election (independent of elections that might occur in the near and distant future), and the confusion of leaders and parties all have contributed to the idea of a "new situation" -- that Mexico is facing an irreversible phenomenon. So as not to complicate this confusing scene even more, this chapter will concentrate on simple electoral facts.

The rise of opposition began in 1973, during the elections for the Chamber of Deputies. Votes for the National Action Party (PAN) appeared in cities with over 100,000 inhabitants and, of course, in the Federal District of Mexico. The leftist opposition, perhaps owing to election laws of that time, was almost non-existent insofar as numbers appearing in the returns. As for other parties, they were not able to capture any votes. The outcome, however, proved that opposition existed. Only future elections would tell whether the number of opposition votes would be maintained, decline, or grow.

The election of 1976, with one candidate, José López Portillo, gave cause for belief in an almost complete reversal. Not since the 1924 election of Obregón had there been an analogous situation. Fictitious or not, the majority had been the constant for forty years, while the PAN had been the "other can-

---

1 Rafael Segovia has been a professor and researcher at *El Colegio de México* since 1962. He has held the positions of editor of the magazine *Foro Internacional*, director of the *Centro Estudios Internacionales*, and General Academic Coordinator. He completed his postgraduate studies at the National Foundation of Political Science of France. He teaches various courses at *El Colegio de México* and at the *Universidad Nacional Autónoma de México*, and has published many articles in magazines and books about political reform. In 1975 he published his book, *La politización del niño mexicano*, and in 1987 he coauthored with Soledad Loaeza, *La vida política mexicana en la crisis*.

didate." This tradition crumbled, either as a result of problems internal to the PAN or the rigidity of the election code.

In regard to this turn of events, Jesús Reyes Heroles, Secretary of the Interior under José López Portillo, successfully undertook the creation of a new elections code: The Federal Law of Political Organizations and Electoral Processes. The spirit of the law was intended to circumscribe political problems within Parliament -- more specifically, within the Chamber of Deputies -- in order to remove political problems from the universities, the refuge of the left, as well as from the streets. To open the door to the left would mean having to come to an agreement with it, and, apart from what one would suppose, it was the rightists who capitalized upon this reform. In 1982, after the constitutional elections to renew federal powers, the PAN returned vigorous and with a new face -- neopanism. Its political aggressiveness and new program aimed toward the electoral ground signaled the alarm that became conflict in Chihuahua.

Two lessons can be inferred from the Chihuahua conflict: 1) The PAN maintained its regional character, but this regionalism appeared and became entrenched in Northern Mexico, where the most modern and developed Mexican states are located; and 2) the vote for the PAN was a vote for protest, as evidenced by its limited powers to mobilize after the elections. The Institutional Revolutionary Party's (PRI) real problems lay in areas apart from the elections, such as the foreign press's support of the PAN, the militant and combative position of the church, the deliberate silence on the part of and open censure of intellectual groups, and the constant public attention focused upon the election. For the first time, the PRI had to face a real danger able to spread across the country. If on top of all this economic crisis occurred, the situation could become a disaster.

President de la Madrid's response was to promise more open elections in 1988, a recurring theme in his political speeches during the last two years of his term. The 1986 Election Code, carefully read, was created so that the PRI could lose, or, more exactly, was created to minimize the PRI's losses, considered inevitable ever since that year. The changes paved the way to the PRI's limitation of itself.

PRI's Presidential Selection

In 1987, the PRI had to "disclose" its candidate. Breaking with party tradition, it did not wait until October to inform, through internal judgment, the lucky winner. It designated six "distinguished" PRI members and called upon them to appear in an unusual public conclave -- not before the National Executive Committee -- to expound upon possible programs for the government. This operation, supposedly democratic, consolidated the split within the PRI and confirmed political sides. Options and interests had to be made public: The party's fragile unity, threatened on the left by the rise of the Democratic Current, dissipated. The candidacy of Carlos Salinas, disputed until the very morning of the day of "disclosure," signaled discord. It was not pulled off with the customary unanimity. Not only did the left -- or presumed left -- of the party break away to establish a nucleus which in turn would join the *Cardenistas*, but the latent conflict between politicians and technocrats was brought to the surface.

In 1963, Raymond Vernon described an obvious split in the Mexican government, with an acuity unsurpassed to this day. The division resided in the conception and use of power to increase control throughout not only the government but also the whole political system. Vernon used the dominant political theory, modernization, to interpret his ideas. As Mexico became modernized, political roles concretized, society moved towards secularization, and the economy towards industrialization. Following this line of reasoning -- and everything appears to affirm it -- Mexico modernized. The presidencies of José López Portillo and De la Madrid were uncontestable triumphs of the technocracy that had reached heights unheard of before then. The men of the new and modern Mexico were economists and engineers -- in one word, the *technocrats* of Vernon. And following, on the other hand, Juan Linz and his theory about authoritarianism -- also used almost exclusively to explain the Mexican political system -- *the party* (read the PRI), by being the unnecessary part of the system -- as Peter Smith verified in *The Labyrinth of Power* (1979) -- became impoverished and ran the risk of disappearing: any path was better than the PRI if one wanted a political career.

While a political theory rarely predicts an absolute situation, it possesses the power to create an intellectual climate that spreads through the press, television, radio, and political science studies until it becomes a system of belief. This was the consequence in Mexico, so it seems, of these North American works -- at times simplified, at others acute and deep. They became a *self-fulfilling prophecy* accepted like cash by the interested party -- in this case, the politicians. Everyone else, appalled by the trends, had no need of the books either in English or Spanish but could simply observe the reality of daily political life. Technocracy had won the theoretical field and the journey.

The Campaign

In the electronic age, election campaigns of eight months are an anachronism and a nuisance. Candidates obligated to give fifteen-hundred speeches, no matter how short, end up only contradicting themselves and wearing themselves out. Their political goals become watered down, their platforms and programs weakened so that their pure physical image is juxtaposed to political intentions based merely upon rumor and supposition. No human or political attention is capable of lasting two-hundred days, especially when bombarded by the media. Hence, the reduction of political space in the world of political professionals. One may expect the most unforeseen results and the most crass ignorance. The role of the politicians, whose imagination is put to the service of conquest and the maintenance of power, becomes crucial. To think of political ends, to keep up an intellectual position in the face of political fact, may lead to absolute confusion and the most categorical errors; to reason by analogy results in errors. True, the intellectual always will come up with a reason for his mistakes to demonstrate that what he actually thought was right. "Perverse mistakes" do not exist for him.

Written documents intended for the parties' major reports and resulting from laborious study are, during the campaign, ignored when not despised. The least important party platforms prove this: Incoherent, scornful, and ignorant about the economy, so abundant with silences, omissions, and generalizations that even the press, radio and television will not report them. Only two or three key ideas -- the default on the debt and the reduction of presidential powers -- appear in program after program and determine the formation of blocs. Frank readings of the various platforms reveal certain intentions, such as the desire on the part of the Mexican Socialist Party (PMS), to eliminate enemies on the left or to establish a candidacy of unity -- the old and familiar demon of the Popular Front.

From the beginning of its campaign, the PRI imposed a strategy based on an erroneous reading of the social and political reality, although, in all fairness, the majority of those concerned made the same reading. The PRI was concerned most of all about the rise of a conservative, Catholic, non-partisan middle class that voted for the PAN in the absence of a more attractive political organization. Chihuahua seemed to confirm this worry. Before the passivity of worker and peasant groups -- the authentic vote -- the voter franchise in dispute was the urban middle class at which speeches were directed.

The theme centered around modernization. A society dominated by the middle class is always modern. However, before the presence of other classes, no matter how passive, this central theme had to be changed in order to cross class lines and to promote unity. Everything became modern, yet one decisive concept superseded the idea of modernization: The president of the Republic would not abandon a single one of his prerogatives -- one of the causes most sought by the opposition, as much the left as the right.

The four fundamental speeches about the future government of Carlos Salinas emphasized the central role of the State in the life of Mexico. It did not matter if another type of government were offered. Attention was fixed upon the central role of the State.

The opposition did not follow suit. Cuauhtémoc Cárdenas and Manuel Clouthier obscured, in fact ignored, the content of their programs and directed public attention primarily toward their own personalities, and only then to the battle against the PRI. With negativism and surprising undertones of utopia that at times merged on the ridiculous, they condemned the indefensible economic and social situation and so met with approval. They simplified critical issues to the point of exaggeration: Their future economic programs went no further than to default on the debt. Their anti-imperialist response was just a conditioned reflex. Clearly, the content of the programs took second place. Much more important were the moments, the times, the places where the programs were described. Under these conditions, the election, or, more properly the elections, became plebiscites.

Candidates for senator and deputy faded beside the five contenders for president, of which actually there were only three. Whenever a candidate for senator or deputy stood out, the result was only a backlash. Such was the case with Joaquín Gamboa Pascoe. Nominated by the PRI in the Federal District, he was dragged down by incalculable consequences. Other candidates were not seen as anything more than shapes in the background, without relief or profile.

The Parties

No democracy exists without parties. A great part of the confusion surrounding the July 6th elections arises from the historical lack of Mexican political parties. Sixty years of rule by the revolutionary party destroyed any initial constitutional intent for a party *system*.

Nevertheless, the original party organization, stronger on the right than on the left, made way for itself, thanks to what may be called an *awarded democracy*. Successive election codes, always restrictive, allowed for a limited electoral atmosphere in which they openly outlined the PAN. The impossibility of an open contest with equal conditions for the contenders, including even intellectual and ideological views, pushed the university groups -- center of political debate in Mexico, turf of Trotskyites and Stalinists, and focal point for other manifestations of socialism -- toward the left. These same conditions and consequences were present in the 1988 election.

The PAN was able to present a unified front with a candidate unquestionably from within and without, who, in spite of his violent and common tone, captured the imagination of the Mexican right, although the progress of the campaign made clear the natural and cultural incapability of Manuel Clouthier to govern the nation. But he fulfilled his campaign of protest, opposition, and negation in grand style. The PAN possessed characteristics of a tributary party; its presidential candidate was a champion of the people more popular than the left's candidate, quiet and restrained, distant and alone.

The heirs of anarchy, grouped behind the emblematic rooster of the Mexican Democratic Party (PDM), completed the group on the right. Excessively archaic, plagued by internal and personal quarrels, the PDM's ancient appeal in what were the *cristeras* zones was known to be in danger because of its principles.

The chapter about parties in the Mexican election code has always been ambiguous. The code calls for, on one hand, a tractable, predictable contest, and on the other, an open contest in which candidates show their true colors by way of debate and confrontation. For the PAN, the PDM was merely an annoying younger child; the proliferation of leftist political organizations was much more serious, and, for that reason, the settling of accounts more bloody.

Already the platform of the Mexican Socialist Party (PMS) asked for a higher election threshold. No doubt, such a pious intention had a name: The party asked for the liquidation of the Workers' Revolutionary Party -- refuge of Trotsky's followers. A party internally dominated by communists does not support socialist heretics anywhere, least of all to the right, and especially not when there is a question of a historical schism. The selection of the PMS candidate created one more internal conflict. Next to Cuauhtémoc Cárdenas and his initial triumphs, a candidate from PMS was going to carry little weight and the party could head straight for disaster if left stranded. The selection of Heberto Castillo by internal election went against the wishes of the party hard core. Castillo was too independent, his ideas excessively personal and he turned out to be too rigid to negotiate for a single, unified candidacy. It remains to be seen why traditional allies of the PRI -- Party of the Authentic Mexican Revolution (PARM), Socialist Workers' Party (PST), and Popular Socialist Party (PPS) -- left that coalition to unite themselves with Cárdenas's movement. One may suppose the reasons were the same as those which brought about the split within the PRI.

After sixty years of continual power, the political-electoral machine of the PRI became routine. The old professionals stayed chiefly on the sidelines. Carlos Salinas did not find, faced by criticism from the opposition, the fitting and requisite tone with which to speak to a country in crisis. Modernity and modernization sounded like a new form of austerity, or, even worse, a reaffirmation of the same. The opposition did not offer an economic program: It limited itself to negating the political economy of President de la Madrid's regime and criticizing the PRI's candidate, whose propositions they considered "more of the same."

The spread of propaganda, a neutral press, and television controlled by the PRI had a boomerang effect. On top of this, the electoral consequences of the Pact of Economic Solidarity and the stock market crash of October 1987 were catastrophic in the Federal District, or, more accurately, the Valley of Mexico, where the inhabitants had been the appeased victims of the government's economic policy.

Another trial for Carlos Salinas was not to break with his predecessor. Defending his own performance presented additional costs: Salinas was one of the authors of the economic policy, and by accepting a proportional responsibility he broke with tradition. Echeverría never hesitated to heap the blame for the repression of 1968 upon the shoulders of Dias Ordaz, launch a populist policy, and call upon the same youth that had been punished only months before. Political morality had nothing to do with bourgeois morality.

The Electoral Surprise

The battle for numbers, in the eyes of the public, still is undecided. While in the legal sphere there is no question as to who is the president of Mexico, the opposition will continue to agitate, perhaps for the next six years. The opposition wants to settle the conflict through the people, but the PRI intends to reduce it to terms of legal procedure. There never will be an absolute winner. All parties will lose in this confrontation.

The first great surprise was the new arrangement of the parties, which, for this precise case, are more aptly called movements. No longer is there the PRI-PAN dilemma, but a triangular conflict: center-left-right, in which the right, the historic, privileged and sole rival of the PRI, won a modest third place and was surpassed by a left that garnered double the votes of the right. The 31% obtained by the *Cardenistas* remains the mystery of the 1988 election.

Cuauhtémoc Cárdenas led a front, an unusual coalition of parties, a movement -- whatever is less than a party. He was not able, therefore, to achieve unity upon command or merely at will. In either case, even if he did not want to negotiate with his followers, he could not ignore their volition. The formation of the electoral party lists and the nomination of candidates were completely outrageous. For example, his faithful ally and *ame damnee*, Porfirio Muñoz Ledo, senatorial candidate in the Federal District, faced another candidate from the PMS who refused to withdraw from the list. It is not in this second level of senators and deputies where Cárdenas finds his strength, but in a personalized election, a plebiscite. Manuel Clouthier[2] will find himself in a similar situation: He will be the PAN. The other PAN candidates will count for little. The same situation, with few exceptions, will happen in the PRI.

In this occasion, the parties' machineries are going to demonstrate their strengths and weaknesses. The PRI crosses the entire country, from the *Bravo* to the *Suchiate*. It has the support of the federal government and the local governments, and, through radio and television, an unlimited logistic support. The middle ranks, on the other hand, stay with the party with great difficulty: In the Federal District, an alarming number of followers are defecting. Only in the rural areas does the PRI maintain an uncontested presence, but in some

---

2 This was written before Clouthier's death (editor's note).

hinders the machinery: President de la Madrid and candidate Carlos Salinas's desire, expressed on infinite occasions, to achieve "transparent" elections. The PRI will not conduct the traditional "operation"; they will deny preparing frauds. The PRI's conviction of being boss of the political scene, its faith in its historic missions, and a mistaken reading of the will and orientation of a very important part -- one half -- of the electorate, put it in a dangerous position on July 6th.

The composition of the *Cardenista* electorate is not even known. Only future studies will explain its distribution within Mexican society. For the moment, it is not possible to risk making hypotheses based on numbers too large to establish precise correlations. In spite of the lack of precision, one is able to say that the Cárdenas wins either were at the expense of the PRI or produced by voters who took refuge in abstention until 1988.

The electoral campaign of the Front moved with military precision. It made use of the principal points in the PRI and the PAN offensives and projected itself upon states with uncommitted voters: A strip of land from Veracruz to Guerrero, whose center is in the Valley of Mexico. With the notable exception of Baja California, the North turned its back upon Cárdenas while, for obvious reasons, Michoacán sided with the general's son. The followers of Cárdenas are as regionalized as were those of the PAN. Did they respond for the same reasons?

The results of July 6th were defined by the nature of the parties, but even more by switches among political personnel. Seeking more fruitful ground, the old allies and subordinates of the PRI went with arms and equipment to the opposition. Those that occupied the first files and seats in the proportional elections were all known names: There was Gotha from the old guard of the PRI. Others were allies, with rare exception. The most notorious exception was Heberto Castillo. An absolute opponent and prestigious writer, inflexible and apocalyptic in his stances, he tried unsuccessfully, and against the party nucleus, to win through an internal election the PMS candidacy for the Mexican presidency. The politicians, especially those from the old PCM, felt tempted from the beginning by a familiar demon -- the popular front. Three candidates from the left were enough and the PMS sacrificed its candidate in honor of unity. The remaining parties, sheltered by the name and figure of Cárdenas, defined their men more than their ideas.

From a strictly political point of view, the PMS was right: It was not facing a situation that might be able to change the "bourgeois morality." The interests of the most solid and consistent formation of the left, the possibility of abandoning the political and social ghetto where the left were contained, and, above all, the possibility of heading a coalition, federation or new fusion was too tempting. Heberto Castillo, from his splendid isolation, would not be able to counterbalance the decision of the oldest and best organized party in Mexico which boasted the most experienced politicians. The electoral results would only be disastrous.

Unlike the PMS, the old satellites of the PRI, frightened all the way to election day, considered the election figures of July 6th a relief and tidings of undreamed of possibilities. They were a divine surprise. The other side of the coin was the perpetuation of the leadership of those parties. First, they had never been truly autonomous: Their decisions, or pseudo-decisions, depended as much upon the will as the economic support of the government. Second, they lacked real parliamentary experience. Third, the interests of those parties were not distinguishable from those of their leaders. The consequence of this situation will be a future at times comical, at others intolerable.

The PAN committed different mistakes. Handing the candidacy to Manuel Clouthier implied a break with a tradition of respectability and formalism, the "decency" that so seduces the PAN voter. It also meant that the party would be represented to the public by a single idea, whereas the PAN has always been a strict party, arranged hierarchically, respectful of the direction of the group, the majority and collective decisions. In sum, by avoiding the spiritual violence of neopanism, they were swamped in programmatic confusion and a verbosity repellent to the typical PAN voter.

The old guard -- Vicencio Tovar, González Hinojosa, Bátiz and other politicians -- surrounded in the conflicts and debates, were not able to contain or direct the PAN. The announcement of a possible cabinet, composed largely of men who did not belong to the PAN (they offered Rosario Ibarra the position of *ombudsman* or *ombudswoman*!) ended up by disconcerting loyal members. The charismatic leader was placed above the professional -- although it is true that in the PAN ranks there are few professionals -- above those who have a solid political formation acquired among the people, the committees, the press, and books. The group was possessed by an uncontainable desire to speak, and the repetition and contradiction led to boredom. Certainly, more than one speaker made his audience yawn.

The record of De la Madrid's presidential term pushed the PRI into a defensive position. A truly threatening opposition, for the first time in the PRI's history, and above all, the crisis that permeated the country, did not auger well for a triumphant campaign. Carlos Salinas sought a rational tone; his fundamental speeches were read, his most important declarations were made during press conferences; he never let anyone speak for him. He placed his political future in four speeches based on the idea of modernity and modernization, from which he drew his economic, not political, program; to declare the PRI a central progressive party was the same as acknowledging the defection of the left within the government party. The rightists in the PRI were enchanted, the remainder of the liberal wings, less so; the authoritarianism of the brotherhood, resting upon a base becoming more and more reticent, felt that its candidate had ceded everything. That base, on the other hand, believed its luck abandoned to a future in which it trusted little.

An Electoral Disaster?

Accustomed for more than sixty years to winning by 70-99% majorities, the PRI experienced the tremendous surprise of finding itself with less than 51% of the vote. Another surprise was the candidates' winning order, which altered the outcome even further. The fact of Cuauhtémoc Cárdenas's coming in ten points ahead of Manuel Clouthier introduced into Mexican politics unheard of elements. Or, more correctly, it introduced something new and unwanted: The electorate.

The opposition vote, be it left or right, rises above the candidates and parties and is, above all, a vote of protest, a vote against the PRI, and in this case, a vote of punishment. The flimsiness, if not the internal contradiction or absolute vagueness, of the programs, platforms and listed parties, permits the supposition that the orientation of the citizens' vote -- when not a captive vote -- answers to motivations foreign to doctrinaire positions. This phenomenon can be observed in the PAN victories: The PAN has a tradition behind it and a presence in the public mind. It is, along with the PRI, the only party identifiable by the electorate, including children and adolescents. What caused its retrogression, even among its bulwark of voters?

On July 6th, the electorate showed an instability most notable among the urban vote. The majority of cities were divided as to the opposition vote, giving the prize to *Cardenismo* and abandoning PAN where least expected, such as in Nuevo León. The experience showed the PAN's inability to mobilize its voters. Only a portion of the truly faithful followed the slogans and advice -- the PAN rarely gives orders. And the agitation in the streets, going against the PAN's spirit and principles, was followed enthusiastically merely by this handful of the convinced. When expressed, the protest was individual, reasoned, and always within the limits of sacrifice.

Neopanism changed the PAN's conduct. Populism, agitation, and the taking to the streets and plazas only came after Clouthier. The tone of the speeches also was different. The change in political style was superimposed upon the debates and even the internal conflict. More than a democratic posture internal to the life of the party, the electorate saw populism among the right, a belated agitation and hesitation in the face of power. More people belonged to a traditional right than would deny it. Within a nation and political system in which the right had become discredited during the past century and burdened by all the sins of this century, there remained in 1988 the possibilities that, in principle, the right hoped would turn into political and electoral facts. If, with its name, its progressive and generous image, its asphalt politics and tradition of fight and sacrifice (the PCM always has paid for the consequences of social movements), *Cardenismo* is about popular agitation, then it beat the PAN to the punch. The dubious past of party bosses who forced the coalition, the non-existence of programs and the internal and external vendettas did not matter. Resentment and personal interest were forgotten before one of the indisputable heroes of the Mexican Revolution. The symbol, the great saint created by official history, was abducted and he changed sides. That which had been nothing but an inherited *Cardenismo* converted, in public opinion, into a *Cardenismo* for the here and now. The blocs of the political parties and the parapolitical organizations accomplished the rest. The supposedly loyal vote fell into the hands of the dissidents.

The change in orientation by 30% of the voters and the rise of abstentionists become participants did not materialize only through sage and calculated maneuvers in the major political states or because of national symbols. An unending economic crisis, and instability that engendered intolerable quotas, the inexplicable stock market crash, the dismissal of bureaucrats, inflation, and the wage freeze made protest inevitable. The Valley of Mexico, victim of all this, and almost sole headquarters -- Mecca -- of all the parties, fell, as if a ripe fruit, to the side of the opposition. The disaster was near absolute for the PRI in this region; only one district in the city of Mexico remained with the PRI. Only one. The fall of the PRI was cushioned by its control of the rural vote, the only true union, and by the PAN/FCRN (*Partido del Frente Cardenista de Reconstrucción Nacional*) rivalry.

The Protest

Let an example suffice. The PPS saw its votes rise from one election to the next by 680%, an almost unthinkable situation in a stable political system. The composition of this party, the lack of a solid, permanent framework and the lack of militants placed it in a situation, as much within the Federal Electoral Commission as the Electoral College, which it had neither the means nor the manpower to resolve. The same may be said of the other *Cardenista* parties, with the exception of the PMS and, partially, of the PFCRN.

The Federal Elections Code, approved in 1986, had two political objectives: 1) To keep the verification of the elections in the hands of the PRI and 2) to limit this party's losses. It was a law focusing on past inconsistencies and election results which should have been rejected by force because of those very inconsistencies. To establish the simple majority in the Chamber of Deputies ensures the PRI's privileged position, a privilege that would have multiplied had it been faced with a series of smaller parties and not two blocs. All in all, the gain of 200 for the opposition across the proportional elections satisfied the wishes of the parties. The liquidation of the PRT, openly asked for by the PMS, and the PAN's costly wish for the liquidation of the PMS, raised no more protests than those of the interested parties.

The disunity within the opposition and the inconsistency of the Federal Elections Code and the Electoral College resulted in more strength than hoped for. The PRI lacked persuasiveness in the debate and so accepted a simple majority. The major portion of the opposition's protests revolved around appeals to the principles of political philosophy, the spirit of the law, and the principle of equality. Thus, the letter of the law was imposed.

For the first time since General Henríquez had sought the presidency, popular manifestations and the press reflected the protest. *Cardenista* demonstrators, en masse, crushed the members of the PRI and the PAN who abandoned the physical public space. This was nothing but one more feature of the open battle to win public opinion.

One of the inexplicable points of the election on July 6th is the defeat of the PRI in the camp of credibility, popular sympathy, and public opinion throughout numerous states in the Republic. Unexpectedly, television proved to be ineffectual. The press in Mexico scarcely covers the national elites. The reaction against television demonstrated by the opposition cannot even now be satisfactorily explained. In any case, television's fall to the daily press and the rise of *La Jornada*, an impartial organ open to the opposition, revealed the problem of credibility in other dailies and weeklies.

As popular as the feature writers, editorialists, chroniclers and followers sympathetic to Cuauhtémoc Cárdenas were, the printed media did not create the climate of opinion. There were unexpected channels of communication that supplemented the formal channels. From now on, it will not be possible to lose sight of, or even less ignore, the politicization of some cities. And the politicization worked against the PRI.

What Lies Ahead?

The difference between the current protest and those led by Almazán and General Henríquez is not by degree but by its very nature. It would be difficult to prove that the undeniable popularity of Cuauhtémoc Cárdenas and Manuel Clouthier was the base and motor for the disunity. As indispensable as ever, the parties fulfilled a lesser role, especially on the right. The new actor was -- will be -- the urban voter, freed from partisan and ideological bonds, moderately informed and possessing objections, and still to realize its political will. Hence, its link with the charismatic leader -- today, popularity is confused with charisma. Divisions marked by class, group or regional interests are not defined, and, of course, in no way correspond with vague and confused party lines. If the PRI, in spite of its defensive situation, commands a formidable machine, the opposition, with the exception of the PAN, exists immersed in an incomprehensible magma.

To the left there is one figure, that of Cuauhtémoc Cárdenas. But he is a politician about whom the parties, anxious to preserve their unexpected victories and to increase their successes in every region if feasible, are doubtful. The calls for unity, for a federation of all the parties, for the abandonment of the PMS, are seen not only with fear, but are openly rejected. Disunity and the latent breach, soon to become open, rule the day. Lack of confidence defines the left, which, nevertheless, knows its only possibility of parliamentary continuity and political presence lies with Cárdenas. Once more it runs toward the precipice without troubling itself about anything more than three years of the current legislature.

In the foreseeable future, the principal function of the PAN is to assimilate and analyze its retrogression. Having incurred this retreat in the populist sphere had advantages. For the first time, the PAN encountered its true, popular opposite. The drawbacks were major, when seen clearly. Clouthier turned out to be excessive and even exaggerated for the PAN arena. Perhaps not for the voter. And here lies the dilemma of this party.

The protests of the PAN's candidate, aimed at the masses, contrast with the political caution and parliamentary posts of "his" deputies. The test of modernity and of assimilation into a democracy more European than North American will come from these differences between parliamentary, directive, affiliated, supporter and voter groups. Together, these groups will have to decide who is the true leader of the PAN. The party has, at this moment, the advantage of knowing how to quiet its differences and avoid a public debate in which outsiders intervene.

The fear on the part of a diffuse and abstract left, as it appears with Cárdenas, is one more lifesaver for the PAN. Mexican society on the right has exhibited more fear of the left than willingness to reject the PRI. Any notion of a union between left and right is impossible under current circumstances. In the face of the disassembling of the left -- origin of ineffectuality -- the protesting voter will look again towards the PAN, if he does not, once more, take refuge in abstention. For the opposition, the Congress of the Union will be the *aqua regia*.

Reference

Smith, Peter H. 1979. *Labyrinths of Power: Political Recruitment in Twentieth-Century Mexico*. Princeton, N.J.: Princeton University Press.

5

Mexican Policy and Its Implications for United States- Mexico Relations

By Tonatiuh Guillén López[1]

Introduction

Relations between Mexico and the United States have had a significant historical importance, which greatly explains both countries' present situations. These relations are asymmetric, due to unequal development. The greatest impact of the bilateral relationship has been felt by Mexico, which has had to define, especially with respect to the United States, its individuality as a nation on the basis of that impact.

Both countries recently went through a common phase in their political cycle -- presidential elections, in which many of the compromises and relations between society and its government are renewed. However the similarities end there. The particularities of this juncture have radically different meanings in each country. In Mexico, the present situation will have long-term effects due to the fact that the current repetition of the six year ritual coincides with the process of establishing -- or rather, attempting to establish -- a new political structure. Unlike in the United States, in Mexico it is more than a matter of presidential succession and reaffirmation of an already established political system. On the contrary, Mexicans are debating the definition of new rules of

---

1 Tonatiuh Guillén López; is a chair of the Department of Public Administration at *El Colegio de la Frontera Norte* (COLEF) in Tijuana. His recent sociological research concerns ideology and politics in the northern border region, and some of his results have been published in COLEF's *Cuadernos de Trabajo*. A recent article appears in *Estudios Sociológicos*.

government, and the construction of a new political structure. This debate has not been exhausted by the 1988 electoral process.

Under the new conditions, Mexico's national policy defines the limits and duration of the process of national change, which is regarded as a departure from the country's history. In the search for alternative solutions to national problems, the recent presidential succession has expanded Mexico's political horizon. Among the issues susceptible to change is Mexico's international policy, particularly with respect to the United States. In this sense, Mexico's national policy and the course it might follow are the best parameters within which to approach the question of future bilateral relations between Mexico and the United States.

It would be convenient to explain that I assume the Mexican perspective, although I do not disregard the fact that the United States also will adopt its own national and international policy, and this in turn will influence to some extent the terms of the current in Mexico. For the time being, however, the United States perspective with regard to what is happening in Mexico and the actions that might be derived from such a perspective are beyond the scope of this chapter. From the wide range of relations between Mexico and the United States I will consider only those closely related with the economic program of the De la Madrid six-year presidential term which ended in 1988.

National Policy and Mexico's Relations with the United States

Out of the complex universe of United States-Mexico relations, those pertaining to economic matters have been the most impacted by changes. The economic policy implemented by Miguel de la Madrid's administration has incorporated a large number of changes into the relations between the nations.

The presence of the international market has been a high priority as part of the "structural change" strategy of Mexican economics. In the past few years the Mexican economy has become more open to direct foreign investment, and this has translated into Mexico's adherence to the General Accord on Trade and Tariffs (GATT). The international market now represents about 65%[2] of

---

2 Taking into account indicators for international trade in 1987, 65% of the total exports went to the United States, and a comparable percentage of imports came from the United States. Regarding direct foreign investment, a similar percentage is of North American origin.

Mexico's market. The economic policy of Mexico's recent past and, potentially, of the Salinas administration involves an ever growing relationship between both Mexican and North American economies, although the long-term drawback of losing some independence has been recognized.[3]

On the other hand, just as the economic program put into practice by Miguel de la Madrid's administration redefined Mexico's international relations, it has also led to significant transformations in national policy. It was precisely during the recent electoral campaign that the future of Mexico's political system and, at the same time, the future of the country's economy were debated.

Not withstanding the promised long-term benefits, the government's response to the economic crisis during the De la Madrid administration resulted in drastic reductions in the purchasing power of the working class. Although the political effects of the economic crisis were latent during the 1983-1986 period, they became radically evident during 1988. The main political force with the capacity to utilize the critical potential that was latent for years was the *Frente Democrático Nacional* (FDN). Contrary to the democratization of the political system which achieved some moderate success, the FDN deemed social struggle as it concerns a more even distribution of wealth as a higher priority than the liberalization of the political system. The FDN economic policy became the fundamental thesis around which diverse tendencies -- from extreme left to moderate and right wing but all opposed to the government's economic program -- converged. The extraordinary force generated by the FDN during the electoral process made the demand for democracy a fundamental issue. The FDN maintained and also expressed its critical attitude towards economic policy and its commitment to the Mexican State's revolutionary tradition.

Within this national and external context, the economic "structural change" program has established an intense link between national and international policy, and between Mexico's national policy and its relations with the United States. Economic policy has been essential in the formulation of national policy, as has Mexico's relation with the United States. As a result of these links, the perspectives for a satisfactory bilateral relationship with the United States are directly involved in the future of Mexico's economic policy.

The structural change policy implemented by De la Madrid's administration has no parallel with past administrations. It has set precedents that reach further than United States-Mexico relations, encompassing the most important na-

---

3 In a recent session at the Board of Advisors of the Bank of Mexico on International Trade, De la Madrid stated that "it is not in Mexico's interest for its economy and foreign trade to depend so excessively on the United States" (*La Jornada*, July 26, 1988, p. 18).

tional issues. In particular, it tends to redefine the government's relation with the economy and social classes. These changes are vital in the history of contemporary Mexico and have been hastened and made more complex by recent political events. I now will focus attention on a subordinate but at the same time essential aspect of this process: Mexico's relationship with its neighbor to the north.

The Leading Actors and Their Respective Positions

With respect to United States-Mexico relations, it must be acknowledged that the fundamental changes have taken place already, as implicated in the economic program of the present administration. Therefore, the question of continuity and the possible risks facing the administration permeate the bilateral atmosphere. And it is not because these changes were designed with the United States solely in mind or under guidelines set outside of Mexico.[4] The link was established in an implicit manner due to the importance of Mexico's economic relations with the United States. As the Mexican economy's participation in the international market changed progressively, so United States-Mexico relations were modified. The steps taken towards making Mexico more accessible to direct foreign investment take on particular significance as well as the country's adherence to GATT, and the veering of the economy into the control of private capital.

In fact, the "structural change" policy has as its main goal a stronger link to the world market, which means a stronger bond with the United States economy. Leaving aside the logic of economic analysis (which is measured with variables of an identical nature), political indexes define the importance of economic changes brought on by the present government. From this perspective, the discourse which has been part of the conflict between the *neocardenistas* and the government, as well as the attitudes that other important sectors have assumed with respect to the present economic policy are proof of the importance of the "structural change," both nationally and in the area of Mexico's international

---

4 Although international pressures should not be discarded, especially those attributable to the foreign debt and its negotiation, where the influence of the creditor banks and organizations such as the IMF are considerable.

relations. Below is a description of the attitudes prevalent in the United States and Mexico.

The United States Perspective

A major part of the external context is the concern of the government and private sector in the United States with respect to the continuity of the economic program established by President de la Madrid. The new director of the State Department's Mexican Affairs, with a few legislators, expressed his desire that Mexico continue with the economic strategy designed by the De la Madrid administration.[5] In the same vein, the now former United States ambassador to Mexico, Charles J. Pilliod, forecasted an increase of foreign investment in Mexico.[6] David Rockefeller, in his capacity as head of America's Council, visited President de la Madrid whom he congratulated for his economic policy, and especially for Mexico's becoming a member of the GATT and its flexibility with foreign investment.[7]

The De la Madrid government received a great amount of attention in the United States. This is true in spite of the fact that in other areas there is still serious friction in bilateral relations, such as drug trafficking and the Mexican attitude towards Central America. In the economic field, on the other hand, the consensus in the United States seems to demand the continuity and broadening of the course that has been set. Extremely optimistic positions that favor the program are nothing more than an extension of the United States

---

5 Those who participated in the reunion included, among others, the director of Mexican Affairs of the State Department, John St. John, and two members of the House of Representatives, the Republican from Arizona Jim Kolbe and the Democrat from Texas, Ronald Coleman (*La Jornada*, July 9, 1988, pp. 36 and 14).

6 *La Jornada*, July 28, 1988, pp. 1 and 8; and *La Jornada*, August 3, 1988, p. 5.

7 *La Jornada*, September 21, 1988, pp.1 and 28.

model in Mexico which was proposed some time ago as a solution to its financial difficulties.[8]

It is clear that among the current problems that most concern the United States in its relationship with Mexico is the continuation of the current economic policy. The presidential succession in Mexico and the strengthening of the opposition parties has cast shadows over my expectations; I shall try to define their magnitude.

The Business Perspective

Positions on the De la Madrid economic program are sharply contrasted in the interior of Mexico. The business sector has supported the general thrust of the regime's economic policy. Its criticism has been for not fully carrying out the program, especially as it concerns the economic contraction of the government. There are some differences concerning foreign trade as expressed by the industrial sector that has not been able to take advantage of commercial opportunities and which demands a slower pace.[9] In spite of these differences -- and these are not the only differences with the government -- the dominant position within the private sector has been not to question the general thrust of the official economic program, especially when it is compared with the last months of the previous administration.

At the end of the De la Madrid administration, the private sector's position concerning the Mexican government changed from angry criticism -- after the experience of the nationalization of the banks in 1982 -- to a conciliatory stance, which encourages the continuation of the program undertaken by De la Madrid. Mexico is far from embracing an extreme economic policy, such as the nationalization of the banks in 1982 which was "a definitive coup against the ac-

8 This is according to a recent report on Mexico of the Counsel for Hemispheric Affairs (*La Jornada*, August 6, 1988, pp. 11). In the same vein, an analysis of the Mexican elections which appeared in the *Washington Post*, signed by Stephen S. Rosenfeld, points out that the economic policy of De la Madrid was directed by Reagan. "This pains the Mexicans, whose extreme nationalism has been hurt (necessarily and inevitably) by the structural reforms that were promoted by the government of President Reagan when he helped Mexico manage its debts after 1982" (*Excélsior*, July 16, 1988, p. 28 [from the *Washington Post*]).

9 The president of the CONCAMIN, Vicente H. Bortoni, has asked De la Madrid to slow down the pace of economic liberalization. "This policy, which may be useful in conjunctural contexts, must be revised very soon. Industry cannot continue to function under these conditions for much longer" (*La Jornada*, September 15, 1988, p. 6).

tivities of the private sector and a clear signal that the country was entering socialism."[10] The private sector's most recent declarations emphasize the adequacy of the government's economic program and demand its continuation in the Salinas administration. For example, the president of COPARMEX, Bernardo Ardavín, considered it fundamental that the Salinas government "goes deeper into and accelerates the process of privatization of the economy" and that it avoids at the same time the growth of the social sector.[11] Several others have come forward following the same logic of support for the "reprivatization." Among them, are the president of CONCAMIN, Vicente H. Bortoni,[12] as well as José María Valverde, president of CANACO in Mexico City, who "congratulated the Mexican government for having set aside slowly the growing interventionist economic policy." He also pointed out that "the reprivatization of the Mexican economy stands out as praiseworthy."[13]

The Perspective of the Frente Democrático Nacional

The main organized opposition to the current economic program and, consequently, to the current state of affairs with the United States, is the FDN.[14] If the FDN is considered as an offshoot of the Democratic Current (*Corriente Democrática*) of the PRI, the decisive importance of economic policy in the political movement can be appreciated. The first formal step in the formation of the *Corriente Democrática* was the so called "First Working Paper," signed by a larger number of members than any communiqué since. This paper was a synthesis of the criticisms of the economic program of the De la Madrid government. It specified the following: "We are alarmed by the progressive foreign dependency, the tendencies that lead to the dismantling of the industrial base, the reversal of the nationalization of the economy and the decapitalization of

---

10 Statement by Manuel J. Clouthier, then president of the *Consejo Coordinador Empresarial* (*Excélsior*, September 3, 1982, p. 21).

11 *La Jornada*, August 13, 1987, pp. 1 and 16.

12 *Excélsior*, July 16, 1988, pp. 1 and 10.

13 He participated in a reunion of the International Council of the Chamber of Commerce which took place in Turkey (*La Jornada*, September 21, 1988, pp. 1 and 28).

14 This is not to say that this is the only point of contradiction of the FDN with the governing bureaucracy. It is important to make clear that in the FDN's conflict with the political bureaucracy there exist more important issues than those regarding bilateral relations with the United States; however, here I focus my analysis on the relationship with that country.

the country, as well as the exorbitant interest rates that choke the public treasury, concentrate the income and discourage the productive impulses by giving preference to speculation."[15]

Within the institutional arenas of political action characterized by the possibility of influencing the economic policy of the country, the FDN was not able -- or was not allowed -- to obtain sufficient positions in the government, neither in the presidential election, nor for senators and representatives. Its possibilities are reduced even more if we consider that the strength that the opposition parties had acquired by joining forces in 1988 tended to disintegrate in economic discussions. The PAN party may play a central role here, taking into account that its social project is closer to that of the federal government than the *Cardenismo* of the FDN.

Although the Chamber of Deputies is going to be the principal institutional place for the debate concerning economic policy, the FDN does not have enough deputies to impose its social project. It is possible that its greatest strength resides in the diffusion of its critique, which will accent its nationalist tone in proportion to the internationalization of the Mexican economy. The means of mass communication could become its most powerful ally, exerting more strength than the votes it obtained in 1988, although insufficient in face of the state's power. Outside of the space of governmental positions -- even within the institutionalized means -- the mobilization of the masses is one of the FDN's alternatives. However, in the short run the results seem to be limited to winning positions in local governments, and that is a far cry from influencing economic policy. In these conditions, it is most likely that the new opportunity for the FDN to change the central aspect of economic policy should wait until the next legislative election in 1991, which will take place in a very different political environment.

The appearance of the *Corriente Democrática* was justified precisely from the instant the economic budget proposal of the De la Madrid government was rejected. The main demand of the *Corriente* was a change in the economic policy direction.[16] When the demand was transformed into an internal opposition, outside the unwritten rule of the party which threatened to challenge those in power, the *Corriente* reduced its original members. Due to a different reason, the majority aligned themselves with the "party discipline," although they maintained their differences. An interesting case is that of the CTM; although it

15 "Working Paper Number One," in Cuauhtémoc Cárdenas, et. al., *Corriente Democrática. Alternativa frente a la crisis.* Mexico, Costa Amic Editores, 1987, p. 9. It was signed by César Buenrostro, Cuauhtémoc Cárdenas, Leonel Durán, Vicente Fuentes Díaz, Armando Labra, Severo López Mestre, Ifigenia Martínez, Janitzio Múgica, Porfirio Muñoz Ledo, and Carlos Tello.

16 Octavio Paz strongly criticized them ("Historias de ayer. Ante un presente incierto," *La Jornada*, August 11, 1988, pp. 1 and 12).

never sympathized with the *Corriente*, when Carlos Salinas's presidential candidacy was anounced, the CTM asked him, through the Labor Congress, to change the country's economic policy (*La Jornada*, October 7, 1987, pp. 1 and 12). This statement did not contain anything new: From very distinct forums and sectors of society involving both popular organizations as well as academic analysis, the government's economic program had been the object of strong criticism. The uniqueness of the *Corriente Democrática* was that the criticism took place inside the official party at the leadership level. This broad criticism, both inside and outside the PRI, is precisely what permitted the formation of the FDN.

The formation of the FDN as the main opposition force to a regime that has sustained itself for decades as the absolutely dominant power should be analyzed from a broad perspective. The essence of the FDN's proposal lies in its social aspect and its ability to call people together. Even if the FDN has not been formalized in a program,[17] it neverthless exists. Even with its lack of definition, there is no doubt that this opposition movement against the government and the official party follows *Cardenista* ideology; however it should be clarified that it did not take this form due to the leadership of the son of Lázaro Cárdenas. The FDN was a viable movement whose representative at that time was its leader Cuauhtémoc Cárdenas.

By inverting the sequence in the relation between the leader and the social aspect of the movement, the latter emphasizes its content which was most essential within the country's political tradition to confront the economic program of the De la Madrid administration. The point is not to minimize the importance of the leadership of Cuauhtémoc Cárdenas, which was indispensable in explaining the broad ability of the FDN to pull people together. However, for the moment, it is necessary to deal more with the ideological content of the movement and less with its social strength.

Briefly, if *Cardenismo* can be revitalized today and used as the ideology of a broad opposition movement, it is because of the economic policy applied during the De la Madrid administration. During this time, the political tradition of the revolutionary swung to an opposite extreme position. The importance of considering the ideological horizon of the FDN is that it permits us to highlight

---

17 The *Cardenista* form of the FDN also is due to the genesis of the *Corriente Democrática*, that is born as a division of the political bureaucracy. The origin of the movement, that in the beginning tried to be an integral part of the governing group, did not break with it; it tried to remain within the political tradition of the Mexican Revolution. In this way, the ideological spectrum was limited for the *Corriente* from the beginning, and had to find within it a representative who would express its project. *Cardenismo* was appropriate as the period in which the identities of the Revolution's ideals and governmental policy were most similar.

its ability to contradict totally the economic policy inaugurated by the De la Madrid government.

With respect to this objective, *Cardenismo*, as the dominant ideology of the FDN, has the capacity to oppose frontally measures such as the growing presence of foreign investment and the opening of the national market, which in turn have been defined as the main changes in Mexico's relations with the United States. Another aspect of *Cardenismo* is its extensive popular support as shown by large public meetings called by the FDN and, above all, by electoral results.

Contrary to the other main opposition party, the PAN, which concentrates its criticism on the antidemocratic features of the political system, the *Cardenista* ideology extends its range to economic policy, in particular to the instruments the government uses to determine the direction of economic development. Regarding the thesis of economic set-back, *Cardenismo* emphasizes the thesis of governmental intervention; opposing opening the market to foreign investment, it stresses nationalism; and it supports the protection of national industry. The *neocardenista* ideology and movement thus have been converted into the principal obstacle to the extension of the economic program of "structural change" and, consequently, to the increasing integration of the Mexican economy with that of the United States. By contrast, the PAN opposition -- even more now with the control of the *neopanista* faction -- generally agrees with the strategy of the economic restructuring and public financing undertaken during the De la Madrid administration. As opposed to control by the FDN, political control by the PAN would not represent a substantial change in current bilateral relations with the United States. The proposal of the FDN, in contrast to the concern expressed by the national businessmen and by representatives of United States interests, opposes the proposal of continuing with the economic development program initiated by the De la Madrid administration.

Taking into account the political attitudes it has generated, the economic program set forth by De la Madrid indeed initiated a new period in Mexico's national economy and policy. The program's original proposal for "structural change" has been put into practice consistently. The first steps have been taken to break the link between government and the economy, and with it -- although we should evaluate to what extent -- the foregoing relation between government and social classes. At the same time, the economic program has redefined the relation between Mexico's national economy and the world market of goods and capital, redesigning Mexico's economic relations with the United States.

The main fault, however, of the modernization and structural change project is that it lacks the support of a social movement. This project has failed to generate a positive consensus; on the contrary, it has generated a negative one which expressed itself in the 1988 presidential election. On this matter the analysis made by Héctor Aguilar Camín is very clear: "Under the shelter of the

Cardenista convergence, the July elections have raised questions with respect to the path to modernization that the present administration has followed and they urge we turn to the past -- a populist inefficient past that is however seen as better than the present -- in search of a way that is not so far removed from the country's traditions and history as that initiated in the 80's with the economy and government's readjustment."[18]

The same opinion has been expressed in the words of eight Mexican intellectuals with respect to the electoral experience: "Mexicans voted and in fact we have kept on voting since the sixth of July in favor of democracy. We could also perceive a demand that had remained under control and therefore manifested itself in a novel way. It was a demand in view of the uneasiness caused by the recent economic policy, and in favor of a credible and lasting opening of the political system."[19] In view of the lack of a social base to serve as support -- with the exception of the business sector -- the origin of the modernization proposal seems due in great part more to the schedule the external debt has imposed on the government than to any other determining factors.

The result of the confrontation between the FDN and the elite of the political bureaucracy will undoubtedly be reflected in the economic policy that the Salinas de Gortari administration will undertake. In the meantime, Salinas has made public his interest in continuing, in a broader sense, the path set by the government of Miguel de la Madrid. This means establishing a continuity of the economic relations with the United States which generated much interest among United States representatives as well as Mexico's business sector. Now the question is what are the chances for success in establishing that continuity, as these changes are now equivalent to the FDN's force.

The Continuity Thesis and Its Perspectives

Carlos Salinas de Gortari, Mexico's new president, has been associated by his backers and detractors with the continuity of Miguel de la Madrid's economic program.[20] An abstraction of the PRI's answer to the future Mexico-United States economic relation is quite clear: More of the same, with respect

18 See Héctor Aguilar Camín, "La reforma de los electores." *Cuaderno de Nexos*, in *Nexos*, No. 128, 1988, p. X.

19 See Rolando Cordera Campos, Arnaldo Córdova, Gilberto Guevara Niebla, Pablo Pascual Moncayo, Adolfo Sánchez Rebolledo, Raúl Trejo Delarbre, Arturo Whaley Martínez, José Woldenberg, in "Para una transición democrática," *Perfil de La Jornada*, August 28, 1988.

20 In spite of the fact that in the same moment, as an emerging candidate for the presidency in search of his own political personality, Carlos Salinas declared that he had no commitment to continuity. "I am not committed to continuity, except that which strengthens the fundamental principles of Mexican society" (*La Jornada*, January 8, 1988, pp. 1 and 6).

to what has been established in the past six years. In particular there is an expectation of an increasing integration into the world market. The main characteristics of this integration would be a greater opening to direct foreign investment and the liberalization of international trade. The presidentialist structure of the political system would favor the continuity of this development model.

However, after the 1988 federal elections the presidentialist structure is lacking its former style. With such a fundamental deficiency the road to continuity for the economic policy is not an easy one: The forces the policy has generated now constitute its greatest obstacle. Thus, at the initial stages of the new administration there was a growing debate centered on economic policy and the changes that can be introduced in it -- as it cannot remain indifferent to the new social forces arising in the country. There are several factors that must be considered. The first, of course, is the political force of the contenders; the second, the hierarchy indicating which elements of the policy are subject to negotiation and which are not. Below is a review of the second factor.

The economic program of the Salinas administration, as described by Carlos Salinas during his presidential campaign, consists in a broadening of the path followed by the De la Madrid government. Although the Salinas program has been advertised as a new economic development model, its basic foundations had already been laid.[21] Direct foreign investment is still a priority, as well as the "reprivatization" of the public sector. The main objective of the economic proposal consists in increasing the economy's exporting capacity, especially in the manufacturing branch, which is where foreign investment is concentrated.

The determining characteristics of the economic policy -- inasmuch as they constitute the basic characteristics of the administration -- probably are not subject to negotiation. Salinas does not intend to give up these characteristics, just as he did not give up political control in those instances where it was subject to debate. There are certain aspects of the economic policy that Salinas will not modify no matter how hard the FDN presses for changes. Any changes that could take place will depend on the FDN's being able to assume political control of the country. In this classification are found those aspects involved in the economy's and the government's own "structural changes." These aspects have in fact been deemed irreversible by Carlos Salinas. This involves a redefinition of the public sector and the decentralization of economic activities. The open-

---

21 Textually, "A new strategy of modern economic development." Carlos Salinas de Gortari, *El reto económico: crecimiento sin inflación y con equidad.* Mexico: Partido Revolucionario Institucional, 1988, p. 7.

ing to foreign investment includes international trade as well as direct foreign investment.[22]

In this way, the most important changes introduced by the De la Madrid administration in the relationship between Mexico and the United States administration maintain their priority within the economic strategy of the new administration. This is not to say they will be carried out without difficulty, but they are not under negotiation with the FDN; they can be imposed more easily than they can be agreed upon. They could only be altered by political changes within the country and these are not occuring at the moment.

On the other hand, there are certain aspects of economic policy that have been openly subject to debate, with some restrictions.[23] Among them are those related to the foreign debt, as alternatives can be proposed short of a direct confrontation with Mexico's creditors. There is also the question of extreme poverty which has become worse in the last six years. However, these aspects are not an essential part of the new economic development strategy. The foreign debt, which is the major obstacle confronting economic growth, is essential to economic policy. A reduction in foreign debt would be the greatest help that the Salinas administration's economic policy could receive, but it is clear that the policy's implementation does not depend upon such a reduction.[24]

The first factor on which the economic policy changes depend is the relation of strength of the contenders which can be evaluated by taking into consideration the 1988 electoral experience. In the first place, although certain advances were made toward democratization that even established limits to presidential absolutism, political power did not change hands. The notable changes in the distribution of governing positions, particularly within the Chamber of Deputies, did not reduce the government's capacity to impose its decisions in the long run. That is the way it has been during the entire electoral process. Political bureaucracy is still the dominant force in the country; it has yielded certain spaces within the government's structure, but it has maintained a limit which allows for its own reproduction.

Along the same line as what happened during the electoral process, the political bureaucracy can set the general terms of economic policy, its "irreversible" elements. The presence of the PAN in the Chamber of Deputies and its agreement on the general terms of the economic policy could be the instance that gives legitimacy to these decisions, even with the FDN's opposition. With respect to the negotiable aspects of the economic program, even if the govern-

---

22 See footnote 21, p. 14.

23 *La Jornada*, September 13, 1988, pp. 1 and 6.

24 It could be said that between the foreign debt and the policy of structural change there exists an inverse relationship: The greater the weight of the debt, the more insistence there is to take this path.

ment obtained results contrary to its expectations, it would regain in the political arena what it lost in the economic.

The immediate possibilities of the FDN are limited to participation in the secondary features of the economic policy that might include problems with far reaching effects for the country. Among them is the foreign debt, on which the FDN agrees with the government in the search for alternatives to reduce it. Paradoxically, if this goal were achieved it would strengthen the economic program's possibilities for success. Even more, a successful renegotiation of the foreign debt could be presented as a nationalist aspect of the government's modernization project, counteracting the criticism it has received in this respect.

On the other hand, although the solution to the foreign debt problem is not essential in carrying out the economic program of the Carlos Salinas administration, it is essential to achieve its economic growth goals and an increase in the population's income. Up to now the economic policy during the period of crisis has not generated social consensus, but quite the contrary. This is where the elements of international policy might exert some influence, in particular the attitude of the United States government if it considers it in its best interest to help promote a solution to Mexico's foreign debt problem. The travels abroad of the PRI Secretary General Manuel Camacho, tended towards a solution along these lines, as he has expounded in several forums the important role that the reduction of Mexico's foreign debt might play in the Salinas administration's economic policy and its main problem, lack of consensus.

In conclusion, even if the FDN should continue to increase its capacity to call people together it has limited power to modify the central aspects of the Salinas administration's economic policy.[25] In terms of United States-Mexico relations, this means a period of at least three years for the government to establish the continuity of the De la Madrid program; this might set a factual precedent that may be even harder to revoke. The assumption is that the political debate in Mexico will remain, with its ups and downs, within institutional channels.

In relation to the overall view that has been presented in this chapter, the immediate future of bilateral relations between Mexico and the United States might be characterized as follows: An even greater economic integration, through trade and foreign investment, which might mean a greater dependence on the part of Mexico. With respect to Mexican national politics, the FDN and the ways it manifests itself will remain the essence of nationalism, preparing the circumstances for the 1991 electoral confrontation.

---

25 That begins to meet its limits, like the failed attempt to transform the FDN into a single party.

References

Aguilar Camín, Héctor. 1988. "La reforma de los electores." *Cuaderno de Nexos*, in *Nexos*, No. 128.

Butler, Edgar W., James B. Pick and Glenda Jones. 1990. See chapter 2 of this volume.

Cárdenas, Cuauhtémoc, et. al. 1987. *Corriente Democrática. Alternativa frente a la crisis*. Mexico: Costa Amic Editores.

Cordera Campos, Rolando, Arnaldo Córdova, Gilberto Guevara Niebla, Pablo Pascual Moncayo, Adolfo Sánchez Rebolledo, Raúl Trejo Delarbre, Arturo Whaley Martínez, José Woldenberg. 1988. "Para una transición democrática." *Perfil de La Jornada*, August 28.

Excélsior. 1982. September 3.

Excélsior. 1988. July 16.

Guillén López, Tonatiuh. 1989. "La cultura política y la elección presidencial de 1988: hacia un análisis del neocardenismo," *Frontera Norte*, No. 1, El Colegio de la Frontera Norte.

La Jornada. 1988. January 8; July 9; July 26; July 28; August 3, 11, 13; September 13, 21.

Paz, Octavio. 1988. "Historias de ayer. Ante un presente incierto," *La Jornada*, August 11, pp. 1 and 12.

Salinas de Gortari, Carlos. 1988. *El reto económico: crecimiento sin inflación y con equidad*. Mexico, Partido Revolucionario Institucional.

Washington Post. 1988. July 16.

6

Mexico's 1988 Elections, A Turning Point for Its Political Development and Foreign Relations?

By Roderic Ai Camp[1]

Introduction

Mexico's 1988 presidential elections mark a turning point in the fortunes of the Institutional Revolutionary Party (PRI), the governing elite, the political opposition, and the electoral process. Heavy United States media coverage of the July elections popularized a number of general assertions about Mexico's political process and the history of the governing party. These assertions, while truthful as far as they go, have not accurately portrayed historical trends in the Mexican electoral process, and unfortunately, they have tended to focus on Mexican political behavior as a unified entity, rather than as many Mexicos.

The election results not only imply many consequences for Mexico's political development, but they have important implications for Mexican-United States relations. However, it is important to emphasize that the results themselves, and how they are interpreted by government officials in the United States, are not the sole source of influential consequences. A clearer understanding of historical trends, and differences among all Mexican voters, clarifies some misperceptions which many observers in the United States share.

In the first place, although there is no doubt that the 1988 election represents a landmark in the Mexican electoral process, the distribution of votes and

---

1 Roderic Ai Camp is chair of the Latin American Studies Program at Central University of Iowa and contributing editor on Mexico to the Library of Congress' *Handbook of Latin American Studies*. He has carried out field research in Mexico for two decades and has studied Mexican politics under the auspices of numerous fellowships. He has published many articles and ten books on Mexican politics, including his novel, *Memoirs of a Mexican Politician*. An examination of entrepreneurs and politics in Mexico is in press (Oxford).

the PRI's apparent weaknesses have strong historical precedents extending back to the 1940s. Second, economic modernization, as measured by urbanization, income levels, and education, is the single most important determinant of support for opposition parties. Third, despite their notable successes, opposition parties in Mexico to date are structurally weak, having limited geographical, ideological, and occupational support. Fourth, geographically the Mexico with which most North Americans, including government officials, are least familiar, is most supportive of the PRI. Fifth, and finally, the United States media has a tremendous responsibility in educating the North American public and leadership about Mexican politics, but has not presented the larger picture clearly.[2]

A word of warning is in order. Since 1984, many Mexicans and North Americans have become infatuated with Mexico's elections. An emphasis on elections is, of course, a concern of all democratic political cultures. Mexico incorporates certain democratic features in its political process, but elections and vote counts have not been notable elements of its culture in the past. The credibility of reported votes, both past and present, is questionable. Election fraud at the local level, and the national government's ability to manipulate reported election results, make it difficult to draw conclusions about Mexican election data and their comparability over time. Without ignoring these serious impediments to electoral analysis in Mexico, what may be most remarkable about the 1988 election is that it is the first presidential election for which pre-election data are available in the form of voter polls and from which voter intentions can be compared with actual results. These voter polls, in general terms, reinforce the credibility of the present election results.

Geography, History, and Development in Mexican Elections

As any election buff in the United States knows, North American elections always produce a lengthy discussion about the strength of the Republicans and Democrats in the most populous states. Analysts of the Mexican political scene, for the most part, have never focused on populous versus less-populous states. The reason for this is understandable. The legislative system, dominated by the Chamber of Deputies, has since the 1930s been uninfluential in the policy process. Moreover, Mexico's electoral process has served more to legitimize the party in power and to educate its presidential candidate, than to determine

---

2 For example, see Buzenberg's (1987: 253) statement that "North American press coverage of Mexico's midterm elections suffered from significant errors of exaggeration and distortion. Essentially, these errors stemmed from lack of understanding of Mexico's political reality and biases on the part of U.S. reporters."

who shall govern. Consequently, on the surface, it has not been particularly significant if voter preference for the PRI is stronger in some states than the others. Nevertheless, the distribution of votes by state is significant, not because it has determined the outcome of the election, but because of what it reveals about the competing parties' strengths and weaknesses.

The PRI generally is strong in the most populous states. If we examine those states or entities in which more than 600,000 citizens voted (the Federal District, México, Chiapas, Guanajuato, Jalisco, Michoacán, Nuevo León, Oaxaca, Puebla, Sinaloa and Veracruz), the PRI won eight of eleven of these states in the 1988 presidential balloting (See Table 6-1).

The National Democratic Front (FDN), a coalition of leftist parties and a splinter group from the PRI, won the three populous states lost by the PRI: México, Michoacán, and the Federal District, and had a fairly strong showing in Veracruz. The National Action Party (PAN), traditionally the most important opposition group, and representing the ideological right, won none of these states, although it had a fairly strong showing in Guanajuato, Jalisco, Nuevo León, and Sinaloa. In fact, Mexicans who voted in just six states in 1988, in order of the most populous, the Federal District, México, Veracruz, Jalisco, Puebla and Chiapas, accounted for slightly more than half the total votes cast (9.7 million). These six states, out of a total of 32, could conceivably determine the outcome of an election.

Although the PRI continues to dominate the vote in Mexico's most populous states, location, political relations with the center, level of development, urbanization, historical existence of opposition, and not size, are the most important variables. The prominence of these variables can be seen by looking at where the opposition is strongest. In the 1988 elections, the combined opposition parties actually beat the PRI in seven states: Baja California, the Federal District, Guanajuato, Jalisco, México, Michoacán, and Morelos. Of those states, the opposition carried Michoacán and the Federal District by a margin of three to one, the states of México and Morelos by two to one, and the others by lesser amounts.

Have these patterns always been true, or are these results, as some would have us believe, entirely new? Since 1946 the level of opposition present in Mexico in 1988 had not existed. The presidential elections of 1946, 1952, and 1982, where the reported results for the opposition were strongest, nevertheless reveal a distinct geographic pattern in support for the PRI. Eight states in those three elections, on the average, have historically supported opposition parties. Specifically, the combined results reveal that more than 30% of the vote was against the PRI. Those states are Baja California, Chihuahua, the Federal District, Guanajuato, Jalisco, México, Michoacán, and Morelos. With the exception of Chihuahua, these states are precisely the same ones which voted against the PRI in the 1988 elections.

Why have these particular states had at least a forty-five year history of strong opposition to the PRI? The reasons vary. Growth, income level, urbanization and development are variables for Baja California, Chihuahua, the Federal District, and México, which are among the six states with the highest levels of per capita income in Mexico. Geography and proximity to the United States help explain the success of the opposition in Baja California and Chihuahua, where the PAN historically has been strong. History plays an important role in the cases of Guanajuato, Jalisco, Michoacán and Morelos. Morelos, although bordered by México and the Federal District, is relatively undeveloped, with a strong historical aversion since the 1910s to Mexico City domination. Under the leadership of the radical agrarian revolutionary, Emiliano Zapata, it produced the strongest and most persistent resistance in southern Mexico to the Porfiriato, and even to the immediate revolutionary governments. Guanajuato, Jalisco, and Michoacán produced the anti-government movement in the 1920s known as the *Cristero* rebellion, a political-religious uprising opposed to the governing elite's heavy-handed persecution of the Catholic Church during this period.

A state's proximity to the United States has also been important to recent political developments. Although surveys and analysts typically have not attempted to connect concretely this proximity with voting, there is little doubt that where people live affects their views of the United States and its political system, and consequently, their political values.[3] Repeatedly, the United States is the country most admired by Mexicans, and the political system in the United States is part of what is being admired. Both Mexican and United States surveys demonstrate that the closer Mexicans live to the United States, and the more they travel there, the more they admire that country.[4]

The United States undoubtedly has a tremendous impact on Mexico culturally, and our political culture and values have been part of that larger cultural influence. Consequently, it is not surprising that the northern states, which are also among the most highly developed, and which have been characterized since the 1930s by a large influx of recent migrants, historically have been opposed to the political influence of the center. They produced the dominant leadership of the Mexican Revolution of 1910, and the initial generation of post-revolutionary leaders in the 1920s. Today, many contemporary opposition figures, including Manuel Clouthier, the PAN candidate, are products of that border culture, and indeed, the United States culture itself. Clouthier, for example, studied at Brown Military Academy in San Diego and the Black Fox Military Institute in Los Angeles (Camp, 1988:3).

---

3 See the recent analysis of Hernández Hernández (1987).

4 Numerous studies support this conclusion. See, for example, Alduncín (1986); Hernández, et al. (1987); Millard (1981).

Historical voting data, which demonstrate both the longevity and geographical continuity of opposition in Mexico, suggest that the existence of the National Democratic Front did not produce these centers of opposition in 1988; rather Cárdenas's party enhanced the vote favoring the opposition in states or regions where long-term dissatisfaction has existed with the PRI and the federal government. If anything, the historical patterns voting data tend to support the view that disgruntled voters in these regions long have sought alternative parties for which to cast their votes, and the FDN finally provided them a viable alternative to the PRI and the PAN.

This can be seen in the data presented in Table 6-2. Historical voting patterns cannot be generated for the FDN because each leftist party currently affiliated with the front operated separately in 1982. But if those districts won by the PAN in 1982 are compared with those in 1988, a definite pattern is apparent. Generally, the PAN already had established itself as a strong contender, winning over 30% of the vote, and in seven districts actually receiving 40% of the vote, when its national congressional average was only 18%. Consequently, with the introduction in 1988 of the FDN, whose vote essentially came from the PRI, the PAN easily became the plurality party in these districts. This is significant for several reasons. First, De la Madrid's election definitely established the position of the PAN six years prior to the 1988 contest. Second, its strength changed very little. Third, although analysts generally have assumed that a large percentage of the PAN's vote is a protest vote against the PRI, in most cases voters do not seem to have fled from the PAN to vote elsewhere, since support remained fairly consistent between 1982 and 1988.

The 1988 electoral data, when broken down on the basis of the three parties, reveal additional patterns in the geographical distribution of the vote. The oldest of the major opposition groups in Mexico, the National Action Party, is actually quite limited in its appeal to Mexican voters. In 1988, the PAN did not carry any state, either by a majority or plurality of votes. In fact, even in those states which are traditional strongholds of the right, Baja California, Baja California Sur, Coahuila, Chihuahua, Guanajuato, Jalisco, Nuevo León, San Luis Potosí, Sonora, and Sinaloa, the PAN never came close to winning (See Table 6-1).

Even on the legislative district level, which indicates a much firmer notion of the party's grassroots support, the PAN did not do well. An examination of legislative districts in the 1988 elections reveals that of the 31 seats it won in the Chamber of Deputies, 25, or 81%, were located in just five cities: Mexico City; Guadalajara; Jalisco; Ciudad Juárez, Chihuahua; Tlanepantla, México; and León, Guanajuato (Table 6-2). Each of these cities have been strongholds of the PAN since the 1960s.

Data for 1988, which generally are repeated for the past three presidential elections, suggest that the PAN is not a national party, nor is it even a state party. It is a city party, with pockets of strength in a small number of regional, urban centers. The PAN lacks breadth geographically and also appears limited ideologically. In the first place, electoral data over time clearly show that the PAN's vote is essentially stagnant. It has ranged consistently from 11-16% for president since 1964. In polls completed after the 1982 election, only 10% of the population indicated it was sympathetic toward the PAN.[5] Although the vast majority of Mexicans think of themselves as having right-of-center values, they do not identify with the PAN (Hernández, et al., 1987:102).

Moreover, support for the PAN is limited to certain occupational sectors of the Mexican population. Those individuals who most frequently describe themselves as supporters of the PAN are businessmen, interest group leaders, students, white collar-workers, and professionals, all of whom, for the most part, are middle and upper middle class groups (*Prospectiva*, 1988). The PAN, consequently, despite its leadership's denials to the contrary, tends to be a class oriented party, and appeals to a selected occupational strata who numerically are among the smallest groups in Mexico. Moreover, higher percentages among each of these occupations vote for the PRI than the PAN, with the exception of students, who express equal sympathies for both parties.

Finally, critics label the PAN as the party of businessmen and the Church. The data actually contradict the view that the PAN is a party appealing primarily to businessmen. One out of three Mexican businessmen are sympathetic to the PAN, but slightly more than one out of three businessman are sympathetic to the PRI. It is true that businessmen are more attracted to the PAN than any single occupation group, but it is not true that more businessmen are attracted to the PAN than any other party (Basáñez, 1987:193). In fact, it is interesting to note that in 1988 one out of four businessmen sympathized with the National Democratic Front, whereas in 1983, only one out of ten sympathized with the left. In the case of religion, the relationship between Catholicism and the PAN sympathies is blatantly spurious. Religious affiliation does not determine whether a Mexican votes for or against the PAN. More importantly, the intensity of Mexican religious beliefs, as measured by frequency of church attendance, is not reflected in voter preferences. Those Mexicans who attended church more than once a week did not prefer the PAN to the PRI, nor did these same individuals show any disproportionate preference for the three leading parties, the PRI, the FDN, and the PAN.

The newer of the two opposition parties, and consequently more difficult to analyze, is the National Democratic Front, dominated by Cuauhtémoc Cárdenas's own Front for National Reconstruction. The FDN is difficult to analyze because it joins many smaller parties together, including the Authentic Party of the Mexican Revolution (PARM), a traditional splinter group from the PRI that never was described as sympathetic to the left; the Popular Socialist

---

5 *Partido Revolucionario Institucional, Encuesta nacional de partidos políticos.* April, 1983.

Party (PPS), another traditional splinter group from the PRI, self-described as orthodox Marxist but in practice essentially pragmatic; the PMS, Mexican Socialist Party, a leftist party of intellectuals, labor, and students; and the Unified Socialist Party of Mexico (PSUM), an amalgam of traditional leftist and communist groups. Consequently, although the *Cardenistas* have been commonly labelled "leftist," that is somewhat of a misnomer. Cárdenas himself could more accurately be described as representing the populist wing of the PRI, and the reasons people voted for Cárdenas range from ideological, to personal, to the desire to cast an anti-PRI vote.[6]

Election results for the FDN, however, reveal some very significant voting patterns. The National Democratic Front, although more evenly represented geographically than the PAN, especially considering its recent origins, is not yet a national party. However, it is much stronger on a statewide basis than the PAN, having won five states for the presidency: Baja California and the Federal District with pluralities, México, Michoacán, and Morelos with majorities (Table 6-1). The FDN, like opposition in general, has done well in the first three states because of their level of development, growth, and urbanization. Michoacán, although historically a state favorable to opposition movements, was overwhelmingly *Cardenista* because it was his father's state, as well as his own home state. In Morelos, where Cárdenas also won a majority of the votes, the strong heritage of the *Zapatistas*, whose agrarian movement had the sympathies of Cárdenas's father, help explain his success.

On closer examination, at the congressional district level, the strength of the National Democratic Front seems diffuse and weak. In the states or entities it won at the presidential level, with the exception of Michoacán, it did not fare well among congressional seats. In the case of the Federal District, where it received 1.4 million votes (49%) for president to the PRI's 792,000 (27%) and the PAN's 639,000 votes, it carried only three seats out of forty (8%), which represents a tremendous shortfall in support at the grassroot levels (Table 6-2). Furthermore, the PRI and the PAN swept all seats in the new Mexico City assembly. In the state of México, with thirty-four seats, Cárdenas's party only carried three seats. Importantly, in the districts of Netzahualcóyotl, which now forms Mexico's second largest city, heavily populated by workers and marginals, the National Democratic Front did not carry any seats, although one is under formal dispute before the Electoral Commission. In the case of Morelos, the results were much better. Cárdenas himself attracted 58% of the vote, and his party carried two of the four congressional seats. The FDN won no seats in Baja California. Only in Michoacán, Cárdenas's home state, can it be said that the FDN has breadth: That is, it not only took all but two of the thirteen seats, cor-

---

6 Survey by PEAC, commissioned by the author, June, 1988.

responding to Cárdenas's personal overwhelming majority, but it was equally well-represented in both urban and rural districts.

It is true that the FDN was not able to unify its candidacies on the congressional level. In addition, it remains to be seen whether Cárdenas can transfer his own personal appeal, in a sort of coattails effect, to his party's congressional candidates. The task is likely to be difficult because Cárdenas appeals to occupational groups which, while fairly broad, rely heavily on two categories having limited potential: Intellectuals and students. These groups, admittedly strong in organizational skills and media influence, are quantitatively not very significant. Furthermore, the lowest income groups, without regular employment, support Cárdenas, and their present political impact is limited. The FDN's strength also lies among blue-collar workers, and 41% of these voters say they support Cárdenas compared to 37% for the PRI and only 14% for the PAN (*Prospectiva*, 1988). It has also done well among peasants, but the PRI is still ahead among that occupational group. In order to create broader support, Cárdenas will have to appeal more significantly to housewives, the largest single group of Mexican voters; to white-collar workers, whose sympathies still lie with the PRI; and to bureaucrats, an influential portion of the middle class.

Cárdenas also appeals to one other group in Mexican society, those without a formal religion or who are atheist. These Mexicans account for only 9% of the population, a large percentage of whom are intellectuals, and this group is inclined strongly toward the FDN.[7] Again, although they favor Cárdenas, quantitatively they are not significant enough to have a future impact.

What is most important about the groups who favor both opposition parties -- the FDN and the PAN -- are income levels. According to the data published by PEAC, and reflected to a great extent in the occupational support analyzed above, 65% of the FDN supporters are in the lower income category (less than double minimum wage weekly), which is true of only 50% of the PRI's supporters and 45% of the PAN's. Naturally, a disproportionate group of the PAN sympathizers come from the highest income groups, and to a lesser extent, middle income families. The PRI's strength is that it appeals strongly to the middle classes, whereas Cárdenas does not receive his fair share of their support.

An analogy to Mexican politics may be drawn from the British political system more readily than from the North American polity because of the degree to which the Mexicans identify with liberty over equality (Hernández, A. M. et al., 1987:101). The British Conservative Party, operating in the context of one of the most industrialized nations in the world, has been far more successful in winning general elections than the Labor Party since 1945. Numerous reasons exist to explain this phenomenon, but one explanation is the fact that the Conservative Party does well among the middle classes and among workers who

---

7 Survey by PEAC.

take on characteristics of the middle classes. These working class voters are generally citizens who place a high value on social deference. In other words, in a society where social inequality is more visible and tolerated, and social conservatism more acceptable, a party of the middle-right is likely to gain long-term success over a party of the populist left.

If Mexican psychological studies are correct, Mexicans see themselves firmly on the right of the political spectrum. Their self-label, although not clearly defined in terms of political values, would not seem to auger well for a leftist political movement. On the other hand, a right of center political movement, to appeal ideologically to the sympathies of the average Mexican, obviously needs to be grounded more firmly in centrist philosophies, and not readily be identified with special, minority interests, as is the PAN. At present, it is the PRI which has the potential of playing a role similar to the British Conservative Party.

The left has an uphill battle in Mexico because most Mexicans still favor moderate change (Hernández, A.M. et al., 1987:103; *New York Times,* 1986). If the FDN presents itself as a radical alternative to the PRI in the governing process, it is more likely to repel than attract more voters. The same can be said of the PAN. Even immediately prior to the 1988 election, most Mexicans were still optimistic rather than pessimistic about their future. Whereas 39% believed that their personal situation would improve, only 26% thought it would worsen, while 22% believed conditions would remain the same.

Economic conditions, of course, affect voting behavior. One of the most important long-term trends in Mexico which has had and will continue to have a persistent impact on voting behavior is economic growth (see Tables 6-3 and 6-4). Eighteen years ago, Ames (1970), in the first North American article to statistically analyze Mexican election data, argued that a relationship existed between economic development and electoral results. Essentially, he demonstrated that through 1964, those states with the highest income per capita were, contrary to what one might expect, those giving the least support to the government party. In other words, favorable economic growth, while it encouraged stabililty, did not translate into political rewards for the party in power, measured in terms of votes. The Federal District has always been a classic case of this assertion, receiving a disproportionate level of federal investment. Historically, the PAN, and more recently the left, have done well there. Ames's original study has been followed up by Paulina Fernández Christlieb and Octavio Rodríguez Araujo's (1986) analysis, which demonstrates that the lowest income states give the highest votes to the PRI, and the highest income states give the lowest votes to the PRI.

These patterns between income and support for the PRI are quite consistent and clear. As states urbanize and develop, and as income increases, residents become more sophisticated and less satisfied with the government party (Klesner, 1987:135; Molinar, 1987:26). Moreover, urban areas have demanded, and have been more successful in achieving, a more fair vote tally. This explains why for years the National Action Party has done very well in the Federal District as compared with elsewhere. But as a long-term trend, the consequences are significant. As Mexico develops, the PRI increasingly loses support among the more developed sectors of society. Modernization, slowly but surely, is taking the vote away from the PRI. To survive this process, the PRI itself must modernize, as Carlos Salinas himself has argued, presenting an image as the leader of Mexican development, not as an impediment to change.

All high income states with the exception of México and the Federal District are located in the north, in close proximity to the United States. Thus, development, urbanization and geography have intertwined to produce stronger levels of opposition to the PRI. In terms of direct federal investment, the Mexican government has favored not the least, but the most developed states. Thus, government policy, ironically, has reinforced these patterns, benefiting those regions which have given the PRI the least support (Camp, 1976).

Finally, one important remaining variable is the age of the voter. Insufficient attention has been paid to this variable. The PEAC survey demonstrates that 50% of the FDN support comes from voters under 30, while the PRI receives only 35% and the PAN 42% of its support from that age group. The 30 to 39 year old group is the largest age group of registered voters (*Mexico Journal*, 1988). Mexico is a youthful nation. Nearly half (44%) of its population is under the age of 18. Statistically, the opposition parties, particularly the FDN, might seem to be in an advantageous position. However, youthful support brings certain disadvantages as well. Historically speaking, in other countries, youths do not register or vote in large numbers compared to older voters. Second, it is risky to make predictions about the behavior of voters as they age. Many tend to become more conservative, a pattern which has been demonstrated in studies of Latin American and Mexican students (Liebman, et al., 1972). Thus, while the FDN may appear to be the wave of the future, that support may very well dissipate as these younger generations marry, take on positions of responsibility in the work force, and mature.

Conclusions

What do the results of these elections mean for Mexico, and for Mexican-United States relations? The most extraordinary consequence of the election is that Mexico has entered a new phase in its political development, a phase in which Mexicans are likely to witness an era of political pluralism. The 1988 elections mark an end to the traditional majoritarianism of the PRI, imposed or earned. Although Salinas won slightly over 50.3% of the votes, even conceding some government manipulation of the results, this percentage is not substantially different from the expressed intention of the voters prior to the polls. Assuming the polls were in fact accurate, Salinas's actual vote may have been closer to 45%. Even if true, the outcome of the election would not change, but rather it reinforces the notion that the PRI is essentially a plurality party.

As a plurality party the PRI will need to readjust its behavior in the policy process. First, it cannot survive as the dominant party much longer unless it regains a stronger sense of legitimacy, especially as alternative choices become increasingly available. Second, despite the executive branch's predominance over Mexican policymaking, the legislative branch is becoming increasingly significant. The vast majority of Mexicans believe they are badly represented in the Chamber of Deputies, and the Deputies themselves, in the 1985-88 legislature, including many from the PRI, want the legislative process to function democratically.[8]

Opposition parties are bound to use the legislative branch as a focus of their policy contributions. The fact that PRI now only has 256 (249 majority, and seven plurinominal) seats out of 500 to work with, suggests future difficulties in approving legislation. Four of those seats are also in danger since the Electoral Commission will hear formal complaints of irregularities before approving the selection of those deputies. More importantly, the PRI is far short of the necessary 60% to make constitutional amendments, a frequent process used by the government to implement and legitimize the most politically significant legislation. Naturally, wide-ranging differences among the opposition make a united front in the chamber difficult to achieve; nevertheless, it is also not unreasonable to expect a small percentage of the PRI deputies to be mavericks, and vote against their own party. The PRI, as well as the opposition parties, therefore, is going to have to stress political compromise to succeed.

The increasing importance of the legislative branch also complicates Mexico's relations with the United States. What the United States must understand is that it will be dealing with a divided legislative body, but a unified executive branch. Whereas it is true that policymaking will continue to focus within the Mexican executive branch, the increased visibility of the legislative branch, the media attention paid to debates in the legislature, and its role as the most representative institution of the new pluralistic culture, gives it increasing influence politically. Because the executive and legislative branches' relationship during the next six years is likely to be tense, the United States risks controversy by ignoring the increasing power and policy perspectives of the legislative branch.

As a value in the political culture, pluralism and participation are here to stay. What is less apparent, and extremely significant, is Mexicans' understanding of political opposition within the context of a democratic culture. Cárdenas and Clouthier's behavior in claiming absolute victory and treating the

---

8 Unpublished document, Chamber of Deputies, 1985-1988.

PRI as an enemy, instead of as a respected adversary, is not encouraging. Before Mexico can entertain a working system of political democracy, it has to accept the concept of loyal opposition. Studies demonstrate that Mexicans value many of the significant elements essential to a democratic political culture, excepting tolerance of the opposition (Booth and Seligson, 1984). Mexicans have admitted, for example, in the CREA survey, that they would be extremely intolerant of individuals with leftist views (Hernández, A.M. et al., 1987: 247). It is ironic, therefore, that it is Salinas who has publicly recognized the advent of pluralism in Mexico, whereas Cárdenas and Clouthier have taken an all or nothing posture (Rubio, 1988).

Political pluralism has advantages and disadvantages for United States-Mexican relations. Among the advantages to the United States is that it can appeal to diverse interests represented by the organized opposition in Mexico, giving it more room to maneuver in the face of a PRI-government foreign policy decision it opposes. Naturally, even historically, United States officials have found diversity useful, except that these conflicting interests formerly were represented within the government, rather than outside of it. Among the disadvantages to the United States is that political pluralism always complicates the dealings of one government with another. The Mexican executive branch's own ability to maneuver is limited by the narrow legitimacy of Salinas's mandate, and by the strength of the opposition, not only in the Chamber, but among various interest groups and organizations.

One of the most important foreign policy decisions facing Mexico, with implications for United States-Mexican relations, is the question of the debt. Since the posture of the FDN has been opposed to the present government's position of gradual renegotiation, it poses serious limitations on Salinas's ability to maneuver in future debt arrangements with United States and foreign bankers. The FDN will maintain constant and public pressure on the government to radicalize the PRI's position on a debt moratorium.

Before the 1988 elections, the only strong opposition in Mexico was from the right. But if historical precedence suggests that the right, as represented by the PAN, had limited political prospects, does this now mean that Mexico's political future lies within the left? Probably not, since as suggested earlier, the FDN is at best shaky because of what each of the front's parties represented in the mind of the voters, and because of Cárdenas's personality. Instead, the majority of Mexicans want moderate changes. Furthermore, those surveys which show Mexicans as identifying themselves as sympathetic with the right seem essentially correct, provided that in political terms one thinks of the PRI as representing the center-right.

Voting statistics in the 1988 elections demonstrate that slightly more than two-thirds of the population voted for center-right and rightist parties. What most Mexicans are really searching for as an alternative to the PRI is not a party of the right, such as the PAN, nor a party of the left, such as the PST or the

PSUM, but a party of the center, preferably center-right. But no such opposition party exists. Cárdenas initially offered a party of the center-left, but his image is blurred by the association of far left parties with his front. Cárdenas's major impact on the PRI has been to weaken the populist faction within the government leadership, and to make it more likely, with his electoral successes, for younger, strongly committed politicians sharing these views to join his movement rather than remain within the PRI. If such a trend does occur, the PRI will become increasingly narrower in focus, more accurately representative of its own right-center label, and opportunities for a center-left alternative outside the PRI will be enhanced.

Opposition parties, as argued above, are structurally weak because of their geographic imbalances and limited occupational support. Moreover, the FDN is limited by its leadership. Personal popularity can be an asset in the short run, but if it dominates the image and fortunes of a party in the long run, it is not useful. The press has made much of Cárdenas's popularity because he inherits the mantle of his father's name. Although today General Cárdenas is the most well-remembered president since 1920, he was extremely unpopular with many groups during his administration, especially the middle classes (Lajous, 1988:19). Interestingly, the most important features of the centralization of political authority in Mexico City -- the dominance of the executive branch, and the establishment of government controlled interest groups, all opposed by the FDN -- were set in motion by former President Cárdenas himself. Finally, questions need to be raised about the motivations of the FDN leaders like Porfirio Muñoz Ledo, winner of a Federal District senate seat, who as the former president of the PRI was primarily responsible for preventing the PPS from winning the governorship of Nayarit, coopting the party's president with a senate seat. In other words, are Cárdenas, Muñoz Ledo, and others reformers, or are they merely ambitious for power, having been deprived of it in a party where their ideological and personal factions are not in vogue?

The other major consequence of the election is apparent within the government leadership and the PRI. Although it can be argued that Salinas actually may have received even fewer votes than reported, his historically small margin of victory had to be imposed on recalcitrant party leaders who most likely would have resorted to manipulations far greater than those of which the PRI is accused. Salinas's designation marked a sharp split within the government leadership. Many of the PRI leaders, disappointed with Salinas's candidacy, have given lukewarm support to the party, or have actually supported Cárdenas. Within hours after the close of the elections, high PRI officials opposed to the Salinas faction deliberately leaked information in Mexico and the United States that Cárdenas had actually won the election, creating increasing difficulties for Salinas's leadership (Baer, 1988).

The fact that loyalties are divided within the government leadership further limits Salinas's maneuverability against the opposition. Although Salinas has demonstrated a willingness to make tough decisions, and to take his own party, kicking and struggling every inch of the way, along the path of political modernization, regardless of short-term losses in the electoral arena, he faces a difficult task in maintaining consistent economic and political decisions, which could have implications for Mexican-United States relations. The United States government will need to be very sensitive to the limitations placed on Salinas as leader of a house divided, not only nationally, but with his home team. Consequently, the United States will have to be very careful not to misread every cue as indicative of a long-term policy direction, provided Salinas has the skill and courage to sustain his goals.

Regardless of whether one sees Salinas as pushing Mexico into a pluralistic political arena, or the opposition forcing him into it, or both, political pluralism, especially in a transitional period, generally introduces behavior associated with political instability. These characteristics should not be looked upon unfavorably by United States analysts, but rather they should be perceived as welcome growing pains of a society moving from democratic adolescence to maturity. Moreover, various political factions, including those within the PRI, will attempt to manipulate the United States government for their own benefit. Consequently, the United States should not hope wishfully for "the good times" of the past, when our relationship with Mexico seemed clearer and more consistent. There is no turning back for Mexico, or for the United States. As Mexico resolves its political future, the United States must consciously allow it room to maneuver, limiting its public judgements of the efficacy of Mexico's political modernization, as it strikes out on the rocky path of democratic pluralism.

Table 6-1
1988 Mexican Presidential Elections:
Percentage of Vote for Major Parties, by State

State	PAN (%)	Party PRI (%)	FDN (%)
AGUASCALIENTES	28	50	19
BAJA CALIFORNIA	24	37	37
BAJA CALIFORNIA SUR	19	54	26
CAMPECHE	12	71	16
CHIAPAS	3	90	7
CHIHUAHUA	38	55	7
COAHUILA	15	54	30
COLIMA	15	48	36
DURANGO	17	63	19
FEDERAL DISTRICT	22	27	49
GUANAJUATO	30	44	22
GUERRERO	2	61	36
HIDALGO	6	65	28
JALISCO	31	43	24
MEXICO	16	30	52
MICHOACAN	10	23	64
MORELOS	7	34	58
NAYARIT	6	57	37
NUEVO LEON	24	72	4
OAXACA	5	64	30
PUEBLA	10	72	18
QUERETARO	19	63	16
QUINTANA ROO	10	66	24
SAN LUIS POTOSI	21	68	9
SINALOA	32	51	17
SONORA	21	69	10
TABASCO	5	74	20
TAMAULIPAS	10	59	30
TLAXCALA	6	60	31
VERACRUZ	5	74	20
YUCATAN	31	67	2
ZACATECAS	11	66	22

SOURCE: Adapted from *Mexico Journal*, July 25, 1988, pp. 16-17

110

Table 6-2
Comparison of Selected Legislative Districts,
1982 and 1988 Mexican Elections

1988 Districts Won by Opposition		1988 Winning Party	1982 Percent Vote (b)
CHIHUAHUA			
#3	CIUDAD JUAREZ	PAN	38
#4	CIUDAD JUAREZ	PAN	40
#8	CIUDAD JUAREZ	PAN	40
FEDERAL DISTRICT			
#1	CUAUHTEMOC	PAN	34
#7	CUAHTEMOC/JUAREZ	PAN	31
#9	AZCAPOTZALCO/HIDALGO	PAN	26
#10	GUSTAVO MADERO	FDN	9
#16	BENITO JUAREZ	PAN	33
#17	JUAREZ/HIDALGO/OBREGON	PAN	33
#19	AZCAPOTZALCO	PAN	29
#20	GUSTAVO MADERO	PAN	28
#27	COYOACAN/IZTAPALAPA	PAN	31
#29	MADERO/AZCAPOTZALCO	PAN	28
#36	OBREGON/JUAREZ	PAN	11
#37	JUAREZ/IZTAPALAPA	FDN	12
#38	CONTRERAS/OBREGON	FDN	12
GUANAJUATO			
#2	LEON	PAN	40
#3	LEON	PAN	41
#11	LEON	PAN	42
JALISCO			
#1	GUADALAJARA	PAN	40
#3	GUADALAJARA	PAN	36
#13	GUADALAJARA	PAN	40
#14	GUADALAJARA	PAN	39
#15	GUADALAJARA	PAN	(a)27
#20	ZAPOPAN	PAN	37
MEXICO			
#3	LERMA	FDN	6
#6	CUAUTITLAN	PAN	39
#8	TOXCOCO	FDN	5

Table 6-2 (continued)
Comparison of Selected Legislative Districts,
1982 and 1988 Mexican Elections

1988 Districts Won by Opposition	1988 Winning Party	1982 Percent Vote (b)
MEXICO (continued)		
#14 TLANEPANTLA	PAN	33
#16 TOLUCA	FDN	5
#18 NAUCALPAN	PAN	38
#33 TLANEPANTLA	PAN	36
MICHOACAN		
#1 MORELIA	FDN	12
#2 HIDALGO	FDN	3
#3 ZACAPU	PARM/FDN	6
#4 PIEDAD	FDN	2
#6 URUAPAN	PARM/FDN	12
#8 ZITACUARO	FDN	7
#9 APATZINGAN	FDN	17
#10 QUIROGA	PARM	7
#11 JIQUILPAN	FDN	1
#12 LOS REYES	FDN	3
#13 LAZARO CARDENAS	FDN	7
MORELOS		
#1 CUERNAVACA	FDN	5
#3 YAUTEPEC	FDN	3
SAN LUIS POTOSI		
#1 SAN LUIS POTOSI	PAN	27
SINALOA		
#3 CULIACAN	PAN	17
VERACRUZ		
#15 COATZACOALCOS	PARM/FDN	3
YUCATAN		
#1 MERIDA	PAN	37

SOURCE: District data are from Volker G. Lehr, *Manual biográfico del Congreso de la Unión* (Mexico City: UNAM, 1984); *Diario Oficial de la Federación*, Vol. CDXV, No. 5, April 7, 1988; and *El Financiero*, July 14, 1988, p. 55.
(a) PRI received only 37% of the vote in 1982, with 30% going to PSUM.
(b) Data for FDN in 1982 are percentages for PSUM alone, the PST alone, or in some districts, a combination of leftist parties.

Table 6-3
Mexican Congressional Elections
by States' Per Capita Income and PRI Vote

Election Years	1979 %	1982 %	1985 %
Percent of Vote for PRI			
National	74	69	68
Low Income States	81	83	81
Medium Income States	78	71	68
High Income States	55	56	52

NOTES: High income states were: CHIHUAHUA, MEXICO, SONORA, NUEVO LEON, BAJA CALIFORNIA, BAJA CALIFORNIA SUR, and the FEDERAL DISTRICT; low income states were: OAXACA, HIDALGO, YUCATAN, CHIAPAS, PUEBLA, SAN LUIS POTOSI, ZACATECAS, and TLAXCALA. The remaining states were classified as medium income states.

Table 6-4
Mexican Presidential Elections
by States' Per Capita Income and PRI Vote

Election Years	1976 %	1982 %	1988 %
Percent of Vote for PRI			
National	86.9	68.4	50.3
Low Income States	92	82	75
Medium Income States	93	73	56
High Income States	78	55	37

SOURCES: Adapted from Paulina Fernández Christlieb and Octavio Rodríguez Araujo, *Elecciones y partidos en México* (Mexico: El Caballito, 1986), pp. 218, 223-24; and Joseph Klesner, "Changing Patterns of Electoral Participation," in Judith Gentleman, ed., *Mexican Politics in Transition* (Boulder: Westview Press, 1987), pp. 130, 135; and for an expanded discussion of these and other variables, Joseph Klesner, "Electoral Reform in an Authoritarian Regime: The Case of Mexico," unpublished Ph.D. dissertation, MIT, February, 1988; 1988 election statistics, *El Día*, July 16, 1988, p. 8.

References

Ames, Barry. 1970. "Bases of Support for Mexico's Dominant Party," *American Political Science Review*, 64: (March): 153-167.

Alduncín, Enrique. 1986. *Los valores de los mexicanos*. Mexico: Fomento Cultural Banamex.

Baer, M. Delal. 1988. "Post Election Analysis," Report No. 2, Latin American Election Study Series. Washington, D.C.: Center for Strategic and International Studies. August 15.

Basáñez, Miguel. 1987. "Elections and Political Culture in Mexico," in *Mexican Politics in Transition*, Judith Gentleman (ed.). Boulder: Westview Press.

Booth, John A. and Mitchell A. Seligson. 1984. "The Political Culture of Authoritarianism in Mexico: A Reexamination," *Latin American Research Review*, 19: 106-124.

Buzenberg, William E. 1987. "The 1985 Mexican Elections and the North American Press," in *Electoral Patterns and Perspectives in Mexico*, Arturo Alvarado (ed.). San Diego: Center for U.S.-Mexican Studies, University of California.

Camp, Roderic Ai. 1976. "A Reexamination of Political Leadership and Allocation of Federal Revenues in Mexico, 1934-1973," *Journal of Developing Areas*, 10:100-202.

Camp, Roderic Ai. 1988. *Who's Who in Mexico Today*. Boulder: Westview Press.

Chamber of Deputies. 1985-88. Unpublished documents.

Diario Oficial de la Federación. 1988. CDXV (No.5) April 7.

El Día, 1988. July 16, p. 8.

El Financiero. 1988. July 14, p. 55.

Fernández Christlieb, Paulina and Octavio Rodríguez Araujo. 1986. *Elecciones y partidos en México*. Mexico: Ediciones El Caballito.

Hernández, Alberto Median, et. al. 1987. *Como somos los mexicanos*. Mexico: CREA.

Hernández Hernández, Alberto. 1987. "Political Attitudes among Border Youth," in *Electoral Patterns and Perspectives in Mexico*. Arturo Alvarado (ed.). San Diego: Center for U.S.-Mexican Studies, University of California.

Klesner, Joseph. 1987. "Changing Patterns of Electoral Participation and Official Party Support in Mexico," in *Mexican Politics in Transition*, Judith Gentleman, (ed.). Boulder: Westview Press.

114

Klesner, Joseph. 1988. "Electoral Reform in an Authoritarian Regime: The Case of Mexico." Unpublished doctoral dissertation, MIT, February.

Lajous, Adrián. 1988. "The Politics of Mexican Democracy: The 1988 Presidential Elections," in *Mexico and the United States: Leadership Transitions and the Unfinished Agenda*, M. Delal Baer (ed.). Washington, D.C.: Center for Strategic & International Studies.

Lehr, Volker G. 1984. *Manual biográfico del Congreso de la Unión*. Mexico: UNAM.

Liebman, Arthur, et al. 1972. *Latin American University Students: A Six Nation Study*. Cambridge: Harvard University Press.

"Mexican Election Facts." *1988. Mexico Journal*. July 11, p. 15.

Millard, William J. 1981. *Media Use by the Better-Educated in Major Mexican Cities*. Washington, D.C.: United States International Communications Agency, December 18.

Molinar Horcasitas, Juan. 1987. "The 1985 Federal Elections in Mexico: The Product of a System," in *Electoral Patterns and Perspectives in Mexico*, Arturo Alvarado (ed.). San Diego: Center for U.S.-Mexican Studies Center, University of California.

New York Times. 1986. October 26.

Partido Revolucionario Institucional. 1983. *Encuesta nacional de partidos políticos*, April.

Prospectiva Estratégica. 1988. A.C., "Encuesta," *La Jornada*. July 5.

Rubio, Luis. 1988. "El dilema del futuro de México," *La Jornada*. July 29.

7

The Postelectoral Conjuncture in Mexico and Mexican-United States Relations

By Carlos Rico Ferrat[1]

Introduction

The results of the 1988 Mexican presidential and legislative elections captured the imagination of a good number of national and foreign analysts. This is because of the magnitude and novelty of the modifications in the Mexican political panorama that the elections caused. To attempt an analysis of the present political conjuncture (the circumstances which define the political scene) is difficult precisely because of the new factors that have rendered irrelevant any exercise based on the simple extrapolation of trends. In fact, it seems easier to specify certain features of what has occurred than to predict what the immediate future may offer.

In this chapter, I examine the major factors in the Mexican political scene for the purpose of relating them to an analysis of Mexican-United States relations which since the beginnings of the 1970s suggests they are the principal sources of and limitations to the intergovernmental conflict. Before beginning, I must clarify that the Mexican political situation is only one of the variables that would be incorporated into a more complete analysis. To complete the picture described here, ultimately it will be necessary to incorporate election data from the United States electoral conjuncture.

1 Carlos Rico Ferrat is a professor and investigator at *El Colegio de México*. He received a doctorate in political science from Harvard University. He has been advisor to the Mexican Secretary of Foreign Relations; founder and director of the Institute for Studies of the United States at *Centro de Investigación y Docencia Económicas* (CIDE) of Mexico; Walter J. Levy fellow of the Council of Foreign Relation (New York); and visiting professor at various universities in the United States and Latin America. Among his recent publications is "The Contadora Experience," *Latin America and Caribbean Contemporary Record 86-87*.

The Postelectoral Political Conjuncture in Mexico

The postelectoral political conjuncture in Mexico is extremely rich and contains many possibilities. The accumulation of unpublished incidents after the election offers only the most convincing proof. The temptation, implicit in the wealth of material available, is to analyze, summarize, and reduce the meaning of the recent election to its impact on the immediate economic crisis. However, it is imperative to adopt a point of view that permits the greatest perspective.

To introduce an evaluation of the possibilities of and limitations to the *apertura democrática* (political liberalization), it would be ideal to outline the long process of change in electoral influence that the country's many political forces have experienced over the last eighteen years. However, this would be impossible in the brief space of this chapter and with my even more limited capabilities. Thus, after simply noting that the Institutional Revolutionary Party's (PRI) "electoral debacle" last July was no more than the last installment (of such pronounced characteristics that it would have been impossible to anticipate from the sole projection of what had occurred in the last two decades, although undeniably related) in a much longer and more complete history, I must resign myself to summarizing briefly the most immediate incidents, particularly the experience of Miguel de la Madrid's government.

After examining these preceding events, this chapter summarizes the principal results of the electoral process and its implications for, on the one hand, the opposition's strength, and on the other, the potential responses that the Salinas government as much as the PRI can attempt in the face of the new set of realities that defines the country's political conjuncture.

Some Fundamental Antecedents

Perhaps the major point of departure for evaluating the extent of the events of July 1988 might be to return mentally to the political conjuncture at the end of 1982 when Miguel de la Madrid assumed power. The economic crisis appeared to be of such a magnitude that many foreign observers asked themselves not if a major political crisis would occur, but when. For their own part, no few Mexican analysts, in response to persistent news foretelling almost immediate disaster, indicated that the Mexican political system still had, in spite of its gradual decline, strong and functioning bases. The history of De la Madrid's term both confirmed this assertion and also helped to undermine it.

The government's project, announced and in good measure implemented by the De la Madrid Mexican government, had considerable social and economic costs. These are summarized in a series of statistics on the level of real wages, per capita product, etc. that have become common in any discussion of the national situation. It is not necessary here to repeat the statistics. Nevertheless, it behooves one to recall that the most recent comparative estimations, juxtaposing the Mexican reality with the rest of the region (every Latin American country suffered economically during the last years), shows that former priorities in such areas as health and education have suffered a considerable setback. In competition with all of Latin America, Mexico takes last place in terms of budgetary allocations to these areas.

That which I will simply call "De la Madrid's project" depended, in fact, upon the functioning of the structures of political and social control upon which for decades the stability of the Mexican system was based. But at the same time, and in spite of being able to find indications of political sensitivity concerning some budgetary cuts, the project tended to undermine profoundly the lines of party adherence upon which such control was based. When the cuts affected even the state bureaucracy at its lowest levels, it became necessary to ask with which political recourses the "new national project" would confront the series of conflicts and tensions that, at least in the short run, it seemed doomed to generate.

It is true that the country for which the previous project had been created, and the mechanisms of political and social control associated with it, exist no longer. But this does not eliminate the problem: In the short run at least, the necessities of the government program severely struck these mechanisms without simultaneously generating other plans to maintain the conflicts brought about by the state project. For example, the corporatism of the labor union proved essential to maintain the rigid policy of a wage freeze. But in the end, the union had to pay the price caused by the increase in salaried workers.

Perhaps this conflict is summed up more clearly in the problems the De la Madrid administration had by combining the political and economic liberalizations into one project, which, at least in the short run, had a high cost. In that short time, the eminent symbol of "political liberalization" was many times substituted for economic and social demands. But in the final analysis, through the very advancement of that liberalization, the possibility of the state's maintaining the same type of costly measures in a controlled framework was limited. Thus, the worth of symbolism diminished in light of the growing need for concrete action; at the same time symbolism contributed to new arenas in which withheld demands could be put forth and defended.

I do not seek to imply that the administration's "political liberalization" contained great breadth and depth. The severity with which it confronted practically every important labor strike during the six years provides the first reason to doubt such an affirmation. It is not even necessary to examine the social arena. After the experiences from 1983 to 1985, the De la Madrid government increasingly tended to close ranks, even in that area where it principally had waved its *aperturista* banner -- the electoral.

Some observers had sought to find an explanation to the political liberalization complication in the survival and strength of the most sluggish and reactionary sectors of the official party, those today called "dinosaurs." This interpretation tends to exaggerate these sectors' autonomy from the president in the conduct of public policy. More important, it ignores the fact that there existed (and still exists), at least in the short run, a real, profound tension of new importance between the economic and political dimensions of the *aperturista* project.

Many new and old conflicts were engendered and deepened in this manner. Such conflicts occurred within and outside the party and state arenas. Within the opposition parties a more aggressive leadership less disposed to respect the formal rules of the "loyal opposition" was growing. The case of the National Action Party (PAN) is, in this respect, particularly interesting. But outside the partisan game new realities also were being born. The social conflict increased notably, although its manifestations always were maintained so that frequently it would not excite the attention of the journalist or casual observer. Not only did the conflict grow, but, fundamentally aggravated by the experience of the weeks and months after the 1985 earthquake, it tended to express itself in a manner increasingly independent of the traditional structures of corporative state control.

Anyone who has given a lecture before the intermediate leadership of PRI in its *Instituto de Capacitación Política* also knows that a great deal of friction occurred between the government (this government with its economic and social policy) and a good part of the party's middle groups. To some degree, these "family conflicts" had to do with the confrontation between "technocrats" and "politicians." But this angle of observation usually offers a narrow perspective of what really happened. The problem was not restricted to the disagreement of some traditional and antidemocratic politicians to the *aperturista* program of the "young technocrats." To this disagreement (that in fact existed and still exists) there often was added another which occurred over what the party's own middle groups considered to be implications both *entreguista* (conceding industries to foreigners) -- particularly to the United States -- and "antidemocratic" (in the sense that they negatively affected the greatest majorities of the country both socially and economically).

The Election Results and the Realities of the Ratification Process

Even up to this moment, it is practically impossible to have a definite opinion about the truth of the election results of July 6th. A seemingly well-founded doubt exists concerning the degree of fraud both on election day and the days immediately subsequent. It is alleged that fraud took place on three distinct occasions, each one bearing different implications for political analysis. First, one can think that the irregularities of election day occurred more through local or state initiative than through a centrally designed and conducted program. Second, it remains difficult not to think that in the succeeding days, the "cover-up" and "alchemy" were systematically and coherently implemented through central decision. The difference suspected (upon which were based all the disagreements, petitions and eventually the self-condemnatory denial over whether all the boxes be opened, or at least, subsequently, a sample) between the real contents of the electoral boxes and the results set down in the available records perhaps offers the most significant demonstration. The third occasion of fraud refers to what happened before the elections in the confirmation of the electoral roster. Cases such as in Chihuahua, where an important number of the PAN militants were removed from the register, make one think central authorities were involved.

Why was fraud committed? This is the really important question. Only those on the inside who knew the truth about the facts and the three above-mentioned instances would be able to answer adequately. In my opinion, the object of the fraud was simply to widen considerably the margin of victory for the official candidate. By this I mean that I do not think Salinas would have been defeated, but that the vote for Cárdenas could have been significantly larger; Clouthier was certainly the principal object of the fraud committed before the election.

Without a doubt, official information now reveals changes of primary importance in the country's political panorama. Among the most significant facts the following stand out: (A) In the north, the geographical base for the PAN's support, the PRI recouped a considerable number of votes; (B) the center of the country and in particular the metropolitan area of Mexico City voted for the FDN candidate; (C) also favoring the FDN were those districts in which important labor union forces, such as the Oil Workers Union formally linked with the official party, have an undeniable political presence; (D) without the vote of the least "modern" (and most susceptible to electoral manipulation) sector, the official candidate -- who received from this sector his principal percentage of support -- would have obtained the majority with difficulty, even in the official tally; and (E) the sectors that lost many votes are those directly related to the aparatus of corporative control, in particular the unions. The most paradoxical fact is that Salinas's "modernization" proposal encountered significant opposition in the most "modern" regions, yet those sectors the proposal tended to displace were precisely the ones that allowed his electoral triumph. In the face of persistent doubt about the level of electoral fraud, nevertheless, it is necessary to ask whether the sectors that voted against Salinas were made up of "the most modern" of the country or simply the most "watched over" by the opposition.

One also may find interesting considerations, not in the official data on the election results, but in the ratification procedures followed afterwards. The first concerns the categorical opposition of the government and official party to "opening the boxes." This made it difficult, even for observers most disposed to keep the ratification open, to doubt declarations of centrally orchestrated fraud. The second would recapitulate the change in attitude from Salinas's initial, conciliatory statements to the behavior of the PRI bloc in the Electoral College, based on the open use of its scant, yet existent, numerical majority. The second of these two indicators appears the most relevant for clarifying some of the possibilities that surround the present political conjuncture.

Three implications of this conjuncture appear worthy of mention. The first is that the election results already have introduced a significant change in the relationship between the chief executive and the legislature. The PRI majority in the Chamber of Deputies is so narrow that, for example, the president will not be able to introduce changes to the constitution through a simple majority such as was used for his verification. One ought not to exaggerate the importance of this point. Salinas must be able to govern without having to resort to such an expedient, widely used by his predecessors. In fact, in the present political conjuncture, the opposition surely would be more interested in such constitutional modifications. This is because the principal resolutions of the electoral law in force since the reform of 1986 (and the guarantee, for example, that even without a majority vote the PRI would maintain control of the Chamber) have become part of the constitution.

The second implication of import is the monolithic behavior, customary until now, of the PRI bloc in the Chamber and College. The expectations of desertion by the PRI legislators in favor, for example, of the FDN, chiefly have not been realized. The net result of desertions from one camp to the other have tended to cancel each other out. But this is not the most important point. Politically, that which is really crucial is the necessity of maintaining that unity, leading to a situation in which even the smallest of the PRI factions is essential for implementing the legislative dimensions of the Salinas proposal. Salinas has ended up being a hostage to everyone in the PRI. Certainly, each one of these factions will at least try to demand something of him in exchange for its support.

The third implication concerns the great importance for the PRI of again having to achieve collaboration with some of the forces that today are part of the FDN coalition, in particular those accustomed to collaboration through previous partisan experience. It is not difficult to foresee that the "temptation" for many deputies from PARM, PPS, or the new PFCRN,[2] for example, will be considerable. Thus, it is essential to explore, even rapidly and superficially, the situation that now appears to maintain the opposition and its most important future possibilities.

---

2 For a description of these political parties, see chapter 1.

A New Opposition

July's election results have relatively different meanings for the two principal opposition forces. For the PAN, the basic outcome is that it clearly has lost to the *Cardenista* coalition its position as the second electoral power in the country. This has various implications. The first concerns the PAN's former ability to attract a good percentage of the "protest vote." In the final, total vote, the PAN did augment its percentage, but only by a small margin. In regards to a country-wide crisis (seeming to set the almost ideal stage for any proposal by an opposition party), the increase was without a doubt disillusioning.

Among the reasons for this are some that, in my opinion, have not been adequately covered in the post-electoral analyses. The most interesting to me is directly related to the plan put forth by the PAN. Without wanting even to note all its various aspects, some of which clearly are different from the PRI's, it is essential to recall one point. As far as the basic outline for an economic policy (in which, as I will point out later, can be found some explanations for the *Cardenist* vote), the PAN did not propose any alternative to the model created and implemented by the De la Madrid administration and proposed by its official candidate. In fact, the PAN basically proposed to do the same, although more efficiently and, above all, without corruption. The PAN's monomania in the political arena over democracy and morals within government was not enough to make its appeal reach further than the ranks of its traditional supporters. Perhaps for the same reason -- and for its *de facto* proposal in favor of an economic program "such as De la Madrid's, but efficient and morally administered" -- the PAN clearly became consolidated as the party whose principal electoral support lay with the "modern" sectors.

Internal to the PAN is an argument which seems to give new life to the dispute between its principal factions (apparently overcome by the "neopan" hegemony under Clouthier) concerning the type of campaign its candidate conducted. In the opinion of some members, the "populism on the right," aggressive and with a messianic purpose, that dominated Clouthier's campaign could have been among the reasons for his thwarted presidential ambitions.

Along with these negative elements, nevertheless, it is necessary to point out the possibility of a coherent action; for example, among the congressional seats won by the opposition. As a *party*, the PAN remains a second force. None of the parties grouped within the FDN possesses the combination of internal party coherence and widespread electoral support that characterize the PAN today.

What are the future possibilities for this party's development? Two basic types of argument may be presented in this respect. In one, the clear "modernity" of the PAN's electoral base would lend optimism to its future. Through the uncontainable process of economic and political modernization one may anticipate that both the bases for potential and electoral support for the party will increase. Nevertheless, it must be remembered that because of these bases, the PAN will have to compete with the official party whose current, hegemonic proposal also embraces such modernization. It is not unusual that in the course of the election campaign the principal forces of private enterprise are directed clearly to the official candidacy. This will certainly tend to be reinforced at the same time that pressure from "the left within the constitution" as exercised by the FDN clarifies the PRI compromise with Salinas's version of modernity.

The other side of the coin would be the limitations -- that a country with the shortages and social inequalities that characterize Mexico is able to have -- to the attraction of an economic proposal that, at least in the short run, necessarily has an inflationary impact upon the majority of the population. This limitation is relevant to both modernity proposals (Salinas's and the PAN's), but undoubtedly it will be more difficult for the PAN to assimilate. It is not the same for the PRI to go ahead with it, making use of the instruments of social and political control the regime still employs and making up its face with a revolutionary tradition that, although remote, still dominates official speech, as it is for the opposition to present it unadorned and clear and without more support than that of the appeals largely from the so-called "middle sectors" of the country -- those which, in terms of their place in the distribution of the national income, are not in the "middle."

The National Democratic Front also has strong and weak points which derive in good measure from the wide coalition that supported the candidacy of Cuauhtémoc Cárdenas. What brought together all these forces? Why did the electorate decide to support them in such a significant manner? There have been many interpretations. Here I only want to add a point. Since 1973, and in particular during De la Madrid's term, the most relevant partisan debate in the country seemed to take place in an arena artificially small when compared with the political options being discussed at the societal level. Practically every opinion poll available during that period demonstrated a clear division over, for example, protectionism or the continuance of the state's role in the economy. There was practically the same percentage (always over 40%) of those in favor of the *apertura* and a significant reduction in state control as there was opposed. Nevertheless, in the partisan debates, it seemed that this was limited to the positions of the PAN on the right and of the PRI government on the "left," both, as we already have recalled, basically in agreement with the first groups of those polled. It seemed that the second, those who did not want the "dismantling of the state" and the "end of protectionism for national industry" did not have a form of expression on the eminent partisan level.

The disagreement between government and party to which I referred before was concerned, at least in part, with this same problem. It should be remembered that in a Gallup poll conducted during the weeks before the election, practically one fourth of those pledged to vote for the official candidate considered, at the same time, the proposed economic policy of an "opposition candidate" to be preferable. To this disagreement over the economic proposal and, in particular, over the implications that for the majority sectors were formulated under De la Madrid, was joined a second worry. In this instance, it was concerned with the implications the same project held for the autonomy of the country from the rest of the world. Beyond official pronouncements to the contrary, it became clear to many, even the PRI militants, that an open market left to its own devices would result in an increase in the "silent integration" of the Mexican and United States economies and the eventual deterioration of Mexico's power to make governing decisions. Sometimes we forget the complete name of the PRI faction that constituted the true backbone of the FDN coalition: Democratic and *Nationalist* Current.

It often has been commented that because of the multiplicity of original and considerably different governmental programs that the electoral forces had integrated in the FDN, this party had not presented a clear economic proposal. This is true. There was no such precise proposal. Nevertheless, this is not the most important consideration. The *Cardenista* coalition appealed to something known to the electorate and which did not need great precision: The clearest traditions of the so-called ideology of the Mexican Revolution. These were the governing role of the state, preoccupation with the economic and social interests of the major groups, and emphasis on the internal market and defense of the national sovereignty. Even that which has been called the "magic factor" concerning the name of the FDN's candidate, referred precisely to this inheritance. One did not vote for only a Cárdenas but a clear-enough version of the Mexican revolutionary heritage. In this sense, it is extremely simplistic to attribute the FDN vote to an otherwise rational reaction to the specific economic situation of the country. In my opinion, it better represents the persistence in the people's imagination of a program well-known and therefore unnecessary to specify. That such a program should have real viability during the current conditions of the country and the restructuring of the capitalist world with a more global emphasis presents another problem.

To what point will it be possible to institutionalize that which was won? The first sign is that undoubtedly there will be the desire to do it. The very history of the Democratic Current and, in particular, its decision to abandon the PRI in 1987 instead of accepting internal defeat, clearly points out this sentiment. The history of the other real force that exists today in the country (PMS) and especially the long march of PCM towards the unification of forces of an important faction on the Mexican left, also clearly indicates that there will be groups pledged to the task. Nevertheless, the process will not be easy.

Of late, the preferred form of such an institutionalization has become clarified as much as have its foreseeable difficulties. After the election it became clear that at least part of the FDN presidential candidate's attitudes and positions was directed, on one hand, to maintain the unity achieved by a series of undoubtedly very diverse political forces and, on the other, to "raise itself" above any of the parties that formed the coalition. It could be speculated that the intention was to form a party without having to depend upon negotiations with the party authorities. After all, it was commonly agreed that the increase in electoral wealth of such parties as PARM and PFCRN clearly was related to the candidate and not the party's strength. Nevertheless, it was foreseen that the same party directions, raised together by the very electoral results, would not find it easy to join such a proposition. Indeed, the subsequent events have shown this to be the case.

To what point will Cárdenas and those party forces favorable to unification be able to advance in the face of the alternate to maintaining a coalition? I believe that a central factor will be the creation of a new party. An individual affiliation (although not only individual) would have considerable impact independent of what other party structures maintained, at least in the short run. It is not difficult to think that a good part of the militants who on this occasion joined, for example, PARM would transfer their affiliation to the new organization. Nevertheless, the process necessarily will contain not only the sum of the forces but also some subtractions. The net result, in the short run perhaps, diminishes the joined forces of the new organization. But if it is carried out to good end undoubtedly it will establish the bases of that which was announced clearly not only by the same election but also by the revision of data about public opinon, and to which I have made reference already: The existence of real room in the country for a center-left party.

One of the motives that may contribute greatly to this end will be awareness that by having presented single candidates to the legislative elections, the Front would have had a considerable number of victories. In fact, in the metropolitan area of the city of Mexico it would have become overwhelmingly the major force. There is a period of three years until the next legislative elections, and during this time the centripetal and centrifugal forces of the coalition ought to be exaggerated.

The key to the strength of the leftist opposition shaped after the election is defined by its capacity to dispute the very heritage of the Mexican Revolution. For the first time, the Mexican government will have to contend with a real force from the left that underscores and illuminates the contradictions and inconsistencies among, on one side, this heritage and the official rhetoric through which it is expressed and, on the other, the specific policies followed by the administration. In this manner, the left will be able to establish itself in what has constituted historically the center of the national political consensus. Not even the process of again co-opting some of the Front's forces or the left's departure from the official party has been completed.

Two very different and precise clarifications must be made. First, the numerical force among the FDN's social bases of support is not the same as its political force. The official party unilaterally verified the presidential elections not only because it held the barest majority necessary in Congress but because it is backed by the real force of the most important economic and political actors. Thus, it is predictable that, for example, the FDN forces will move from a strictly electoral competence to active competition in the social and unionized arenas of the organization.

The second clarification raises doubts as to how long the leftist coalition will be able to avoid being succeeded by the independent mobilization of diverse social groups. This is another very important component of the current partisan merger in the country. Growing in strength since the end of 1985, the process of autonomy and independence (as much from the corporative structures of control as the still-weak opposition party alternatives) on the part of important nuclei within the population, especially the urban, defines a factor as crucial for the government as for those forces that intend to articulate politically their demands.

I want to emphasize a point that surely gives an optimistic view of the possible future development of this complex gathering of forces. The political and electoral progress of the conjuncture introduces a greater symmetry between the political party and social debates. Those who had no form of political outlet for their opinions may find an important channel in this new force. Perhaps the left's most difficult problem is precisely to articulate very diverse demands in an organized fashion.

Possible Responses from the Salinas Government

I believe that if he lived in a world without restrictions, Carlos Salinas would decently intend (at the same time) both to continue with the political liberalization (*apertura democrática*) in the country and also culminate the project to open up the Mexican economy (*apertura económica*) initiated by the De la Madrid administration. His world, nevertheless, is full of restrictions.

The first is the tension, already discussed, that inevitably occurs in the short run between both *aperturas*. De la Madrid has demonstrated the limitations to any intention to deny this reality. Salinas comes to power thanks to the least modern sectors of the country and the traditional PRI operations to which -- as of the apparent failure of his original campaign proposal -- he had to resort. The limitations that this defines are simply sharpened by his character of "hostage of everyone." The Mexican presidency continues to possess more than sufficient means to surmount these limitations in the last instance, but one ought not to think that Salinas will be able to act regardless of the opinion of his own party's factions, as some former presidents have accustomed us to expect.

Along with these political restrictions, Salinas must confront others of a fundamentally economic nature; 1988 was the first year of De la Madrid's term in which a deficit in the Mexican current account was expected. The Economic

Solidarity Pact, in my opinion born at least partially of political-electoral considerations, maintained jointly before the complexity of the political conjuncture, and transformed into a kind of business card for the *continuista* project -- inevitably will have to give way to a readjustment process in which only the timing of the inevitable devaluation along with its inflationary sequences is not perfectly clear. In the strictly political sphere, the question is, who will be left holding the bag? Will De la Madrid do as his two predecessors and assume the political cost of the economic crisis? Or will Salinas be inaugurated with this gift? Until now, the political logic on both accounts tended to coincide, but since Salinas is now confirmed as "president," this series of questions necessarily has to be put forward.

During the two preceding presidential terms, the coincidence of "political difficulties on the right" and "problems with the neighbors" caused López Portillo as much as De la Madrid to emphasize the recovery of confidence among the private sector and its North American business associates. An organized and coherent leftist force in the discussion did not exist then. Today things are different. Salinas undoubtedly will not be interested in "sharing the government" as has been demanded by some leftist forces, but it is difficult to see how he will avoid having to make some concessions to these same forces. The question then is, which are the most viable concessions?

In this respect, I believe that one can think of two general factors and a third a bit more precise. The first two would be: (A) The necessity of greater political sensitivity in the management of public expenditure, and (B) the maintenance of a foreign policy within the wide margins that embrace "relative independence." The more particular aspect has to do with the management of the foreign debt. A firmer stance in this respect would have indubitable political benefits and would not necessarily be contrary to the most general features of economic liberalization. One may in fact think that it has been precisely this management of the debt, one of the most important pieces of the *apertura* project, that has tended to increase its difficulties in the short run.

That Salinas might make concessions is not to say, in a strict sense, that he will negotiate these concessions. One of his options will be the simple announcement of policies directed towards "stopping the waving of partisan flags" more than strengthening the public presence of leftist opposition.

Some Final Uncertainties

Three central uncertainties ought to be pointed out. The first is the most difficult to evaluate: Will Salinas, the economist, the undeniably intelligent administrator, be equipped to respond adequately when the policy becomes once more the dominant faction in the political conjuncture? Ever since midway through the 1970s, the coalitionary need has been guided basically by economic difficulties. Today the facts are very different and the type of personality perhaps best suited to resolve the first case is not the most propitious for the second. De la Madrid has given abundant examples of this. Will Salinas rise from his politically unattractive image and presence? It is impossible to make a sensible prediction.

The second uncertainty is concerned with facts outside the Mexican government's control: Among them, the evolution of energy prices and whether or not a relatively open United States economy will be maintained in the political conjuncture of 1989. Today, the country is more vulnerable than a few years ago to negative movements in any of these spheres obviously outside the control of the Mexican executive branch.

The third and last uncertainty concerns the possible reaction of those external forces controlling at least part of the game players; in particular, the United States. Here the central questions are clear: Will such forces understand where their true interests are rooted? Will they be able to arrive at an internal agreement about the same? Will both sides reach a basic understanding that permits them to manage the complex, internal, political, Mexican conjuncture without affecting irremediably the tone of bilateral relations? How much room for movement is available to the Salinas government also will depend on the answers to these questions. In the last part of this paper I propose some attempts at a preliminary answer.

Mexico-United States Relations in the Face of the New Political Conjuncture

The point of departure for the succeeding pages is that, more than the facts of the political conjuncture or my interpretation of it, the crucial element for understanding the potential United States response will be necessarily the evaluation of the dominant perceptions respective of these questions in United States circles. To suggest that the most eminent economic, political and even academic forces in the United States spectrum consider that Carlos Salinas's proposal for government constitutes the best recipe for our country (and, coincidentally, their own) would be the same as to use an inadequately tested hypothesis as the background for this paper. The United States reaction since the unveiling of Salinas as the PRI candidate has been not only positive but also has distanced itself from the bitter tone that bilateral relations assumed in 1985 and 1986. Salinas's nomination was not, of course, the only factor in this change in tone -- even apparent months earlier. But, undeniably, it helped encourage an improvement in climate.

What happened in the Mexican electoral campaign has tended to strengthen this positive predisposition towards the PRI candidate. The purpose of the following discussion is to evaluate at what point this predisposition will be transformed into concrete policy measures granting more political leeway. I will attempt this evaluation through four steps. In the first, I will examine one of the roots of conflict in bilateral relations: The limited overlap among the political debates of both countries. Without a doubt, many other causes of problems and tensions exist, and will continue to come into play. Nevertheless, it is sufficient within the limited space of this chapter to introduce only one -- perhaps that most directly related to the preceeding analysis of the Mexican political conjuncture -- in order to suggest some of the difficuities that must confront any attempt at "good relations."

Then I will attempt to counterbalance this first image through an analysis of one of the principal limitations to the intergovernmental conflict, which I developed through earlier work: The so-called "paradox of the precipice" which suggests that when *the American perception* puts Mexico "close to the abyss," intergovernmental negotiation tends to increase. The next section raises the basic supposition of the paradox: The behavior of the United States government as a "rational, unifying actor." At least part of the bureaucratic, not governmental, complexity of the bilateral relations, is examined. The last section tries to identify some facts concerned with the level of "state priority" that relations with Mexico will assume for the next United States government. The supposition here is that only a high degree of state priority can cause the United States government to attempt to define and impose one version of that which constitutes the United States national interest as much in specific areas as in those concerning the relations.

Based upon this argument, my conclusions will introduce some brief speculations about the other side of the equation -- that which occurs north of the border.

The Non-Coincidental Difficulties of Communication among Political Debates

One of the most profound roots of the conflict in Mexico-United States intergovernmental relations is that, on one hand, the political debate in both countries has been largely consensual (the "liberal consensus" on the United States side and the hegemony of the "ideology of the Mexican Revolution" for south of the border) yet, on the other, has overlapped very little. This is best expressed by the fact that each country's political center is oriented in a position very different from where it would be on an imaginary spectrum embracing both.

The consequences of this for intergovernmental relations are very diverse, but the most fundamental is that all discussion that "sells well" south of the border does not do so well in the north, and vice versa. As postwar experience has shown, this cause for discord can be managed when given two conditions. The first depends on if that which is said south of the border has a limited audience in the north; or if only specialists and government follow the "Mexican developments" with attention. The second depends on, above all, North Americans accepting a significant lack of concurrence between official Mexican talk and actual practice of policy, principally the economic. This was the principal aspect of the series of "implicit accords" that governed relations during the postwar period.

Ever since 1973, and particularly during De la Madrid's term, as I already have suggested, the political debate in Mexico seemed to increase the overlap between it and its United States counterpart. This process was limited principally by the movement "to the right" in the United States. In some senses, the Mexican debate ran after that in the United States without ever being able to catch up.

Facts about the political conjuncture examined in the first section of this chapter introduced a change, taking place across more than three lustrums, of major import in this situation. It is not necessary to repeat them here. For an equilibrium most like the old hegemonic ideology and which makes room for the left in the debates that dominated public discussion in the latter years, it is necessary that the pendulum swing back towards the left. In this case, "the movement toward center" in the north is not sufficient to compensate for this change.

On the other hand, significant changes also have occurred with respect to actors in the United States. At least one of the two conditions proposed above appears difficult to recover. Today, that which is said south of the border is listened to and followed by the growing numbers taking part in the debate in the United States. In the future, it will be very difficult to avoid a negative reaction in some eminent North American circles to the type of declarations that the political conjuncture often will impose on the Mexican government. The open question refers to the second of these conditions and already has been put forth in the preceding pages: Will the implicit understandings be revived at least among the political/governmental United States elite? The second part of this section attempts to furnish elements of an opinion in this regard.

The "Paradox of the Precipice" and the Limits of Conflict

Just as there exist deep roots to the conflict in Mexican-United States relations, there also exist factors generally limited to the level of intergovernmental relations. In an earlier work I tried to identify the principal characteristics of one of these factors and it is neither possible nor necessary to repeat them here. It suffices to indicate that the deep and growing links between the economies and societies on both sides of the border -- like the continuity of a project that fundamentally coincides with what the North Americans identify as *our* interests as much as *theirs* -- many times help lift the Mexican government to the rim of the "abyss," but do not give the final, great push.

It is necessary only to clarify that the general restrictions of the argument that I noted above also operate here. It is not important for the purpose of my "heuristic toy" whether or not the country is objectively in the abyss or if that is what we estimate, but that North Americans perceive the situation as critical. In the financial sphere, for example, it is not necessary to be extremely precise in making such distinctions. In the political sphere, though, in which the deciding factor would be developed from what, in the opinion of eminent North American actors, constitutes a "political abyss" for Mexico, precision is crucial.

To clarify this point, one may refer to current bilateral relations. Given the mutilated national debate that predominated in the last five years, the effect any policy of "North American toughness" could have was seen as limited and actually restricted to strengthening the PAN option that, as I have already indicated, established very little room for debate about those themes truly central to the United States concerning the position of De la Madrid's government. In the North American opinion, Mexico seemed very far from the abyss, and so there existed considerable room in which Mexico could push itself without running the risk of falling in. In fact, the best possible world was the consolidation of some terms of debate in Mexico in which the two "extreme" positions became clearly "sensible and responsible."

Today, the situation is very different, and without being exactly on the precipice, the country is able to have taken -- *through a new reading with the North American stereoscope* -- considerable steps in this regard. In the new conjuncture, an image of conflict may help define an identity politically more attractive to the new Mexican president, but also may (especially if they identify important discrepancies between rhetoric and practice) consolidate the positions of the coalition that today dominates the left side of the Mexican political spectrum. Many influential North Americans certainly will ask themselves if it is worth playing with fire. Many also will emphasize the need to compare their country's national security and interest with the specific interests that in diverse spheres would be able to be sacrificed on the altar of a more "comprehensive" policy toward the Mexican government. Nevertheless, it is not realistic to think that they can reach this objective, as I intend to show in the following paragraphs.

Is It Wise to Hope for Coherence?

The new presidents of Mexico and the United States are only two, although the most important, of the numerous actors that weave the tangled web of Mexican-United States relations. The governmental and non-governmental complexity of this, on the other hand, is not limited to the number of interests involved, but also to the fundamental fact that these very interests are many times contradictory, not only between the countries, but also domestically. It is already common to indicate that on both sides of the border there are winners and losers in practically any issue of bilateral relations and that, as a consequence, a good part of those relations are intimately linked with the domestic political realities of both countries. Until now, this has been analyzed particularly concerning the United States side. From now on, it also must come into play south of the border.

This third element raises the supposition of "rational, unified action" upon which the domestic logic of the heuristic toy employed in preceding paragraphs depends. The question that inevitably arises is whether relations with Mexico will assume on the United States agenda a level of sufficient importance so that the central United States authorities will be disposed to pay the undeniable cost of imposing only one policy upon all these actors. This constitutes the fourth and last stage of my argument.

What Priority Will the United States Government Give Mexico?

From the beginning of the 1970s, there has been a constant strengthening of the priority assigned Mexico from within the United States government. The Reagan administration's obsession with Central America has obscured, yet not hidden, this process. Today, any United States government is likely to experience the strengthening of priority given Mexico; in the face of developments to the south of its border, it will be impossible for the United States to continue dedicating the fanatic attention to Central America that has characterized the Republican government's Latin American policy. In fact, the documents that circulated among the teams of both United States candidates, and the recent public presentations of the efforts to develop a bipartisan foreign policy, systematically show Mexico to be one of the inevitable points on the agenda. Thus, on principle, it may expect considerable attention. As always, nevertheless, this level of attention must compete with developments in other areas, not only the Latin American region, but also the world; in particular, those areas the United States identifies as critical.

The Other Side of the Equation and Its Impact on Some Preliminary Conclusions

Unlike Mexico, the United States does not now face such differentiated and clear projects as it did during the two former presidential elections. Thus, it is to be hoped that differences incorporated into those projects regarding its neighbor to the south will not be noticeable. Nevertheless, differences exist and, when evaluated from Mexico's viewpoint, both United States presidential candidates had "favorable" and "unfavorable" points.

It can be derived from the argument developed in this chapter that the political climate of the relationship will be particularly important in this case. The disposition of the president of the United States toward developing new understandings ought to be considered a crucial factor. In this respect, it can be expected that Bush represents the continuation of the relatively positive climate of the last two years and not that which predominated until halfway through Reagan's second term. Dukakis undoubtedly would have introduced an improvement in the climate. This could have had positive consequences. But, it could also raise unrealistic expectations that necessarily will be contradicted by the deep roots of bilateral conflict dominating the relationship. Disappointments hit hardest when expectations are set too high; thus, it is not certain that the "inflation of expectations" would necessarily be positive.

Finally, in those areas of the relationship that systematically and slowly have tended to develop great levels of concurrence between the proposals of both governments -- the economic -- it is difficult not to conclude that the social bases of one and the other candidate also bind each of them in different ways. It would be very difficult to imagine Michael Dukakis vetoing protectionist legislation twice. It is conceivable that those Mexican political forces interested in this issue and, in particular, the continuance of the *apertura* program for the national economy, more closely watch the United States vice presidency than the city in which the Mexican president elect -- as all the United States newspapers remind us -- received his "degree training."

8

Political Perspectives of Mexico: Are Salinas and Democracy Compatible?

By Juan Molinar Horcasitas[1]

At the End of Authoritarianism: Dictatorship or Democracy?

At noon on July 7, 1988, "the day after" the journey that many consider the unquestionable boundary line dividing the past from the present in Mexican politics, Carlos Salinas de Gortari, the then-presidential candidate of the Institutional Revolutionary Party (PRI), declared that the single party system had come to an end.

Excessively euphemistic, that affirmation was not the most applauded statement in Salinas de Gortari's speech to his party colleagues. And with good reason; it had at least three defects. In the first place, it was discourteous. Everyone knows not to mention the rope in the house of the hanged man. Yet that is precisely what Salinas did: Go to the party's house (practically the only party) to tell it that the system which had supported it existed no longer. Second, the statement generated unexpected results. Although it irritated house members, it proved too weak to satisfy those on the outside. It is one thing to declare a single party system dead. It is quite another to act accordingly, or at least to say that it continues, it survives and, above all, explain how it will do so. Then, the statement fell flat because it was delivered before an audience that simply rejected it. Thus, without clarity of goals and amongst bad company, Salinas initiated the long postelectoral journey that awaited him. Many of his party mem-

1 Juan Molinar Horcasitas is a political scientist at the *Instituto Investigaciones Sociales* of the *Universidad Nacional Autónoma de México*. He has carried out extensive research on electoral behavior and political parties in Mexico. Among his publications are articles in *Nexos, Estudios Políticos*, and *Revista Mexicana de Ciencias Políticas y Sociales*. He is author of "The Mexican Electoral System: Continuity by Change," *in Elections and Democratization in Latin America, 1980-85*.

bers, who had viewed him with suspicion since his nomination, now were affronted.

In the interim, from the republic of letters and ideas, many distinguished citizens became interested in carrying out their worldly role and contributing their wisdom. For some reason, one of them and the most notable, suggested the tone for the others with a meteorological metaphor to explain the situation: Dawn or twilight, observed Octavio Paz. A little later, Héctor Aguilar Camín announced the dawn, but was watching some clouds on the horizon. Later, Luis Javier Garrido arrived and instead of dawn saw a clouded sky. Finally, to finish the cycle, Magú arrived and he too saw overcast weather, bringing not only clouds but also thunder and dinosaurs. In the long run, even among many *Salinistas*, the observations of Magú and Garrido ended up dominating, although each observer attributed the overcast and thunder to different causes.

Anyone who still doubts Magú and Garrido's prognostication will be convinced if he remembers the election ratification process; or re-reads the multiple declarations of renowned members of the PRI decreeing the illegality of Cuauhtémoc Cárdenas's words and actions; or remembers the warnings from certain members of the Institutional Revolutionary Party (PRI) who threatened the opposition with rectifying "little reforms," such as proportional representation and other "blandishments" associated with *reyesherolismo*. He also should be convinced if he remembers the words of former President de la Madrid indicating he would not permit change in the system or tolerate any questioning of the legitimacy and electoral triumph of his candidate. That is what concerns the PRI.

For the opposition's part, some declared one candidate a winner and others urged the annulment of the elections. Later, the opposition demanded in chorus that the votes be thrown out. Finally, while some candidates supported the legitimacy of the process, accepting it as a fact with which they had to comply, Cárdenas straight out proposed to Salinas that, as a step towards transition, he should renounce his post as president-elect. Unless one thinks the sayings and acts of one or the other groups are nothing but bravado, one will have to accept the correction of the diagnosis: Overcast with thunder . . . and dinosaurs.

Even if it is true that the decades old, Mexican system of a hegemonic party and noncompetitive elections is in its final crisis, the democratic direction of the transition is not clear. The opposite possibility, that of a strict political system, based more upon coercion and control than legitimacy and expression, must not be eliminated -- especially when the majority of the political actors are sufficiently able to abort a democratic process, while, on the contrary, the cooperation of a majority of the protagonists is needed to conduct the transition to a safe harbor. This is particularly true in the case of Salinas. The democratizing will of Salinas, if it truly exists beyond speeches for the people, proves a necessary but not sufficient condition for a peaceful and orderly transition toward democracy. The weakness or nonexistence of his will, will be enough to halt the transition, or else oblige it to cross hurdles that will claim their quota of violence. From what has been seen till now, little strength can be attributed to the democratizing will of Salinas and his team. On the other hand, his ambitions for power seem full of vitality. To err, in this case, would not only be human but desirable.

One note of caution such as this, that well might seem pessimistic, deserves to be presented. I fear democracy alone does not wait at the end of the transition, but that repression will be present too. In any case, a democratic transition depends upon two principles, true acts of faith: First, the belief that some democratizing vocation exists in the *Salinista* programs; second, the belief that Salinas will try to make good that vocation.

Obstacles to Democratization

The first obstacle that will confront those who push for a democratic transition in the current political conjuncture is a profound split in the Mexican political elite, between the PRI and the opposition. Part of the schism stems from the regime's not having been able to assimilate the growing role of political elites not in the PRI (in fact, many members of the PRI simply reject the idea that the opposition leadership forms part of the power elite). Another split arises from the fact that neither has the governmental nor the PRI elite maintained a basic, consensual unity about the rules of competition for power.

This rupture has been evident since 1982. However, it was accentuated in the second half of Miguel de la Madrid's term and became exaggerated after members of the Democratic Current were expelled from the bosom of the PRI through to the September morning battle that led to the ratification -- many times trammelling justice -- of the 1988 election.

The division that exists among Mexican political elites prevented the regime's essential legitimacy through which the entering administration might advance smoothly towards the democratic transformation of the system. In the final analysis, the legitimacy of a regime does not lie solely in the support, or consent, of the citizenry. To an at least equal degree, it rests upon a consensus among political elites. And where there is no consensus, that is, legitimacy, among elites, there will be difficulty in achieving democracy which, in its most basic form, is regulated competition among political elites who appeal to the electorate in order to establish hegemonies.

In this I believe one cannot be deluded: To attempt to recover legitimizing popular support, before reestablishing accord among elites, may prove to be a vain and counterproductive task, scarcely possible if a situation of total confrontation or an increase in revolutionary tendencies are present. The reestablishment of the lost, inter-elite consensus is, then, the first indispensable step toward an attempt to construct a transition to democracy. The adoption of clear and generally-accepted rules for electoral competition is, simply, the first step toward development of a governmental system based on competition between adversaries, the exercise of a politically responsible government, and the vigilance of loyal opposition.

Peaceful and orderly transition toward democracy also is hampered because just as cupolas are restless, so are the foundations. Many citizens today express themselves as voters, as members of neighborhood organizations, as being affiliated with or sympathetic to special interest groups or political parties. They may not be in the street, but they are on the march, taking steps that at times are calm, and at others, agitated. But they keep marching.

Of course, many members of the PRI and governmental officials bet that the popular mobilization soon will go about extinguishing itself until those who remain on the battlefield are only the victims of an exhausted civic insurrection or isolated activists with diverse ideas. That bet would be a bad one. It is worthwhile to remember that the federal government wagered the same after the earthquake of 1985 and was mistaken. A comparison of the votes in the capital in 1985 and 1988 proves this; or a roll call of the neighborhood organizations that, three years since, remain active; or an inquiry of the delegates from the Department of the Federal District whether they consider themselves a more trustworthy source than the masked man -- Superbarrio.

These are the circumstances in the capital. But the list of mobilizing grievances and motives concerning the interior is not minor. The rejection of centralism is, without a doubt, the principle. Also there are old battles against the traditional *caciquismo* (political bosses) in many regions. The 1985 earthquakes left vein marks on metropolitan society in the form of organized activity different from before; the elections of 1988 will do the same for the national society.

Not all observers may be able to accept this. But it seems to me that the behavior of the electorate in 1988 is novel but not new, considering the accentuated prolongation of the historical tendencies of the Mexican electorate. And if the election of 1988 is in good measure the deepening of a process three decades in development, I do not see why it will have to extenuate itself or go backwards in the months to come, chiefly when its structural causes remain present.

On the contrary, I think that the electorate will not stop harassing the PRI until the state party system has crumbled. The anti-system vote that so alarms the PRI and that engenders such scorn among analysts, will continue to be expressed as long as the cause behind it exists. The citizenry will continue voting against the system it despises, or it will abstain. This is unavoidable because these are probably the most effective rational, political options available. Thus, the electorate will vote with Cárdenas against the system when Cárdenas calls upon it to do so, just as it followed and will follow the National Action Party (PAN) when it offers that option, and just as it will join anyone who leads protest against the regime.

Democratization also will be hindered because the election of 1988, like it or not, is for Carlos Salinas a political transgression that gravely hurts his legitimacy. For Salinas it will be very difficult to confront this political fact because, to begin with, many *Salinistas* will not acknowledge it (although they could convince themselves by asking people in the street their opinion about the honesty of the election).

With these beginnings, Salinas de Gortari has no option: If he wants political leadership, he must efficiently exercise the enormous presidential powers. He rapidly will have to build the legitimacy of government that the election did not give him. This will not be easy to do what with the political and economic conditions that afflict the beginning of his term. To build this legitimacy under the current conditions will be arduous labor that may have many fronts, but that accepts as its principal axis the democratization of the country along with all the risks that democracy implies for the PRI and the *Salinistas* (and let us hope not for the nation).

I am afraid, nevertheless, there will be no few *Salinistas* who stubbornly will deny that their leader lacks political legitimacy. I also am afraid that others who recognize that absence will seek to cure the bad with forgetfulness and bread. To ignore what everyone knows would be an arrogant mistake. To think that time will cure the wound and that bread will satisfy the wronged would also be an error. Mexicans certainly demand an economic plan that starts up production, stimulates the labor market, and raises wages. But they also demand other things: Complete citizenship, conditions of justice, and democracy.

Another reason conflicts will characterize the transition toward democracy is it will be very difficult for the National Democratic Front (FDN) and the PRI to find some permanent method of coexistence that permits competition, but not an unfortunate and hurtful dispute leading to the war that ends only with the annihilation of an adversary. The root of these problems of coexistence is that the FDN and the PRI are so perfectly symmetrical that at times they seem to be mirror reflections of each other. It is aggravating that each one sees in the other's image only the worst of itself.

Besides, the PRI really never has been a party, in the sense of being a part of the whole political scene; it always has wanted to be the great, united front of all Mexicans. It has wanted to be, in fact, the society and its state, the electorate and its representative, the people and its government and, at times it even has proposed, although of course without success, to be the government and its opposition at the same time. In sum, the PRI has wanted to be everything that has legitimate claim to represent the nation.

This attitude has reached a level at which, during a recent period, the law intended to allow the PRI to choose its opposition, even though the top ranks of the PRI did not permit those on the bottom even to elect the most mid-level leaders and candidates. Thusly conceived, thusly organized, the PRI was able to tolerate living with the PAN because "it comes from Miramar" (or from

Washington) and the PRI endured the left because it is "exotic." The charge of foreign origin explains this tolerance in both cases: Since they are not "nationals," they cannot govern. "Its victory is morally impossible," although it exists.

But apparently the PRI is not able to tolerate that mirror image that threatens to leave one day and, complete already with body, soul and organization, divide it, split it, confuse it, destroy it. The FDN, for its part, lives permanently in such a situation because the PRI is a constant threat that intimidates, co-opts, corrupts, and confuses the *Cardenista* group. No transition will be possible without coexistence with that new political entity so disturbing to the PRI. Also, it must be accepted that Mexico's foreseeable political future will have to include the PRI. The twins must learn to live together.

The transition may also take steps backwards because of the PRI's internal struggles. This is serious: Although the PRI, by itself, could not guarantee the democratic transition, it could, alone, ensure authoritarian repression. This is important to emphasize because while the heterogeneity and inconsistency of the FDN are continually mentioned with surprise, worry, or discomfort, infrequently is it said that on the other side conditions are no more compact or coherent. In fact, in Mexico there exists a political body more heterogeneous than the National Democratic Front. It is the PRI, better called the FRI: Institutional Revolutionary Front.

In essence, the sum of ideologies and mentalities, even opposing interests, found within the PRI is very vast and incoherent. The only thing that ties this enormous front together is the cement of power and the role of the president of the Republic as the party's real and unquestionable leader. Without this monopoly of power, without the certainty that only through the PRI will one come to power, and without that presidential role, the FRI will disintegrate. And as the years do not pass without change, and as everything, through use, comes to an end, the cement that holds the PRI together shortly will show signs of cracking.

More and more, those aspiring to political power observe new means of access to local and regional power (paths the opposition offers). In fact, in the metropolitan area of Mexico City, or in Chihuahua, Hermosillo, Mexicali, Ensenada, San Luis Potosí, Mérida and other cities across the country, these aspirants have as much chance of success if the opposition nominates them as they do if the PRI selects them. In other areas, such as León, Ciudad Juárez, or Guadalajara, it is better not to stand as candidate for the PRI.

But this does not do the most damage to the cement holding the PRI together. Even worse, the roads to the peak of the pyramid, and the path that leads to Los Pinos (the excutive residence) no longer run through PRI. The shortcut through the Ivy League, Guardiola, Hacienda, and *Palacio Nacional* has been for some time the quick ladder to the top of the pyramid. On the other hand, by taking the path through the party, one encounters rough ground, hazards, funeral urns and dangers, and, to top it off, one does not climb the pyramid, but circles it. Moreover, those who spend a lot of time in the labyrinth of the PRI generally leave with hands filled with votes, and that, it has been seen, stains one's honor.

In fact, the cement that binds the PRI together no longer applies, or is less effective in holding up the structure. The remedy for greater unity does not consist of throwing on more cement, but in changing the structure.

The system also has problems regarding the role of the president as party high dignitary. Salinas's "partisan" origin -- he arrived very quickly and up the short ladder -- the electoral process that carried him to the top, his lack of legitimacy and the frictions evident between his group and project and the important sectors of the Mexican governmental, party, and union bureaucracy, will confound the fulfillment of party functions traditionally assigned to the president. From the point of view of the democratic transition this could be an asset (no democratization is possible if the president "recovers" the role of party leader that the system has had till now), although it is difficult for *Salinismo* to take it as such because it effectively would mark the boundaries of the president's indiscriminate power.

In this manner, if the next government wants to avoid the political and juridical responsibility of leading the country into a serious tightening of the political system, it will have to carry out a lot of maneuvers at the same time. The first will be to recognize that, in effect, the nearly single party system no longer exists and to act accordingly -- separating the PRI from public resources and governmental protection, accepting the end of the state party system, and learning to coexist competitively with the opposition, including, of course, the twin to the left. The second task will be to accept the primacy of the citizenry and the minimum justice it demands: That their votes be counted, all their votes, and nothing more than their votes. Without these actions, no other measure will have value.

How to do these things without annihilating the PRI is the dilemma the *Salinistas* face. To strengthen the PRI as a political party, or rather, as a political institution with a voluntary membership whose interests it represents and by whom it is financed, is indispensable for making the PRI and democracy compatible. But to strengthen the PRI without returning to the tertiary, the age of the dinosaurs, does not appear easy. "That's the *Salinistas*' problem," will be said with reason. But if the *Salinistas* do not settle their problems they will drag the whole country down with them. If the *Salinistas* want both the PRI along with democracy they will have to resolve the conundrum. If they cannot or do not want to, only one path remains them which I do not doubt they are disposed to traverse: The flaring up of authoritarianism, the establishment of a regime of force that lacks a broad consensus, the surrender to the most coercive forms of corporatism. What can they do? Democracy and state party are exclusive realities. Let everyone choose.

The Rhythm of Change

Salinismo will not be able to enjoy a political truce either to measure its forces, regroup, reestablish alliances and isolate opposing factions, or design its strategy and choose tactics and embark upon them. It had to begin before it took over the reins of government because political time is implacable.

On one hand, the integration of its governmental team and the document that it will have to present to the nation on inauguration day are already part of the political process of transition. The reforms of general political arrangements and real political practices will be the lever, not the obstacle, that would facilitate *Salinismo's* task of transforming the relationships between the state, the government, the work and the capital -- national as much as foreign -- that are implicit in its project for the country. Obviously, *Salinismo* already has involved itself up to the elbows in some of these problems. Since the beginning of September, for example, it opened a campaign to appease the interior and to affirm its internal control in the face of foreign interests. Certainly, considering the calculated size of the problem confronting the regime, these actions have been very prudent. The only truce for which *Salinismo* may hope already has come from outside. Nevertheless, the most important front is at home. And at home, *Salinismo* "only" has the support (but not for free) of the monied class. Although quite a lot, that is not sufficient but dangerous because there is no state sanction for the government's support of itself through two allies that expensively condition their loyalty: The men with capital and the dinosaurs.

On the other hand, the electoral calendar of the country promises the government a constant mobilization in diverse parts of the territory. Before the next presidential term begins, many elections will occur: In October, 1988 there were elections in towns in Veracruz and Tlaxcala and for the legislature in Coahuila; in November there were municipal elections in Nuevo León, Chiapas, Colima and Campeche; and in Tabasco, elections for the governorship, the local chamber, and cities. Salinas received all this by electoral inheritance, but then scarcely seventy-two hours after his inauguration, there were city elections in Guanajuato, San Luis Potosí, and Zacatecas, in addition to elections for the high level positions, the governor, legislators and municipal presidents in Jalisco.

As if this were not enough, 1989 presented another full and complicated calendar: Fifteen state legislatures were elected (among these there were elections in Michoacán, Chihuahua and Durango in July, Baja California in September, Sinaloa in November and Guerrero in December). Also, townships in eleven states held elections and the governor's seat in Baja California was renewed.

Many of these states traditionally have been sites of conflict. In some cases, such as Veracruz and Chiapas, the conflict has been characterized by abstention (except in presidential elections, of course) and by factionalism within the PRI and the intolerance or violence that the old *cacicazgos* impose. In others, such as Guanajuato, San Luis Potosí, Jalisco, Baja California, and Michoacán, conflict has arisen from the strong presence of the opposition. And finally, while others have not seen much conflict in the past, change now is promised.

In a situation such as this, it is not possible to expect a truce. Any strategy based on letting time take its course will be condemned to rapid failure. Neither in the federal electoral sphere does the PRI have time, although so it might seem. The next federal election must not be carried out within the same legal framework as before. Because the necessary transformation is profound, and surely will include constitutional reforms, Salinas's team will have to initiate three immediate tasks. Remember, so as not to trip twice upon the same stone, López Portillo launched his political reforms only a few weeks after his inauguration; the reform process of the Federal Elections Code was begun more than two years prior to the election and the legal and parliamentary processes necessary for the maturation of constitutional reform, even at double speed, were scarcely completed. These reforms required several years (two or three), yet took place within political conditions that permitted the exclusion of a consensus among the opposition.

This implies that the task of democratization, if it will be assumed by *Salinismo*, cannot be postponed. Perhaps *Salinismo* would want to be able to have time to fortify itself and begin the task later. That is not possible. It seems to me, in fact, that *Salinismo* and the "renovators" of that team ought to put the affair in reverse: The only means by which they can strengthen themselves *vis-á-vis* the internal factions opposing them is by immediately assuming the offensive in the process of political reform. That process will encounter many setbacks and obstacles of great importance. These are inevitable if the objective of democratization is assumed. To postpone the inevitable would not help those who push democratization in Mexico. Many of the country's political, economic, and social problems are huge today because in their time the responsibility of attacking them was postponed. Once again, time works against the "renovators." If democratization of the Mexican system is an audacious idea, then it requires audacious politics.

Salinismo would have an advantage if it launched itself into the democratization: The sectors of party, union, and government bureaucracies that most oppose it do not have anywhere else to go, because nowhere are they wanted more than in the PRI. If *Salinismo* took the democratic offensive not only would it make progress in the expiation of its original sin, the election, but it would convert the dinosaurs, technosaurs and tyrant-osaurs into hostages of its politics, instead of *Salinismo* being the hostage of the most retrogressive, political forces in Mexico.

9

Morality and Democracy in Mexico: Some Personal Reflections

By Samuel I. del Villar[1]

My purpose here is to establish the link between the fundamental morality of the Mexican people, the outcome of the July, 1988 presidential elections, and the basis for confidence in Mexico's democratic future. Since I am writing for a United States audience, the prevailing United States interpretation of Mexican morality and politics serves as the reference point for my analysis.

Perhaps the best known book in the United States about "modern day" Mexico is Alan Riding's *Distant Neighbors: A Portrait of the Mexicans*. Mr. Riding is neither a United States citizen by birth nor a naturalized citizen. Nevertheless, no other book about Mexico has been more influential in the United States than this best seller by a *New York Times* correspondent.

Distant Neighbors was published in the mid 1980s. However, it failed to anticipate, or to give even the slightest hint of, the constitutional crisis that resulted from the July, 1988, presidential elections. Riding acknowledged that "the system may find in the 1980s that democracy has become both too important a myth to dismantle and too dangerous a reality to tolerate." But, he declared further that this dilemma could be avoided through the use of all kinds of political -- including corrupt -- gadgetry and that it would fall short of democracy. Mr. Riding suggested the Institutional Revolutionary Party (PRI) "can fragment the opposition vote by legalizing more parties with middle-class appeal and secretly financing their campaigns; ... it can pour public investment into regions where support for the opposition is growing; ... it could introduce genuine primary

---

1 Samuel I. del Villar is professor at the *Centro de Estudios Internacionales* of *El Colegio de México*. He received his doctorate in juridical science from Harvard Law School and his research has focused on micro and macro economics, international economic and legal relations, and constitutional law. Del Villar has maintained an active journalistic career with *Excélsior, Proceso*, and *Razones*, and has contributed articles to the *Financial Times* and the *New York Times*. He has served as advisor to two presidents of Mexico in areas of tax reform and anti-corruption measures.

elections to improve the quality of its candidates and to create new transmission belts to carry grassroots sentiments up the bureaucratic pyramid. The PRI could even borrow from the experience of the Democratic and Republican parties in the United States and project a different image in different parts of the country."

The system, in fact, has been following Mr. Riding's recipes. But it failed to prevent the major electoral rebellion in post-revolutionary Mexico. This rebellion broke the system, in effect since 1924, whereby the president selects his successor and the people legitimize that selection through their votes.

All political parties formerly allied with the PRI broke with the system and became part of the real -- not "loyal" -- opposition. Massive public expenditure by the PRI in critical regions did not buy these parties' political support. The order of the primaries, as established by the PRI XII General Assembly, not only increased the bidding, price, and corruption involved in the PRI nominations, but also decreased their popular acceptance. And the different images of the highly-centralized system -- Indian hats in the south of Mexico and Texan-style hats in the north -- did not prevent massive electoral rebellion throughout the country.

Furthermore, the system was politically broken from within. Under the leadership of the heir of Lázaro Cárdenas, Mexico's most significant postrevolutionary president, a new coalition of forces, including the nationalist center-left that had sustained the PRI, took over. This coalition seems to have won most of the vote in most electoral precincts that were under public scrutiny. Mr. Riding had predicted that "the absence of municipal elections in Mexico City eliminates the danger of an embarrassing electoral confrontation." Nevertheless, the system, i.e. the PRI, had to acknowledge officially that Mr. Cárdenas won the core of the country.

The system was also pressured by electoral rebellion from the political right. Under the leadership of a northern entrepreneur, the National Action Party (PAN) reinvigorated both its democratic power base and also its legitimacy as the national center-right party, which had been challenged by the PRI's technocratic leadership.

Mr. Riding's book is, by all means, an excellent collection of the various angles of "a portrait of the Mexicans," and should be a top item in any bibliography of Mexico. Its basic flaw, however, is the moral dimension that it projects for an assessment of the character and spirit of Mexicans. The depiction of this spirit gives life to any portrait, and the artist's ability to paint accurately determines whether he will create a masterpiece. And this is what Mr. Riding's book, and, along with it, the prevailing foreign perceptions of Mexicans and Mexico, have failed to achieve.

Immediately after his chapter concerning the "Loyal Opposition" (which has become so "disloyal" and which questions the legitimacy of the system both from left and right), Riding deals with "Corruption: Oil and Glue." His basic thesis is that corruption in Mexico is "an aberration of the law, but not of society," that it "enables the system to function, providing the perennial 'oil' that makes the wheels of the bureaucratic-machine turn and the 'glue' that seals political alliances." He is wrong. Mexican society is profoundly moral. And corruption does not explain the functionality of the system. Instead, it explains its economic crises, and its imminent political collapse.

The analytical flaw Mr. Riding makes is to deal with the moral and legal dimensions of Mexican culture as something different from its economic, social, and political dimensions. The inefficiency and injustice of corrupt allocative mechanisms, either through the financial, fiscal and regulatory systems, or through PEMEX (*Petróleos Mexicanos*) and other enterprises, is behind Mexico's long lasting economic crises. And bureaucratic plans and corporative pacts, "sealed by the glue of corruption," in Mr. Riding's terms, will continue to make it worse. Electoral fraud, or corruption, is the basis of the political crisis in Mexico. And it certainly cannot be overcome by a government grounded in electoral fraud.

The Mexicans' electoral rebellion in July of 1988 was precisely the expression, from left to right, of the profound morality of the Mexican society that has decided to live under a democratic rule of law. Also, it has decided to reject Mr. Riding's alternative system of oil and glue. It is a basic mistake to confuse the spirit and values that invigorate Mexican society with the vices of a decadent bureaucratic-corporativist system that denies that spirit and those values. The expression of this social morality of Mexicans is not new, although some ignorant technocrats like to present it as their own "modernizing" invention. It was the basis for the founding of the nation and it has provided the motives for Mexico's long-lasting constitutional history.

On July sixth, the majority of the Mexican people exercised their right, as acknowledged since 1857 by constitutional order, to choose a government and to build a democratic government established by that order. This deed did not occur out of the blue. It is the most refined product of Mexico's political-constitutional system. Among its most significant antecedents during this century one may point out the following:

--The prevalence of freedom of expression and freedom of the press as a result of the 1968 Tlatelolco crisis.

--The establishment of the unquestionable constitutional authority of the president as initiated under President Cárdenas and consolidated by the transition to civilian presidents under President Alemán in 1946.

--The consolidation of the constitutional revolutionary principle of "no reelection" of presidents that occurred after the attempt to thwart this principle under President Obregón (leading to his death).

--The uprising of Venustiano Carranza, the first chief of the Constitutionalist army, against the usurper dictator, Victoriano Huerta, that produced the ideological integration -- combining the liberal principles of the XIX century with the justice principles of our new Hispanic heritage -- of the Mexican revolution under our 1917 Constitution.

--And, there is the Mexican revolution initiated in 1910 by Francisco I. Madero under the banner of *sufragio efectivo* (effective vote) which even preceded the motto of "no re-election" and which inspires today the reinvigoration of democratic values in Mexican society.

The fundamental political demand to make the government answerable to the morality of the people was more than evident in the 1982 presidential elections. Moral renovation was a political current within the PRI, headed by Miguel de la Madrid. It attempted to build a bridge between government and people. It was the basis for De la Madrid's nomination in 1981 and for his election to the presidency of Mexico in 1982. It was for me a great honor to have been appointed by him to chair the task force within the PRI which transformed this electoral platform into a constitutional, legislative, and governmental project. Its substance was the renewal of the regime established after the Mexican revolution based upon a radical attack against the corruption that has undermined its political, economic, and cultural institutions, and the ability of these institutions to achieve the values of justice, creativity, and democracy that inspired the Mexican revolution.

Administrative discretion cancelled the moral-renovation political mandate of the 1982 elections. And in the 1988 elections, the Mexican people voted for a change of the system that had failed to renew itself in accordance with the national morality and the popular will. It has been suggested, again without regard for Mexican realities and history, that after the 1988 elections, the Mexican way to democracy will be the Russian way: *Perestroika* and *glasnost*. To the extent that De la Madrid's Moral Renovation and Gorbachev's *perestroika/glasnost* have been reformist currents from within, the analogy might have been relevant six years ago when the Russian concept was still unknown. But, after the 1988 definitive vote of the Mexicans for immediate and effective democracy, the analogy is entirely obsolete for use in understanding the Mexican way to democracy.

If an international analogy is to be established, it seems to me that the Spanish way -- culturally much nearer -- would be more relevant. When the Arias government failed to renew the corporatist-Franco state from within, it was replaced by the interim Suárez government that called for a democratic constitutional Congress, so opening the way for Spanish constitutional democracy. Using this analogy, some people have suggested that Mexico cannot make a peaceful transition to democracy because it does not have a monarch. Fortunately, Mexico has been a firmly established republic since 1864, and it also has something that Franco's Spain did not have: A constitution deeply rooted in its history which truly reflects the national morality and commands the way to democracy.

Reference

Riding, Alan. 1985. *Distant Neighbors: Portrait of the Mexicans*. New York: Alfred A. Knopf.

10

Challenges for Mexico's Opposition in the Coming *Sexenio*[1]

By Joseph L. Klesner[2]

All observers agree that the July, 1988 presidential election in Mexico produced a challenge to the ruling *Partido Revolucionario Institucional* (PRI) unprecedented since its origin sixty years ago. The bare majority accorded to the PRI presidential candidate Carlos Salinas de Gortari demonstrated the dramatic growth in the electoral popularity of opposition parties, particularly on the left. Furthermore, the oppositions[3] grabbed an unexpectedly large share of the seats in the Chamber of Deputies and won their first contested senatorial seats ever.[4] With only 260 of the 500 deputyships, the PRI congressional contingent will be forced to devote more energy to legislative duties than it has been accustomed to in the past: A congressional seat will no longer be a largely ceremonial task. The PRI candidates for state and municipal posts also face the possibility of electoral defeat in the coming *sexenio*, a likelihood about which they seldom have had to worry in the last six decades. Indeed, as many already

1 Research for this paper was made possible by a faculty development grant from Kenyon College.

2 Joseph L. Klesner is assistant professor of political science and director of international studies at Kenyon College in Ohio. He received his Ph.D. in February, 1988 from MIT; his dissertation title was "Electoral Reform in an Authoritarian Regime: The Case of Mexico." He has published several articles on the 1977 Mexican electoral reforms in the context of post-revolutionary Mexican regime evolution based upon research conducted in Mexico under a Fulbright award. He had a recent article in *LASA Forum*.

3 I use the plural "oppositions" to indicate that Mexico's opposition parties are not unified and that they are ideologically distinct even though they do act together at times, especially in defending the sanctity of the electoral process.

4 Jorge Cruickshank of the opposition *Partido Popular Socialista* (PPS) was senator from Oaxaca from 1976 to 1982. However, his election was uncontested by the PRI, which was repaying him for his collaboration in the PRI's defeat of the PPS gubernatorial candidate in Nayarit in 1975, Alejandro Gascón Mercado.

have asserted, the explosive emergence and growth of Mexico's opposition parties clearly reveals that Mexican politics has entered a new era. President Salinas himself admitted on the day after the election, "The virtual one-party system has ended and a new political era has begun with a majority party and intense competition from the opposition" (Salinas, 1988).

The PRI, then, has suffered an extraordinary setback, one indicating that the party system and the political regime are on the verge of transformation into a more competitive electoral order and, possibly, a more democratic political regime. By and large, this portends great opportunities for Mexico's opposition parties, whose leaders have struggled for two decades (and more, in the case of the *Partido Acción Nacional* -- PAN) to force the ruling elite to allow the oppositions to compete for office on a fair and equal basis with the PRI and so they might reject both its parties. The years that the leaders of the left spent in the political trenches seeking the support of enough voters to stay alive as registered parties and the decades that the PAN's leaders spent outnumbered in the Chamber of Deputies and in electoral races seem finally to be paying off with unprecedented electoral popularity and larger-than-ever congressional representation. Yet, this optimism about the oppositions' future must be tempered with realism about the challenges still facing the PAN and the parties of the *Frente Democrático Nacional* (FDN), which supported Cuauhtémoc Cárdenas's candidacy for the presidency. I would like to briefly review three sets of conditions which the oppositions must confront in the coming *sexenio* in their quest not merely to deflate the PRI's margins of victory, but to eliminate its monopoly on power in Mexico. These conditions are (A) the need to build more effective national party organizations, (B) the need to overcome the electoral challenges that the PRI will undoubtedly present in state and municipal elections, and (C) the difficulty of maintaining opposition unity in the Chamber of Deputies.

Building National Party Organizations

If the oppositions intend to overcome the PRI's electoral dominance outside of Mexico City and a few other urban centers (Guadalajara, Ciudad Juárez, and León, most notably), those parties must build organizations capable of presenting and supporting appealing candidacies throughout the nation, including in the more than two-thousand rural *municipios*[5] of Mexico. Those party organizations must also be able to provide and protect poll watchers at the more than fifty-thousand voting places in the country. Until those organizations

---

5 *Municipios* are similar to counties in the United States.

develop such capacities, they can neither expect to appeal to pluralities of voters in the hundreds and thousands of electoral races open each *sexenio* nor hope to defend the victories they believe they have won. However, students of Mexican politics frankly know little about the organizational aspects of opposition parties and the extent to which they reach into the neighborhoods and villages of Mexico.[6] A lot has been written about the ideological tenets of opposition parties, struggles over their leadership, and their electoral fortunes. Most knowledge of the organizational strengths and weaknesses of opposition parties must be inferred from observation of their other characteristics: The distribution of their electoral support, ideological and leadership struggles within them, and the general quality of their campaign efforts. My suspicion, supported by observations of campaigns and electoral results, is that the opposition is weak organizationally, mainly because it lacks members outside major cities. So, while some have remarked that the PRI itself is relatively weak in many parts of the nation, especially that its membership has little role within the party because most members are indirect members of the party, the PRI is overwhelmingly stronger as an organization than the other parties (Garrido, 1987). Based on what is known, what have these opposition parties accomplished thus far and what challenges still face them?

Partido Acción Nacional (PAN)

Of the opposition parties, the PAN has the most extensive organization. Founded in 1939 as a political party that would present a Catholic social philosophy and promote democratic principles, the PAN has far more electoral experience than any other opposition party. These fifty years of political and electoral participation can mislead the observer, however, for the PAN has only presented candidates in the full slate of federal deputy races since 1964. Even in 1973, the PAN ran deputy candidates in only 172 of the 194 federal districts (Klesner, 1988). In the early 1970s, Mabry concluded:

---

6 While one might hope that defending the vote would be unnecessary in a country where democratic electoral practices have been constitutionally established since before the Revolution, and in which recent survey research has suggested a generally democratic political culture exists, nonetheless, democratic rights must often be defended against those who would subvert them for personal gain. As Mexican journalist León García Soler noted, even in the highly competitive Chihuahua elections in 1986, the PAN was unable to present poll watchers at all polling places in the state. As he said, "Nowhere in the world and at no point in time can you trust the competitor to count and recount and then tell you what happened . . . opposition parties suffer from weak organization" (*Voices of Mexico*, 1988: 25). On the political culture of Mexico, see Booth and Seligson (1983).

The state of the extension of PAN organization in Mexico means that the party cannot hope to influence all of the citizenry directly and consistently. Permanent organizations are obviously advantageous for the operation of a political party but the ability to create them is simply beyond the scope of PAN resources. Reliance upon temporary committees at election time is necessary but prevents the party from gaining the experience necessary for the conquest of significant posts of power. Moreover, it aids the claims of rivals that the PAN would be incapable of ruling the country if the party were ever to win a presidential election (Mabry, 1973: 124).

Since the early 1970s the PAN has become a more militant party, with a more conservative and fervently expressed message and a more vigorous electoral effort. In recent years the PAN has further increased its popularity in the northern states, especially in Sonora, Chihuahua, and Durango. The PAN challenges to the PRI in the 1985 federal deputy elections and the elections in Chihuahua in 1986, including the protests of fraud lodged by *panistas* and non-violent demonstrations against fraud led by *panistas* after those elections, showed an invigorated PAN. The 1988 presidential campaign of Manuel Clouthier was the party's largest campaign production ever. Yet, when asked in late May 1988 (less than two months before the election) by the Gallup Organization whether they knew a lot, little, or nothing about the 1988 presidential candidates, over half (53%) of the sample of 2,960 Mexicans said they knew nothing about Clouthier; and 62% of persons without university or technical school education knew nothing about him. This compared very unfavorably with knowledge about the PRI's candidate, Salinas, and even with the FDN's candidate, Cárdenas.[7] Although the Mexican press and mass media must be held responsible for deliberate efforts to ignore the candidacies of Clouthier and Cárdenas, these statistics clearly indicate the continued weakness of the PAN organization, its inability to reach the majority of Mexicans with its message. Until just recently the PAN could proudly point to its refusal to accept the public funding made available to opposition parties as part of the 1977 *Reforma Política* as evidence of its organizational superiority to other parties of opposition which immediately accepted public funding when it became available to them. This did not reflect the class bases of the various parties of opposition so much as the willingness of the PAN volunteers to solicit funding, especially through raf-

---

7 In comparison, 43% of the sample knew nothing about Cárdenas and 23% knew nothing about Salinas. Of those without university or technical school education, 50% knew nothing about Cárdenas and 32% knew nothing about Salinas. ECO/Gallup Mexico Pre-Election Survey Press Release, 16 June 1988.

fles and other small revenue generating efforts. But even these remained limited mostly to the large cities and in the aftermath of the 1988 presidential campaign the PAN has been forced to accept public funding in order to remain solvent (*Excélsior*, October 30, 1988).

The PAN and Neopanistas

Although the PAN had become a Christian socialist party by the 1960s under the leadership of Adolfo Christlieb, Manuel González Hinojosa, and Efraín González Morfín, that reformist ideology came under pressure from more conservative and free-market oriented members of the party, led principally by José Angel Conchello. The latter group, which included Pablo Emilio Madero, the nephew of the apostle of the Mexican Revolution, eventually won the struggle for the soul of the party, causing González Morfín, González Hinojosa, and many of their followers to abandon the PAN (*Proceso*, 1978, 1979, 1984). Conchello and Madero, both of whom had extensive connections in the business community in Monterrey, moved the party to the right and thereby made it more appealing to businessmen and members of the middle class who chose to oppose the PRI after the beginning of the economic crisis and the nationalization of the banks in 1982. Indeed, in the De la Madrid *sexenio,* many businessmen and members of the middle class joined the PAN and became known as *neopanistas* due to their status as late-comers to the party. These *neopanistas* included such prominent leaders of the business community as Fernando Canales Clariond, a Monterrey businessman who put up a stiff challenge to the PRI in the 1985 Nuevo León gubernatorial race; Emilio Goicochea Luna, a former president of CONCANACO, the small business organization; José Luis Coindreau, a former president of COPARMEX, the employers' association; José María Basagoiti, yet another ex-leader of COPARMEX; and Manuel Clouthier, former president of both COPARMEX and the *Consejo Coordinador Empresarial* (CCE) and the PAN's 1988 presidential candidate (Story, 1987; Baer, 1985).

The *neopanistas'* strident demand that the state withdraw from its large involvement in the economy and their more confrontational approach to the PRI in electoral contests initially won the PAN more votes in the 1985 federal deputy elections (in some, but not all states) and in various state and municipal elections, principally in 1982 and 1983. However, the 1988 election results hint that much of that support may have been directed to the PAN in the past because it was the most efficacious opposition; that is, it was a protest vote accorded to the PAN as the most prominent opposition party. Even allowing for the distortions in the official election figures caused by electoral fraud, in 1988 the PAN clearly did not build much on its initial burst in the beginning of the De la Madrid *sexenio*. The appearance of an efficacious opposition candidacy on the left in the form of the *Cardenista* coalition siphoned off much of the PAN's previous electoral support. Polling data supports this conclusion. Table 10-1 shows opinion data from two polls which demonstrate that many voters who previously voted for the PAN were willing this time to vote for Cuauhtémoc Cárdenas. Obviously, the commitment to the PAN by previous electoral supporters was quite conditional.

Why was the PAN unable to maintain the loyalty of these past supporters? I suggest three possibilities: The unusual appeal of the Cárdenas candidacy, questions many voters had about the programmatic statements of the PAN, and reservations voters had about the leadership qualities of the PAN presidential candidate, Manuel Clouthier. The first of these is obvious; the Cárdenas candidacy may be exceptional. In any case, the PAN could do little about it once Cárdenas declared his candidacy. The last two say much about the PAN in the era of the *neopanistas*. The PAN always has strongly defended democracy and undoubtedly received votes because of that. Whether the PAN voters ever voted for the PAN's other programmatic statements is much less clear and certainly put into serious doubt by the fence-crossing that took place in this election. The *neopanistas* not only have moved the PAN more to the right on economic issues, but also toward greater intransigence on some social issues such as abortion and on law and order issues. As polls show, this may appeal to middle and upper class voters generally and more specifically to businessmen, managers, professionals, other white-collar employees, and housewives. However, these groups are also beginning disproportionately to favor the PRI as well because of the challenge from the left (*Prospectiva*, 1988). Who does that leave most firmly in the PAN's camp? Among others, the strong PAN supporters are members of certain "intermediate groups," including *Desarrollo Humano Integral, A.C.* (DHIAC), ProVida, the *Unión Nacional de Padres de Familia*, and the *Asociación Nacional Cívica Femenina*, all of them quite conservative on family and social issues. The presence of these groups in the PAN's campaign likely alienated some less conservative voters who had previously cast their ballots for the PAN candidates (*El Cotidiano*, 1988). Perhaps recognizing the limitations this creates for the PAN as a mass party, PAN President Luis H. Alvarez, an old-time *panista* respected by all for his hunger strike against electoral fraud in Chihuahua in 1986, stated "We should be present in the social movements that come from below, participate more actively in all phases of national life." In justifying a recent PAN decision to accept funding from federal sources, Alvarez seems to have identified the danger to the party's mass appeal created by the strong *neopanista* presence, saying that it was necessary to accept federal funding so as not to rely on "economic groups that want to manipulate the party line," (*Mexico Journal*, 21 November 1988).

Clouthier's candidacy may have handicapped the PAN as well. His campaign quickly became a lightning rod for criticism from the left [8] and by some former *panistas* (Arriola, 1988).[9] His campaign style was undisciplined, populist, and slightly authoritarian. The aftermath of the election suggests that his rhetoric exhorting his followers to civil disobedience was largely bluster and not quite as timely as the civil disobedience movement in the Philippines, which he used as his example of the efficacy of civil disobedience.[10] To his credit, Clouthier ran a high profile, confrontational campaign against the PRI in which it seemed as if he was warmly received by the *panista* audiences he met. However, despite running the most expensive and dynamic race ever staged by the PAN, Clouthier lost. If the *neopanistas* continue to produce Clouthiers as their presidential standard-bearers, the PAN is in trouble.

The PAN as Third Force?

In the wake of the 1988 election, the PAN leadership must carefully consider the party's real electoral strength as the PAN begins to choose the roles it can fill now that *Cardenismo* has apparently forged some degree of unity in the left. On the downside, the PAN leaders must recognize that the party's official national electoral strength remains at about 17% of the voters. This means that in terms of the aggregate electoral result, the PAN performed no better in 1988 than in 1982 or 1985 despite what has been characterized in the press as an unprecedented challenge to the PRI's hegemony. In a number of the PAN strongholds, such as Baja California, Coahuila, Durango, Nuevo León, Sonora, and the Federal District, the PAN made no gain in the three years since 1985 or in some cases even lost ground while the PRI held its own and Cárdenas drew voters away from the PAN (see Table 10-2). If the left remains unified under the *Cardenista* banner, the PAN may be forced to accept a permanent minority status as either second or third force in most or all of the states. *Panistas* of long standing are accustomed to this permanent minority status; the party has a long

---

8 Rodolfo Echeverría Ruiz wrote a series of essays in *La Jornada* entitled "*Clouthier: máxima debilidad del PAN*" (20-23 June 1988) while long-time *priísta* Rodolfo González Guevara earlier had joined the crusade in an essay titled "*PAN, la Contrarrevolución*," *Excélsior*, 3 May 1988. The thesis that the PAN resembled the Nicaraguan contras as a force of counterrevolution was voiced by several journalists (Cepeda, 1988; García, 1988; see also Nuncio, 1986).

9 For example, see the paid advertisement against Clouthier in *La Jornada*, 2 July 1988, p. 13.

10 In May the PAN had staged a trial run for post-election civil disobedience by blocking federal highways throughout the country (*Unomásuno*, May 29, 1988, *Punto*, May 30, 1988). On methods of civil disobedience proposed by the PAN, see *Proceso*, February 29, 1988.

record as a loyal opposition. The party leadership still includes a number of old-time militants such as Luis Alvarez, the party president, Bernardo Bátiz, Jesús González Schmall, and Abel Vicencio Tovar who have played the roles of critics of the regime and civic educators for many years. They may be willing to continue their militancy in the party despite the likelihood that the PAN will not come to power, at least not by itself. However, whether the *neopanistas* who have joined the party and have pushed the party into a more confrontational electoral strategy in recent years will be willing to continue their efforts in the party if its permanent minority status is not likely to change is less clear. Certainly struggles within the PAN's party leadership and mass membership, about its future roles should be expected.

However, the accomplishments of the PAN over the past *sexenio* can be interpreted in another way. From 1982 to 1988 the PAN was consistently in the news, at least in the print media. It has had six years to get its message across to the electorate, to convert voters to its cause, and to build its organization in some parts of the country. As Tables 10-2 and 10-3 show, the PAN has had success in building its core of electoral supporters in some parts of the country, most notably in the west (Aguascalientes, Colima, Jalisco, Nayarit, and Sinaloa) and in Yucatán (including the neighboring state of Campeche, never a hospitable area for the PAN). Furthermore, the 17% of the vote received by the PAN in 1988 also must be interpreted in the following way: In the past, much of the PAN vote was for *an opposition*. Now, because many voters chose FDN, yet the PAN still received 17% means that it may be a firmer 17%. In fact, it must demonstrate some conversion of PRI voters because, despite the introduction of the FDN candidacy, the PAN did not see its vote share decline. In some areas where the FDN did phenomenally well (Baja California, the Federal District, and even Michoacán), the PAN held its own; that is, it did not lose many voters. This suggests that the PAN has a strong enough organization to represent and turn out about one-fifth of the Mexican electorate. The regional concentration of this effort in the north, west, and the Yucatán does, though, suggest that this organization is not yet national in scope. There are still several states in which the PAN cannot get more than 5 to 10% of the official vote.

The conclusion I derive from this past electoral cycle is that while the introduction of the *neopanistas* into the ranks of the party has brought dynamic new blood to the PAN and converted many voters to the party message, the PAN remains weak in some important aspects. If the left coalition stays together, the PAN probably will be only the third electoral force. This will create tensions within the party about its mission in Mexican politics. The PAN's ideological drift to the right may have captured a core of supporters, but may also make it difficult for the party to join a coalition with other elements of the opposition should the PRI's majority slip away in the subsequent federal deputy races. Furthermore, keeping these new militants and voters with the party will be a challenge to an organization which really cannot afford to maintain financially more than a minimal number of full-time party activists and bureaucrats. The PAN, after all, does not have the patronage resources enjoyed by the PRI, but its activists are more accustomed to the middle class lifestyle than many militants on the left. The costs of trying to break out of third place will become increasingly apparent as the PAN begins the long cycle of state and local elections, which I discuss below.

The *Cardenista* Coalition

Making conjectures about the organizational future of the left in Mexico is tricky business. Unification talks have dominated the recent history of the Mexican left. By and large, those unification discussions can only be considered qualified successes. Cuauhtémoc Cárdenas's presidential campaign provided an unprecedented focus for the left's efforts which brought the left together electorally for the first time since Cárdenas's father orchestrated a united front in the 1930s.[11] The challenge for the left, though, is to maintain that unity of purpose in the aftermath of the election. Under Cárdenas's leadership, some members of the left have formed the *Partido Revolucionario Democrático* (PRD) with the intention of giving organizational focus to the coalition effort that took place during the presidential campaign. While I do not wish to downplay the unique opportunity this presents to the left, I would like to highlight some obstacles to the formation of a solid left coalition or party.

The Need for Organizational Development

The PAN may face the challenge of extending its organization into more entities of the nation, but the unified left (whether under Cuauhtémoc Cárdenas

---

11 On the *Cardenista* popular front and the role of the Mexican Communist Party in it, see Carr, 1986;1987.

or not) faces the fundamentally more difficult task of forging an organization where none existed before. There are, among the parties that formed the FDN, some regional organizational strengths. The *Partido Auténtico de la Revolución Mexicana* (PARM), never a party of the left, but the party under whose banner many members of the *Corriente Democrática* ran in 1988, has for more than a decade been the principal opposition party in the northeastern state of Tamaulipas.[12] Alejandro Gascón Mercado, who has spent the past decade and a half in various parties of the left, has had organizational strength in his home state of Nayarit. Cárdenas himself has a very effective organization in Michoacán where he was governor until 1986. Both the *Partido Popular Socialista* (PPS) and the *Partido Socialista de los Trabajadores* (PST), recently renamed the *Partido del Frente Cardenista de Reconstrucción Nacional* (PFCRN), have done well electorally of late in Veracruz. Finally, the *Partido Socialista Unificado de México* (PSUM), which incorporated the *Partido Comunista Mexicano* (PCM), and the nationalist *Partido Mexicano de los Trabajadores* (PMT) have developed extensive organizations in the Mexico City area (including the state of México) and Guadalajara. In 1987, after years of discussion, the PSUM and the PMT merged as the *Partido Mexicano Socialista* (PMS); until June, when he withdrew in favor of Cárdenas, Heberto Castillo, the PMT's founder, was the PMS presidential candidate. To be frank, none of these parties can pretend to have national organizations, but only regional

---

12 The PARM was founded in 1954 by a group of veterans of the Revolution, received its registry in 1957, and has postulated the same candidate as the PRI in every presential election until this one. In ideology it has not differed significantly from the PRI, which has made it a very indistinct presence in the Mexican party system. Perhaps for that reason it has usually been unable to produce significant vote shares, losing its registry in 1982 because it fell below the 1.5% floor for a registered party in a national election. Registered in 1984, some suspecting because of the PRI's desire to obtain another supporter on the Federal Electoral Commission, the PARM won two federal deputy seats in Tamaulipas in 1985. Long a collaborator party, the PARM's postulation of the Cárdenas candidacy has created much ferment within the party, with some former leaders of the PARM being ousted or leaving (Klesner, 1987; *Punto*, 1987; *El Financiero*, 1987; *Proceso*, 1987).

strengths. Again, knowledge of these organizations is scant, but the general wisdom is that the PSUM had the best organization of any of these parties.[13] Even then, organizational inadequacies of the PSUM were very apparent in the presidential campaign of 1982. While over 100,000 people were reported to have attended PSUM's campaign closing event in Mexico City in 1982, in most states the PSUM could turn out only 2,000 or fewer people for rallies for Arnoldo Martínez Verdugo (Hernández and Rock, 1982).

The left has perhaps the most articulate spokesmen on the Mexican political scene today, especially those coming from the PMS, including Castillo, former PSUM Secretary General Pablo Gómez, and Rolando Cordera, past congressional leader of the PSUM deputation. The addition to the left coalition of *Corriente Democrática* members with many years' experience as leaders in the PRI, especially Porfirio Muñoz Ledo, Cárdenas, and Ifigenia Martínez, should be beneficial to the left as well. At the time this was written, though, the left had yet to forge a single, united new party out of the FDN coalition. Cárdenas has founded the PRD, which will integrate members of a number of opposition groups, but the existing parties of the left have not yet dissolved themselves so as to throw their support to the new PRD.[14] However, forming a new party of the united left will involve resolving many underlying divisions in the Mexican left.

---

13 One source of the general knowledge is obtained by simply visiting the headquarters of these parties. While the PSUM's and the PMT's (and later, the PMS's) party headquarters hummed with activity, were adequately staffed, and had party propaganda in abundant supply, the party headquarters of the PARM, the PPS, and the PFCRN in Mexico City were virtually deserted, staffed only by a receptionist and, maybe, idle party milititants who knew nothing of the publications of their organizations. To some extent this may reflect the class and educational backgrounds of the leaders and militants of these different parties, the PSUM and the PMT being parties of urban intellectuals and the PARM, the PPS, and PFCRN appealing more to common workers and peasants from the provinces. However, the suspicion that the votes obtained by the PPS, the ex-PST, and the PARM were not in the past obtained through the campaign efforts of these parties was difficult to suppress. In 1985, unions in the PRI's labor sector were reported to have asked their members to cast their second deputy ballot (for the proportional representation seats) not for the PRI but for the PST (Baer, 1985).

14 Obviously, not disbanding currently registered parties is partly strategic. Under the new electoral legislation introduced in 1986, the conditional registration option introduced with the Reforma Política in 1977 has been dropped. Instead, to become registered, a new party must show evidence of 65,000 members. As the process of obtaining signatures and verifying them takes time and is, in any event, subject to approval by the PRI-dominated Federal Electoral Commission, it is unwise to disband a party until the new one is officially registered.

Resolving Underlying Divisions

The FDN was composed of the PARM, the PFCRN, the PPS, the PMS, the *Corriente Democrática*, and the *Movimiento al Socialismo* (MAS), a splinter from the Trotskyist *Partido Revolucionario de los Trabajadores* (PRT). Each of these parties alone has suffered from severe internal strife in the past -- even the recent past, the last fifteen years or so. Hard feelings still linger among those involved in these struggles. Moreover, there have been serious factional struggles between the parties of the left. To begin, there are longstanding divisions between Communists and Trotskyists and between Communists and *Lombardistas*.[15] The many efforts at unification of the left since 1977 have foundered when *Lombardistas* and Trotskyists have been unwilling to join Communists in a single party. The PMS, as the "united" party of the left, was still for the most part a party of Communists, nationalist populist intellectuals, and former student leaders like Castillo and Pablo Gómez. With some exceptions, it did not include Trotskyists and *Lombardistas*. Personal and partisan conflict from the past compounds these ideological divisions. As perhaps the most prominent example, Castillo and Rafael Aguilar Talamantes, the PFCRN leader, have held a grudge since the early 1970s when Aguilar Talamantes, then a member of the group that eventually became Castillo's PMT, broke away (allegedly bought off by President Luis Echeverría) to form the PST. Struggles within parties have led groups to jump to other parties or form their own parties. For example, within the PPS, the group affiliated with Alejandro Gascón Mercado and Manuel Stephens was ousted in 1976 when they challenged the party leader, Jorge Cruicshank (Lajous, 1985: 118). Gascón Mercado has been a journeyman in the Mexican left since that time, joining and leaving parties, always involved in discussions about unification on the left. Neither he nor Stephens have had good things to say about Cruicshank since then. More recently, in 1987, the then-PST suffered internal strife as Aguilar Talamantes

---

15 Lombardistas are followers of Vicente Lombardo Toledano, founder of the CTM and of the PPS, most of whom have at one point or other been PPS members. *Lombardistas*, while professing to be "scientific socialists" and generally sharing with Communists a Marxist or Marxist-Leninist ideological perspective, have differed with Communists in their interpretation of the PRI. *Lombardistas*, who more strongly emphasize anti-imperialism in their programmatic statements, have tended to see within the PRI a nationalist wing with whom the PPS and other left-nationalists should cooperate. The Communists have been unwilling to grant the PRI that positive assessment. One of the sore points between Trotskyists and Communists is over the role of the Communist Party in the assassination of Leon Trotsky in Mexico City in 1940. On these and other divisions in the left, see Klesner, 1988.

and Graco Ramírez struggled over the direction of the party. Ramírez was expelled and later joined the PMS (*Proceso*, 6 April, 1987; *Unomásuno*, June 11, 1987).

Despite these divisions, these various leftists joined together to support the candidacy of Cuauhtémoc Cárdenas, a former *priísta*, a man from the ruling elite. On what did and do they agree? First and foremost, they agreed with the *Corriente Democrática* that the ascendancy within the PRI of the neoliberals during the De la Madrid administration, which Salinas's nomination promised to continue, threatened to deny the possibility of a return of a populist and nationalist direction to public policy anytime soon. Thus, more than any PRI candidacy of late, the view of the left was that Salinas had to be opposed by a strong opposition candidacy, which Cárdenas could present because of his popularity as the son of Lázaro Cárdenas.

Second, even the *expriístas* in the FDN agreed that the one-party system that permitted the PRI dominance of electoral positions must go because it discouraged the practice of democracy in Mexico. The *Corriente Democrática* had begun as a movement to introduce more democratic practices within the PRI. It moved outside the PRI after its leaders determined that there was no available democratic space even within the party where policy differences and succession struggles could be openly debated. As Porfirio Muñoz Ledo put it, "the PRI has increasingly become subordinate to the government." This trend "reached an extreme under the government of Miguel de la Madrid, who instituted . . . a *coup d'état* within the party, replacing the leading party officials with government officials from the financial sector. This amounted to a clear exclusion not just of progressive currents or those seeking to democratize the PRI, but of politicians. From 1982 to 1985, a great debate took place within the PRI and in public discourse about this substitution of technocratic party cadres for the old guard of politicians. Our movement, the Democratic Current, is the culmination of all these efforts to democratize Mexican politics and the firmest and most urgent expression of such demands to date" (Reding, 1988a). The nomination of Salinas was the last straw for the *Corriente Democrática*, indicating the clear victory of the technocrats even within the party. Other parties in the FDN have been less reserved about the need to end PRI hegemony; after all, they long had suffered the consequences of being minority opposition parties in a one-dominant-party system.

Third, and related to the previous point, members of the FDN coalition agreed that electoral reform was a priority. Only through electoral reform could the PRI be removed from office peacefully since the PRI enjoys tremendous advantages due to an electoral process in which it controls the electoral organs and thus can manipulate the results. Regardless of the past propensity of the PST, the PPS, and the PARM to support the PRI on certain policy issues, they too had suffered from an electoral process rigged in favor of the PRI.

Finally, the FDN coalition was united in its nationalism, especially regarding economic policy. All agreed that the austerity policy of the De la Madrid administration is evidence of the unwillingness of De la Madrid and Salinas to stand up to pressure from the forces of imperialism. They called for a more independent and populist economic program including especially some way of reducing Mexico's debt repayment burden.[16] Now, with the exception of the PMS, it is not clear that most of these parties actually have thought much about policy issues; at least their printed material is not very substantial and their statements not very elaborate. In the material I have read about the PARM, there is practically no discussion of ideology whatsoever, much the less policy platforms. Anti-imperialism is an easy stance to take in Mexico given the proximity of the United States and the clear penetration of the Mexican economy by economic forces from the United States. Populism is an easy stance to take in the context of a 50% decline in real wages in the past six years. Anti-regime stances regarding electoral and other access issues are easy to take when the PRI clumsily has committed widespread electoral fraud. If the new president engages in dialogue about these matters, as Salinas has suggested he might, (*New York Times*, November 18, 1988) how will this coalition respond? When Salinas goes beyond a recognition that these issues must be addressed to submit reform initiatives, will the unity of this diverse leftist coalition dissipate?

Is there Cardenismo without Cuauhtémoc Cárdenas?

Many Mexicans in the street to whom I spoke in June and July expressed considerable enthusiasm for Cuauhtémoc Cárdenas's candidacy. Most of them were excited about Cárdenas because he was Lázaro Cárdenas's son. Lázaro Cárdenas, they told me, had sided with workers, peasants, and the nation in the struggle over control of the petroleum industry. Perhaps, they said, the son would be like the father if he were elected.

Cárdenas conducted a very responsible campaign, not making promises that could not be kept, not inciting followers to violence. In the aftermath of the election he has remained highly responsible, displaying a kind of reserved outrage about the electoral fraud he alleges was perpetrated against his candidacy and, in his movement against fraud, a persistence that personally must be difficult to maintain. He has not engaged in factional infighting and has been willing to share the limelight with other leaders of the left. Despite lacking a dynamic personality and speaking style, Cárdenas has emerged as the leader of

---

16 See the statements of Cárdenas and Castillo in Delgado, 1988: 63-65. Cárdenas carefully skirted the issue of whether Mexico should declare a moratorium on repayment or find some other solution beneficial to Mexico and acceptable to its creditors.

this coalition of left-nationalists that often bears his name. One foreign observer concluded:

> Cárdenas has to have been the least colorful of the presidential candidates. His speeches were delivered in an unvarying monotone, with one hand clasping the microphone, the other held by his side. In content they were devoid of memorable phrases and slogans. As Cárdenas admits, "I am more a doer than a talker." By contrast, both Manuel Clouthier on the right, and Heberto Castillo on the left, were rousing speakers, exhibiting elements of traditional Latin *caudillismo* and *machismo*. But their very belligerence and sensationalism tended to lessen their credibility. Cárdenas, on the other hand, had the benefit of running on two strong records: his father's and his own. The former lent authority to his call for an economic new deal, the latter to his proposal to democratize Mexican political life (Reding, 1988a: 367).

But would this left-nationalist coalition stay together without Cárdenas, either as party leader or presidential candidate, as the focus of the left's efforts? Are other aspiring leaders of the left, including Castillo, Aguilar Talamantes, and Muñoz Ledo, willing to stand back and allow Cárdenas to be the leader of the united left? Castillo, though known to have a strong ego, willingly withdrew his presidential candidacy in favor of Cárdenas in June after waiting years to become the candidate of the left. Aguilar Talamantes has for many years engaged in opportunistic ventures. Muñoz Ledo, too, is known to be a politician who has changed his rhetoric when opportunity knocked. All probably aspire to be king-makers if not kings. But would the Mexican electorate vote for a leftist party without Cuauhtémoc Cárdenas at its head? These questions must be answered in the affirmative before we can expect to see the development of a healthy and permanently unified left.

Focus of Confrontation I: Upcoming State and Local Elections

Despite the centralization of the Mexican state, one should not underestimate the importance to the opposition of winning control of some municipalities if not state governments. The governmental experience gained by opposition mayors of major cities would clearly help advance the thesis that the opposition could govern Mexico if it won the presidency or a majority of the congress. The national attention that an opposition party would garner by winning prominent state and local elections would elevate the simple recognition and reputation of that party. This is not insignificant in a largely apolitical nation in which many potential voters cannot even identify the candidates of any opposition parties, much less the stances of those parties and their candidates. The PAN's experience in the aftermath of its mayoral victories in late 1982 and 1983 in Chihuahua, San Luis Potosí, Durango, and Guanajuato illustrates the possibilities; those victories greatly increased the exposure the PAN received in the national press. The ruling elite itself recognized the danger to the PRI associated with such victories; the notion that a snowball effect could occur in which one or a couple of gubernatorial victories could break the appearance of the PRI's invincibility and cause more and more voters to jump parties, is prevalent within Mexico, including among politicians associated with the PRI and the government. The result in 1983 was that the De la Madrid government closed the electoral opening, permitting the PRI to resort to time-honored practices of producing majorities (Bailey, 1988). Finally, opposition victories in mayoral or gubernatorial races would allow members of those parties to develop experience in interacting with the federal government, experience that will be essential if the PRI's virtual monopoly on executive positions at the municipal, state, and national levels ever ends.

The Electoral Schedule

The electoral schedule presents one of the greatest obstacles to the opposition parties in their quest to break the PRI monopoly on gubernatorial posts. Table 10-4 presents the yearly schedule of gubernatorial races. At the time of this writing, only the Jalisco gubernatorial race remained to be resolved in 1988. The others were won by the PRI as usual. The Jalisco and Baja California[17] races are the only serious challenges to the PRI's stranglehold on governorships in the near future. Jalisco is a stronghold of the PAN but Cárdenas polled well there in July, 1988. As in much of the country, in Jalisco the PRI has been able to divide and conquer; in 1988 Salinas received only 42.6% of the vote, but that was enough to outpoll the PAN by nearly 12% (Clouthier received 30.8%, Cárdenas 23.9%). Baja California may be a greater challenge to the PRI; Cárdenas actually defeated Salinas there in the official vote by a slim margin, 37.2% to 36.7%. Again, there is the danger that the PRI may be able to divide and conquer: The PAN has had a strong presence in Baja California historically.

In any event, the PRI has until September 1989 to prepare to defeat the op-

---

17 Editor's Note: Klesner, of course, correctly divined the election in Baja California!

position candidates for governor in Baja California. It has three years to get ready for the 1991 gubernatorial races, in which the opposition can be expected to put up stiff challenges in Guanajuato, Nuevo León, San Luis Potosí, and Sonora (all are PAN strongholds). There are many more municipal and/or state-deputy contests pending in 1989, some in areas where the PAN has done well (Aguascalientes, Baja California, Chihuahua, Durango, and Sinaloa); others will take place in states where either Cárdenas performed well in 1988 or where parties in the FDN have historically done well (again, Baja California, plus Michoacán, Tamaulipas, Tlaxcala, and Veracruz, in each of which Cárdenas received at least 30% of the vote in 1988). In 1983, the opposition lost 1133 of 1158 municipal contests. Yet, these few victories for the opposition were critical for demonstrating the PRI's vulnerability and for buoying the enthusiasm of the opposition, especially that of the PAN in the north. We can assume that the opposition will win more municipal races in 1989 than it did in 1983. For the PRI to take the *carro completo* in those northern states could lead the north into a state of insurrection.

In general, though, the schedule of state and local elections also will be very challenging to the opposition parties. These elections are sequentially scheduled, which allows the PRI an opportunity to concentrate its efforts on each state election in sequence. The PRI showed in 1985 and 1986 what the results of this could be: It swept all of the races the PAN thought it would win. Granted, electoral fraud was committed in the process. However, even the large demonstrations against fraud that followed those elections, some rising spontaneously, others orchestrated by the PAN or the PAN in concert with other parties of opposition, did not change the official results.

The schedule for state and local races contains two upcoming periods when several elections are bunched together. The first comes with the 1989 elections mentioned above. The second arrives in 1991 at the time of the congressional elections in which half of the Senate seats and the whole Chamber of Deputies will be up for election. Gubernatorial and local elections overlap with these federal elections in Sonora, Guanajuato, Nuevo León, and elsewhere. These are superb opportunities for the opposition. For the PAN, these are particularly important tests of its capacity to effectively challenge the PRI. If the PAN focuses its efforts on winning the elections in these three states, however, serious questions of strategy for the party will be posed: Will the PAN's organizational strength continue to be concentrated in the north and west? Is the PAN going to be primarily a regional party?

For the *Cardenista* coalition, the sequential nature of these elections presents an opportunity to build its organization contest-by-contest in several regions of the country. The scattered strength of the parties of the FDN should allow the coalition more complete coverage of the nation than would the organizations of any single party in the coalition. Moving from one state to the next as the electoral process advances around the country, the *Cardenista* coalition may be able to achieve two accomplishments that will serve to make it a formidable challenger in the 1991 congressional races and the 1994 general election. First, the coalition's national-level leaders undoubtedly will be involved deeply even in local races. This will permit this disparate group of former competitors to learn to work together in an ongoing task, not one that ends the day after the national election or the day after Carlos Salinas takes office. It also will teach national leaders and militants who seldom leave Mexico City more about the nation they seek to govern and about the concerns and abilities of local militants of other parties in the coalition. So, a more integrated, united, and informed national leadership should come at the end of this *sexenio's* electoral road. Second, although the coalition's national leadership will be involved deeply in these state and local elections, it would help itself by leaving in place when it moved to the next state election a local organization capable of challenging the PRI's local organs without the intervention of the national organization. In so doing, a country-wide network of party militants would be constructed, the kind of network the left needs if it is to win a national victory over the PRI.

At this point, the question is whether the FDN national organization can link up to some 1158 local coalition efforts in 1989, or even a large portion of those upcoming races. In many places this will mean creating a local party organization where none existed before and finding candidates in localities where the left has not contested elections recently, if ever. In other places, it will mean striking deals among the local militants of the existing parties of the left so that the feathers of militants who have competed against each other for several years are not ruffled. For example, in any local election, the question of who might be the coalition's municipal presidential candidate will be a divisive issue as will choosing the left's gubernatorial candidate in upcoming races. For instance, the left will have to decide whether its candidate in a major gubernatorial race will be a prominent member of the national leadership, someone like Castillo who is relatively well-known all over the nation, or a local politician who is popular, someone who very likely is a former *priísta*.[18] Tensions within the national leadership and among local leaders of the left are likely to result regardless of who becomes the candidate, but the national leadership must be able to resolve these if it wants to keep the coalition together.

Equally difficult for the left will be the matter of the message on which the coalition will run. Is it possible to continue to rely on an anti-PRI message alone? Probably it is, although the left will have to distinguish itself from the

---

18 In the Tabasco gubernatorial race in November 1988 the left coalition put forward the candidacy of Andrés López Obrador, a former state of Tabasco leader of the PRI who left the party after finding it impossible to reform the PRI from within (*Mexico Journal*, 14 November 1988).

PAN in local and state-level elections because the PAN's message is basically the same -- "throw out the rascals." After victories are won in municipal elections, as they are bound to be unless the PRI refuses to abandon the *carro completo*, the next difficult phase comes: How should the left govern these localities? Resources and positions in local government will have to be distributed. The left coalition will have to develop strategies for rewarding those who contributed to its victory. The Mexican left never has had to face this problem before; while ideological conflicts may have divided the left, conflicts about the distribution of patronage have not because there has been nothing to distribute. Loyalties can be won and enemies made as the result of distributing patronage resources.

Finally, unless deals are struck between the PAN and the left, it is quite likely that opposition parties will continue to divide the opposition electorate with the result that the PRI will maintain its monopoly on statehouses. While they have collaborated to protest electoral fraud and to try to protect the integrity of the electoral process, the PAN and the left have not yet been able to bury their ideological differences to work together to oust the PRI. Recently the PAN President Alvarez suggested that it was time for the two opposition parties to consider cooperating in presenting candidacies, saying, "I would like to think that we Mexicans are capable of reaching a situation like they did in Spain, where representatives of all tendencies sat down together to change the dictatorship to a democracy. In Mexico there is a very open field for action in which ideologically antagonistic forces can and should work together (*Mexico Journal*, November 21, 1988)." Still, agreements of this type will be at least as difficult as agreements within the left about who will be the candidate for a mayorship or governorship.

Focus of Confrontation II : The Chamber of Deputies

Mexico's federal congress has not been a policy-initiating body in recent decades. Rather, it chiefly has served to provide patronage positions to rising (or declining) members of the ruling elite. As Alejandro Portes (1977: 195) concluded: "To recruit, promote, and demote individuals within the Mexican system, a relative wealth of official positions becomes necessary. The apparent advantage of legislatures in this regard is to furnish a pool of strategic posts, characterized by high symbolic prestige and low power, which party leaders can dispose of in fulfillment of the recruitment function." One of the most significant of the measures associated with the *Reforma Política* in 1977 was expansion of the Chamber of Deputies to reserve 100 of 400 total seats for minority parties, distributed under a proportional representation scheme. Those 100 proportionally-distributed seats were increased to 200 in 1986 (with a total of 500 seats), although with the provision that the majority party (the PRI) could win some of them. The quality of Chamber of Deputies debates and the attention paid to them by the press clearly has improved since the opposition first took its reserved one-quarter of the house in 1979. Yet, the PRI's majority consistently held from then until today.

The results of the 1988 election, though, present the oppositions with unprecedented opportunities in the legislature to play roles other than being the persistant critic whose criticism never shapes policy. As the result of the lengthy Electoral Congress proceedings in which the official results of nearly every congressional race were contested, the PRI emerged with 260 of the 500 seats. The parties of the FDN received 139 seats overall and the PAN took 101 for a total of 240 for the combined opposition. The size of the opposition representation in the Chamber of Deputies provides two sources of power: It can prevent constitutional reform and it can force the Chamber to close down for lack of a quorum, both of which require more than a majority. Additionally, its size forces PRI deputies to be consistently present in the Chamber; they no longer can treat their positions as semi-ceremonial and subject to haphazard attendance because to miss a session could contribute to the defeat of a governmental initiative.

In many ways, the effective power of the opposition in the legislature depends on what happens within the PRI deputation. So long as the PRI majority remains disciplined, it will win all votes in the Chamber. If it does not remain a solid pillar of support for the president, however, the opposition will get a chance to affect policy in a positive way. Because the PRI maintains an overwhelming majority in the Senate (sixty of sixty-four seats), opposition initiatives probably stand little chance of becoming law unless some deal is made with the government. Should Salinas present the Congress with an initiative that splits the PRI deputation, however, he may need opposition support on the bill to pass it. Such support will presumably not come cheap. Either the PAN or some element of the FDN would probably demand the opportunity to mold the bill to satisfy its preferences or ask for the PRI support on some other issue such as electoral reform. There are issues on which the PRI majority may disappear, such as debt repayment, an issue which Salinas said during the campaign should be dealt with by the legislature. An agreement between conservative *priístas* and the PAN on one side, or between more nationalist populist *priístas* and some part of the FDN on the other, are conceivable coalitions on economic policy in general, not just the debt repayment issue.

The latter scenario raises a general issue for Mexico's political future that can be phrased generically in the following way: Will opposition parties consistently oppose the PRI in the Congress in a united fashion? Despite their manifest differences on policy issues, especially on economic policy but also on moral issues, will the PAN and the parties of the FDN remain united in their anti-regime stance or will they allow their assumption of large roles in the Chamber of Deputies to reorient their main concerns to policy issues, issues more likely to divide them than unite them?[19]

The oppositions' strength in the legislature depends in large part on their being united against the PRI government. Two factors suggest that they will remain so united. First, despite Salinas's promises to the contrary, the PRI has continued practices that in no way approximate Salinas's ideal of modern politics.[20] These practices, which include efforts to win the *carro completo* in Veracruz, Nuevo León, Chiapas, and Tabasco in the autumn of 1988, are only forcing the opposition parties together.[21] Second, even if after Salinas takes office he is able to bring about change within the governing party, much of the opposition may be unwilling to cooperate with the PRI because of memories of the PRI's past treatment of those parties. The PAN, for instance, is composed not only of *neopanistas* of recent militancy, but also of men like Luis Alvarez, Abel Vicencio Tovar, and Jesús González Schmall who have been in opposition to the PRI all of their lives. Likewise, Heberto Castillo, other former student leaders like Pablo Gómez, and former Communist Party members are unlikely to join in coalition with the PRI regardless of the political stances it may come to take. The most likely source of support for Salinas from opposition ranks may come from former *priístas* and *Lombardistas* of the PPS and PFCRN. To get this support, Salinas would have to move to the left on policy issues, to promote effective political reforms, and somehow reach personal accommodation with politicians who were dissatisfied by De la Madrid's choice of Salinas and who dislike his technocratic style. There are likely to be continued temptations to individual FDN members to defect to the PRI majority in the Chamber of Deputies in return for individualized payoffs to the defector alone or to the group with which he is associated.[22] These defections will become increasingly frequent if other tensions develop within the FDN that cause individual members to doubt the long-term future of the coalition. But the defection of an entire part of the FDN to the PRI majority will cost the ruling elite a heavy political

---

19 Molinar (1988) suggests that the main axis of the present party system is a pro-regime vs. anti-regime division instead of a left vs. right policy-defined ideological spectrum.

20 The two main sources for Salinas's notion of modern politics are his speech "*El reto de la democracia*," given in Puebla, 22 April 1988, and a presentation by Manuel Camacho Solís, Salinas's closest political advisor, to a conference of Mexican and United States journalists and political analysts at the University of California, San Diego, June 1988.

21 See the statement of Luis Alvarez, above, that the PAN was willing to cooperate with other parties to end the PRI's dominance.

22 Three FDN deputies apparently defected to the PRI majority. One deputy was reported to have received a large cash payment; he also asserted that being in the PRI camp would produce positive results for the peasant group with which he was associated (*New York Times*, 11 September 1988).

price either in terms of policy accommodations or political reforms.

One immediate effort of the opposition deputies on both left and right seems to be directed toward undermining presidential authority in general, not just Salinas's personal power. The candidacies of both Cárdenas and Clouthier had emphasized the need to weaken the executive authority in Mexico (Delgado, 1988: 25-28). Events in the Electoral College and the Congress since July have included dramatic acts by the oppositions, especially on the left, designed in part to show that the legislature, or parts of it, can stand up against the president, who has traditionally been accorded great respect. For example, at De la Madrid's final state-of-the-nation address on September 1, one of the most solemn political events of the year, the FDN congressmen led by Muñoz Ledo marched out of the chamber while the PAN legislators yelled "Fraud!" and held aloft ballots they claimed were fraudulent (*New York Times*, September 2, 1988). The qualification of Salinas's victory in the Congress, convened as the Electoral College, was punctuated with uncivil behavior by both *priístas* and opposition legislators (*Excélsior*, September 9, 1988). His final victory in the Electoral College on September 10 included no votes for or against him from the FDN legislators because they had left the assembly rather than approve his election (*Excélsior*, September 11, 1988). These activities received great attention in Mexico and have provoked strong responses from the PRI. They clearly show that the oppositions' enlarged presence in the Chamber of Deputies can be used to its advantage.

Conclusions

The confrontation between the PRI and its oppositions in the lengthy and continuous state and local election sequence and in the Chamber of Deputies raises a key question for Mexico's future: Will either the right (PAN) or the left (FDN) move beyond anti-regime behavior to begin addressing in a concrete way the pressing policy issues of the day? While policy issues could form the basis of the PAN or the left coalition's upcoming electoral campaigns and while they could be the basis of legislative programs promoted by opposition deputies, it seems that the oppositions are not pursuing those policy issues principally. Rather, they are focusing on the nature of the electoral system, making their message primarily an anti-regime message. In part, this may be a strategic decision: The anti-regime activities discussed above could make them winners in upcoming elections. This is a message that is easy to sell, certainly easier than a policy message about how Mexico can exit this economic crisis which certainly will call on some groups to make major sacrifices, either those currently doing so or someone else.

However, what disturbs some Mexican observers is that this message may say much about the nature of the oppositions and about the Mexican political culture. Viewing the prospects for the newly elected legislature, Luis Rubio argued, "To begin with, few members [of Congress] understand, or are willing to accept, the difference between adversary and enemy; all are behaving as if they were enemies for life rather than politicians representing different constituencies." He went on, "What most of the country's political parties do not seem to understand is that Mexicans voted . . . for change, not for a constitutional crisis. But old habits die hard. The people who must take Mexico through that journey of change need a crash course in democratic procedures" (*Los Angeles Times*, September 1, 1988). Octavio Paz echoes that sentiment, writing that

> What the two candidates [Cárdenas and Clouthier] demand is unconditional surrender of their adversaries. In a wink of the eye, they want to tear down the PRI and bring the government to its knees. Once again, *all or nothing*. Possessed by the phantoms of the past, the opposition leaders seek a total conquest, the political annihilation of their antagonists. They do not support a transition or a gradual and peaceful evolution, such as some of us have been seeking since 1969, but rather an abrupt and instant change (*Los Angeles Times*, 28 August, 1988).

Granted, the PRI is not possessed of a deeply ingrained respect for democratic procedure either. Carlos Salinas promises to remake the PRI. However, his will not be the first attempt to reform the PRI. Others have tried and failed to reform this party's behavior from within (Bailey, 1988). A fundamental challenge to the oppositions in this coming *sexenio* is to make the PRI begin to respect democratic procedures. That respect is not likely to be earned, though, if the oppositions engage in anti-regime campaigns that threaten to eliminate the PRI. Moderation on the part of the oppositions will be as important to the future of Mexican democracy as the ability of reformers within the PRI to democratize that labyrinthine body.

Table 10-1
Electoral Preference in 1988
Compared to Self-Reported Vote in Previous Elections

Preference in 1988	Gallup National Sample -- Self-Reported Presidential Vote in 1982			
	PRI %	PAN %	Other %	Total %
SALINAS (PRI)	77	14	12	56
CARDENAS (FDN)	13	29	65	23
CLOUTHIER (PAN)	8	56	12	19
OTHERS	2	1	11	2
TOTAL	100	100	100	100
N =	(924)	(252)	(82)	(1,787)*

Preference in 1988	Mexico City Sample -- Self-Reported Federal Deputy Vote in 1985							
	PRI %	PAN %	PSUM %	PMT %	PPS %	PST %	PARM %	Total* %
SALINAS	59	9	10	0	9	0	10	32.0
CARDENAS	18	41	81	50	64	50	83	32.4
CLOUTHIER	5	33	0	0	0	0	0	13.3
UNDECIDED	5	9	0	17	0	0	17	7.2
OTHERS	13	8	9	33	27	50	0	15.1
TOTAL	100	100	100	100	100	100	110**	100.0
							N =	(855)

*NOTE: First-time voters not reported/not included in above table.
**Error is in original source.
SOURCE: ECO/Gallup Mexico Pre-Election Survey Press Release, 16 June 1988;
La Jornada, 5 July 1988: The latter survey was conducted by *Estudios Electorales del Consejo Mexicano de Ciencias Sociales*.

Table 10-2
Change in Shares of the Vote to Parties, 1985 to 1988

No.	State	PAN %	PRI %	FDN %
1	AGUASCALIENTES	11.9	-18.9	13.8
2	BAJA CALIFORNIA	-1.2	-10.8	24.9
3	BAJA CALIFORNIA SUR	1.5	-13.8	19.9
4	CAMPECHE	9.3	-18.6	14.1
5	CHIAPAS	-0.2	0.3	1.2
6	CHIHUAHUA	2.1	2.4	3.5
7	COAHUILA	-6.9	-13.8	22.7
8	COLIMA	5.0	-34.2	32.1
9	DISTRITO FEDERAL	0.1	-15.4	30.0
10	DURANGO	-9.2	-2.8	13.9
11	GUANAJUATO	10.8	-15.7	17.2
12	GUERRERO	-0.8	-19.4	21.8
13	HIDALGO	0.6	-15.6	18.2
14	JALISCO	8.2	-12.2	13.1
15	MEXICO	-0.1	-26.7	36.4
16	MICHOACAN	-4.8	-47.1	57.1
17	MORELOS	-3.0	-33.7	48.9
18	NAYARIT	8.4	-26.3	22.1
19	NUEVO LEON	0.6	-0.2	2.1
20	OAXACA	0.7	-18.4	17.7
21	PUEBLA	-3.0	-3.2	12.2
22	QUERETARO	4.7	-13.3	12.9
23	QUINTANA ROO	7.4	-19.4	19.3
24	SAN LUIS POTOSI	9.9	-12.8	5.9
25	SINALOA	14.2	-19.7	10.1
26	SONORA	-4.4	0.3	6.6
27	TABASCO	2.9	-13.7	12.8
28	TAMAULIPAS	2.8	-8.8	12.1
29	TLAXCALA	1.6	-23.8	25.5
30	VERACRUZ	-1.6	-0.6	9.1
31	YUCATAN	18.1	-16.4	0.0
32	ZACATECAS	2.6	-18.3	17.2

NOTE: The base for the FDN in 1985 is the sum of votes to those parties in the 1985 federal deputy elections.
SOURCE: Calculated using figures provided by the Mexican Embassy, Washington, D.C.

Table 10-3
Regional Distribution of 1988 Mexican Presidential Vote

	Salinas (PRI) %	Cárdenas (FDN) %	Clouthier (PAN) %
PACIFIC NORTH	51.9	21.0	26.3
PACIFIC CENTER	38.0	37.3	22.4
PACIFIC SOUTH	74.7	20.7	3.7
CENTER NORTH	63.9	12.6	22.8
GULF	63.3	29.5	6.2
YUCATAN PENINSULA	67.7	9.0	23.1
CENTER	58.4	24.4	15.3
MEXICO CITY AREA	28.4	50.4	19.5
NATIONAL	50.7	31.1	16.8

SOURCE: Federal Election Documents

Table 10-4
Schedule of Mexican Gubernatorial Elections, 1988-1994

1988:	CHIAPAS JALISCO MORELOS TABASCO
1989:	BAJA CALIFORNIA
1990:	NONE
1991:	CAMPECHE COLIMA GUANAJUATO NUEVO LEON QUERETARO SAN LUIS POTOSI SONORA
1992:	AGUASCALIENTES BAJA CALIFORNIA SUR CHIHUAHUA DURANGO GUERRERO MICHOACAN OAXACA PUEBLA SINALOA TAMAULIPAS TLAXCALA VERACRUZ ZACATECAS
1993:	COAHUILA HIDALGO MEXICO NAYARIT QUINTANA ROO YUCATAN
1994:	CHIAPAS JALISCO MORELOS TABASCO

SOURCE: Mexican Embassy, Washington, D.C.

176

References

Arriola, Carlos. 1988. "Manuel Clouthier en campaña o la tentación del populismo," *Punto*, February 21.

Baer, M. Delal. 1985. "The Mexican Midterm Elections." Washington, D.C.: Center for Strategic and International Studies, Report No. 4, November 5.

Bailey, John J. 1988. *Governing Mexico: The Statecraft of Crisis Management*. London: Macmillan.

Booth, John A. and Mitchell A. Seligson. 1983. "The Political Culture of Authoritarianism in Mexico: A Reexamination," *Latin American Research Review*, 19, 1, pp. 106-124.

Carr, Barry. 1986 and 1987. "Crisis in Mexican Communism: The Extraordinary Congress of the Mexican Communist Party," *Science and Society*, 50: 4 (1986): 391-414 and 51: 1 (1987): 43-67.

Cepeda Neri, Alvaro. 1988. *La Jornada*. June 22.

Delgado, René, ed. 1988. *La oposición: debate por la nación*. Mexico: Grijalbo.

Echeverría Ruiz, Rodolfo. 1988. "Clouthier: máxima debilidad del PAN." *La Jornada*, June 20-23.

ECO/Gallup. 1988. Mexico Pre-Election Survey Press Release, June 16.

El Cotidiano. 1988. "La derecha en la sucesión," No. 24 (July-August).

El Financiero. 1987. November 3.

Excélsior. 1988. May 3; September 9; September 11; October 30.

García, Ibarra. 1988. *La contra Mexicana: los bárbaros de norte*. México: Comunicación Meridiana.

Garrido, Luis Javier. 1987. "Un partido sin militantes." In *la vida política mexicana en la crisis*, Soledad Loaeza and Rafael Segovia (eds.). Mexico: El Colegio de México.

González, Guevara. 1988. "PAN, la contrarrevolución." *Excélsior*. May 3.

Hernández, Rogelio and Roberto Rock. 1982. *Zócalo rojo*. Mexico: Ed. Oceáno.

Klesner, Joseph L. 1988. "Electoral Reform in an Authoritarian Regime: The Case of Mexico." Ph.D. dissertation, M.I.T.

La Jornada. 1988. June 16; July 2; July 5.

Lajous, Alejandra. 1985. *Los partidos políticos en México*. Mexico: Premia.

Los Angeles Times. 1988. August 28; September 1.

Mabry, Donald J. 1973. *Mexico's Acción Nacional: A Catholic Alternative to Revolution*. Syracuse: Syracuse University Press.

Mexico Journal. 1988. November 14; November 21.

Molinar Horcasitas, Juan. 1988. "El Futuro del Sistema Electoral Mexicano." Paper prepared for the conference on Mexican Political Alternatives. San Diego: Center for U.S.-Mexican Studies, University of California, March 23-25.

New York Times. 1988. September 2; September 11; November 18.

Nuncio, Abraham. 1986. *El PAN: alternativa de poder o instrumento de la oligarquía empresarial*. Mexico: Ed. Nueva Imagen.

Portes, Alejandro. 1977. "Legislatures under Authoritarian Regimes: The Case of Mexico," *Journal of Political and Military Sociology*, 5.

Proceso. 1978. April 10, 17.

Proceso. 1979. April 30.

Proceso. 1984. February 20.

Proceso. 1987. April 6.

Proceso. 1988. February 29, June 20-23.

Prospectiva Estratégica. 1988. A.C., *La Jornada*, July 5.

Punto. 1987. April 6, 13, October 18, November 9.

Punto. 1988. February 21, May 30.

Reding, Andrew. 1988a. "The Democratic Current: A New Era in Mexican Politics, Interviews by Andrew Reding," *World Policy Journal*, 5.

Reding, Andrew. 1988b. "Mexico at a Crossroads: The 1988 Election and Beyond." *World Policy Journal*. 5.

Salinas, de Gortari. *Excélsior*. July 8, 1988.

Story, Dale. 1987. "The PAN, the Private Sector, and the Future of the Mexican Opposition." In *Mexican Politics in Transition*, Judith Gentleman (ed.). Boulder: Westview.

Unomásuno. 1987. June 11.

Unomásuno. 1988. May 20, 29.

Voices of Mexico. 1988. March-May, p. 25.

11

Alternative Mexican Political Futures

By M. Delal Baer[1]

Introduction

Mexico is at a juncture of dizzying possibilities. Since the presidential elections of July, 1988, the Mexican political universe has imploded, unleashing deep forces of institutional decay and political creation. Every feature of the traditional political system, from the single party state to the imperial presidency, is being challenged. New political parties, civic cultures, and social organizations are forming.

The features of this new political universe are far from clear and are unlikely to take definitive shape for years. The dust of ideological realignment, party formation, and institution building has yet to settle. The many scenarios for future political development include muddling malaise, a stable transition to multi-party democracy, unstable Argentine-style populist democracy, liberalized single party rule, repressive rule by the Institutional Revolutionary Party (PRI), low grade insurgency, and full-scale destabilization. Given the nature of political prognostication, the following analysis is an act of imagination, more science fiction than science.

The Demise of Corporatism?

A fundamental shift away from the corporatist organization of state and society to an electorally oriented, multi-party mode of political action underlies

1 M. Delal Baer is a fellow in Latin American Studies at the Center for Strategic and International Studies in Washington, D.C. She has taught and pursued graduate studies in comparative politics at the University of Michigan. She has lived in Mexico where she conducted research on the Mexican media. Baer has written extensively about the Mexican electoral process and has produced a Policy Panel Report on U.S.-Mexican bilateral relations for the Center for Strategic and International Studies. She teaches at George Mason University and is a frequent guest lecturer at the Foreign Service Institute.

Mexico's current electoral volatility and political transformation. Mexican mass political participation traditionally has been structured within the confines of state sponsored, sectoral organizations representing peasants (National Campesino Confederation -- CNC), labor (Confederation of Mexican Workers -- CTM), and professionals (National Confederation of Popular Organizations -- CNOP). These organizations are officially affiliated with the PRI and party loyalty is an obligation exacted of the membership. Corporatist organizations have provided a constituent base of loyal partisan support that has sustained the PRI's electoral dominance. Membership in offical unions brought tangible benefits to millions of members who, in exchange, offered political loyalty to the PRI.

The corporatist organization of Mexican society served to institutionalize, regulate, and defuse the demands of mass society. Corporatism has had its defects. Venal union leaders (*charros*) have made illicit fortunes, with the state turning a blind eye to their excesses as long as they delivered the political support of the rank and file. Legitimate demands and grievances were sacrificed to tight political control. Mexico also was shielded from the instability of more praetorian, less structured Latin American societies. However, the pillars of corporatism are being corroded, and along with them, the single party electoral dominance of the PRI. Not a few observers view this weakening of Mexican corporatism with misgiving, fearing that the absence of replacement institutions will result in a flood of uncontrollable social demands and political radicalization (Grayson, 1989; Wiarda, 1989).

The policies of economic restructuring pursued by Presidents Miguel de la Madrid and Carlos Salinas de Gortari have had the unintended consequence of weakening the very pillars that have upheld the PRI regime. The high social cost of wage austerity, privatization or closing of inefficient industries, and trade liberalization have alienated labor constituencies. Union leaders find it difficult to exact political loyalty from a disgruntled rank and file as patronage resources dry up in an economy of scarcity, austerity, and employment dislocation. More profoundly, the long-term implications of economic deregulation, trade liberalization, and freer markets are decreasing state power and corporatist decisionmaking. Economic opening implies political opening and the disincorporation of Mexican society.

Corporatism is also being undermined by urbanization and social modernization, which leaves a smaller proportion of the Mexican labor force under the control of official organizations. Urban, educated middle classes are not amenable to the hierarchical, authoritarian control exercised in traditional corporatist structures. Rather, individual activism is increasingly seen as a more meaningful style of political action than participation in state controlled organizations. The emphasis on individual choice and freely decided partisan loyalties is characteristic of an emerging Mexican civic culture that was openly recognized by President Salinas in his inaugural address in December, 1988.

Traditional corporatist structures are unlikely to fade away. Rather, these institutions may eventually be prodded into reforms including the more democratic selection of leadership and a softening of the more heavy-handed methods of enforcing obligatory partisan affiliation. However, the electoral system and opposition parties will continue to benefit from the loosening of corporatist restraints, as mass constituencies are freed for mobilization by opposition leaders. The potential for mass realignment of partisan loyalties has created opportunities for the formation of new opposition parties, and the electoral process offers new institutional channels for political participation.

Cárdenas and the Argentine Scenario

The strongest opposition force to emerge from the fiercely fought presidential elections of July, 1988 was that of PRI dissident, Cuauhtémoc Cárdenas. Cárdenas, who garnered 31.1% of the vote according to official statistics, is the son of legendary populist president Lázaro Cárdenas. Cuauhtémoc Cárdenas is symptomatic of the rupture of internal consensus in the PRI and the ideological rejection by the PRI's left wing of the relatively conservative economic strategies pursued by Miguel de la Madrid and Carlos Salinas. Cárdenas claims to be the true heir and representative of the PRI's revolutionary legacy, arguing that the progressive heritage of the PRI has been abandoned by the party's current leadership. Cárdenas's political cause is assisted by the socially painful economic stagnation of the De la Madrid presidency and the quasi-mythical status of his father's name.

Cárdenas's phenomenal populist appeal invites comparison with Peronism and suggests that Mexico may evolve along Argentine lines. The name of Cárdenas provides a charismatic pole around which to anchor mass support for populist policies. The Argentine scenario presupposes that Cárdenas can increase his momentum and establish a new majority or confront the PRI at rough parity. Indeed, the Cárdenas movement appears poised to restructure ideologically the party system, threaten control of the PRI, and displace the conservative National Action Party (PAN) as the largest opposition force.

The permanent institutionalization of a mass party to the left of the PRI could have serious repercussions. A strong Cárdenas movement could slow Mexican economic recovery, shaking the confidence of the foreign and domestic business community. In the domestic arena, the movement could polarize Mexican politics, frighten conservative elements in Mexican society, complicate domestic consensus building, and ultimately jeopardize political stability. Bilateral tensions would likely intensify given the inclination of Cárdenas toward support of Central American revolutionary movements and more autarchic commercial relations with the United States.

Nonetheless, many factors favor a Cárdenas-led realignment of political forces. The election of Carlos Salinas de Gortari was mercilessly attacked as fraudulent. In the war of perceptions, many believe Cárdenas to have been the true victor of the election. The corruption attributed to past PRI presidents such as José López Portillo combined with dubious PRI electoral practices permits Cárdenas to claim the moral high ground in the public relations battle for the minds of the electorate. As a result, Salinas entered office without a honeymoon or a reservoir of legitimacy. Thus, Cárdenas may sustain momentum simply on the basis of the accumulated PRI negatives and the irrecoverability of the PRI legitimacy.

The continued absence of economic recovery would also boost Cárdenas. Mexican purchasing power has slid painfully in the past six years, eroding the PRI's base of support in all sectors of society. The benefits of restored economic growth will take years to compensate for 50% declines in living standards and purchasing power. Cárdenas may find receptive converts among an increasingly restive labor rank and file unwilling to follow the political directives of its union leadership. It is not surprising that chief among Cárdenas's political demands is an end to enforced partisan loyalties among trade unions and the eventual dissolution of current corporatist institutions.

Cárdenas also found mass constituencies among the millions of the Mexico City poor. He mobilized the discontent of the urban poor, who first stirred during the 1985 Mexico City earthquake. The quake triggered the spontaneous growth of popular organizations outside the grasp of the PRI. Cárdenas has offered hope to poor neighborhoods, merchant organizations, tenant's rights movements, Mexico City's quarter of a million students, and dissident unions in the garment industry. The support of the figure of "Superbarrio," a masked Mexico City organizer of poor tenants, lent a folkloric touch of legitimacy to Cárdenas's appeal. Government bureaucrats hard hit by layoffs and wage cuts joined in a lower middle class, urban constituency for populist change (Monsiváis, 1987).

Cárdenas's first task will be to form a single party out of a coalition that spans the ideological spectrum from the repackaged Mexican Communist Party (Mexican Socialist Party), Trotskyites and remnants of the satellite PRI dissident parties -- Party of the Authentic Revolution, and Popular Socialist Party. Overcoming their differences will be a Herculean task. Some have already broken from the coalition, refusing to heed the call of Cárdenas to unify and form a new party, the Party of the Democratic Revolution (PRD). Cárdenas leaders are disinclined to describe themselves as leftist, preferring not to test the conservatism of the Mexican electorate. Cárdenas has distanced himself deliberately from the cadres of the old Mexican Communist Party. However, neither can he abandon socialist causes without losing support and the means of establishing a separate ideological identity from the PRI. Cárdenas will have to walk the tightrope of ideological self-definition eventually.

The ultimate political and economic objectives of Cárdenas are unclear because of the heterogeneous nature of his coalition and key advisors. In the political realm, radicals of dubious democratic persuasion compete with Spanish, Suárez-style moderates who would purge the movement of radicals and form a moderate socialist party committed to electoral democracy. In no other nation in the world do eurocommunist-style activists sit side by side with Social Democrats and APRA-style populists. In the economic realm, the prevailing current favors decisive action on debt, an end to austerity, higher wages, expanded state regulation and nationalization of economic life, and a return to autarky that would slow trade liberalization and slow petroleum exports.

Although it is important that Cárdenas form a political party to sustain his influence, it is not necessary. He is a force unto himself, with the strength to dictate terms to his weaker coalition members. Furthermore, Cárdenas always possesses the option of mobilizing a personalistic mass movement. Cárdenas is an icon whose name, similar to the Kennedy magic, instantly galvanizes the Mexican electorate.

The electoral calendar will determine the pace of political change. The first major test will occur in 1991, when Mexico will hold midterm elections for seven gubernatorial slots, the lower house of Congress and half the Senate seats. Salinas has only three years to restore the economy and reform the PRI. If voters deliver punishing returns in 1991, the regime will be forced into the awkward position of deciding whether or not to permit the results to stand. If election results are altered, the PRI could suffer a downward delegitimizing spiral, setting the stage for a confrontation in 1994. Cárdenas will utilize state and local level elections to expand his electoral base beyond the central highland region, and aim for a commanding presence in Congress. If he gains momentum in 1991, he will be poised for an assault on the presidency in 1994.

Reform and Revitalization of the PRI

Cárdenas's momentum is not inevitable and the PRI will react vigorously to his challenge. It is impossible and dangerous for Cárdenas to sustain protest mobilizations of 250,000 people in front of the National Palace every week. Furthermore, should Cárdenas frighten the Mexican electorate with the specter of a destabilized Mexico, many voters may scurry back to the safety of the PRI. Ironically, since Cárdenas runs on loyalty to the very party that he has rejected by professing to be the authentic heir to the principles of the Mexican revolution, the protest vote may swing back to the PRI if that party mounts a credible reform.

The Japanese model of refurbished single party dominance combined with limited pluralism and a liberal press is attractive to the PRI's political designers.

Economic growth is the critical ingredient to the success of the PRI political comeback. Salinas clearly intends to pursue policies in the areas of debt relief, and foreign and domestic investment that will generate healthy growth rates and renewed attention to social issues. However, the PRI leaders are sensitive to the fact that economic growth alone will not restore the political fortunes of the PRI. Salinas advocates an Aztec version of *glasnost*, emphasizing improved candidate selection, revamped party organization, and a revitalized ideological identity. A faltering Cárdenas and successful reform by the PRI could stabilize PRI's electoral standing at 50 to 60% of the vote.

A Salinas reform will emphasize sensitivity to regional tastes in candidate selection. As one chastened senator commented, "The results of July 6 sent us a telegram. The days of golden parachute candidacies are over." Good candidacies require good infrastructure and effective campaigning. The PRI is likely to experiment with internal primaries to select candidates at the state and local levels. More attention will be devoted to consultation and consensus building with party notables, the recruitment of young political talent, rewarding local party militants, and the gradual elimination of unpopular local strongmen.

Dialogue and grassroots communication are to be the order of the day. The PRI, accustomed to power, had grown fat and lazy. Energetic party reformers believe in throwing the fear of electoral loss to party bosses to *bajarle la arrogancia* (lower their arrogance). Also high on the agenda is putting a halt to defections among party members. A home must be found for party elders, left progressives, and hardworking local party activists. The word is out that those lucky enough to have landed political plums must engage in inclusive staffing. The order seeks to diminish tensions between "ins and outs" and to reduce the temptation of "out" cliques to join the opposition.

Salinas reformers are painfully aware of the decay of corporatism and hope to anticipate the wave of change before their party is overcome by emerging social forces. Young reformers in the PRI would supplant the traditional vertical, class-based sectors of the PRI with horizontal, community-based organization. The enforcement of obligatory partisan loyalty would be supplanted by door-to-door handshaking and freely-made political choices. In short, future PRI candidates must engage in old-fashioned, voter constituent building to sustain power on the basis of electoral competition. Modern campaign organizations must be developed at the district and ward levels.

Vested interests within the traditional corporatist apparatus and labor unions have dug their heels in, resisting any departures from the corporatist organization of the PRI. Union leaders are accustomed to receiving an assured allotment of congressional, municipal, and gubernatorial candidacies from the party. They view the uncertainty of a primary process with dismay. If labor organizations are unable to come up with attractive candidates for electoral office, they may be unable to sustain their presence in a competitive primary system. Even more unsettling is the prospect of electoral losses of labor candidates in fair elections. On the front battle lines of the PRI reform, Salinas's confidant, Manuel Camacho, has felt the wrath of conservative corporatist hardliners. The crusty CTM Secretary General, Fidel Velázquez, dominated headlines with his condemnation of young "pseudo ideologues," describing reformers as scorpions who would devour the body of their own mother, the PRI.

Finally, the PRI must clarify its ideological identity in order to recover political ground. *Cardenistas* have scored points arguing that the PRI has adopted much of the PAN's philosophy, with its focus on private investment over distribution. The PRI may respond by planting itself in the middle of the road, describing its competitors as wild-eyed extremists. A "center progressive" identity may steal support from the moderate wings of both *Cardenistas* and *Panistas*. Already, important sectors of the business community have rallied round Salinas, while more moderate socialist intellectuals have also embraced his presidency. Salinas will engage in a concerted campaign to rewin the loyalties of the Mexican intellectual elite, without whose support all efforts at relegitimization are doomed to fail.

Should Salinas reform the PRI and reverse economic deterioration, he may succeed in extending the life of the PRI's electoral dominance. A PRI capable of winning 50 to 60% of the electorate in free elections can continue to be the fulcrum of political life for years to come. This is especially the case should Cárdenas lose momentum and the PAN regain its former strength. An opposition party system that divides the protest vote into 25% blocs between Cárdenas and the PAN would permit the PRI to engage in congressional coalition building with either force. Thus, the PRI may ally with the PAN to pass legislation aimed at economic reform or with Cárdenas forces to pass socially redistributive legislation. Thus, the need to share political decisionmaking in a more pluralistic fashion would be reconciled with continued PRI dominance.

The Resurgence of the PAN and a Divided Electorate

The traditional preeminence of the conservative National Action Party, the PAN, has been eclipsed by the surprise showing of Cárdenas in the 1988 elections. However, the PAN is ignored by political prognosticators at their own peril. Indeed, it is ironic that the Mexican left, whose democratic credentials are shaky at best, should reap the harvest of an electoral opening that conservatives had sought for so long. The PAN militants have remained true to electoral principles through long years when political fashions were dominated by social engineering and have been the second electoral force since the PAN's creation in 1929. Just a few years ago in 1986, it appeared inevitable that Mexico was headed toward a two party system of the PAN-PRI, with the PAN the principal beneficiary of electoral discontent.

A pre-Pinochet Chilean scenario envisions the PAN rescuing itself as a viable force, dividing the electorate into three roughly equal parts, each with approximately 33% of the vote. Indeed, many *panistas* point to their pre-1988 strength and argue that official statistics suspiciously understate their electoral strength in the 1988 elections. Many are partisans of the Machiavellian speculation that *priístas* worked secretly for Cárdenas to inflate the Cárdenas vote and block the advance of the PAN. The theory holds that the PRI leaders opted for keeping democracy *entre la familia*, a two party system shared with the *Cardenista* left being more congenial to the PRI's traditions. If true, the strategy succeeded beyond anyone's wildest dreams, turning Porfirio Muñoz Ledo and Cárdenas into political Frankensteins that eluded the control of their handlers. Both the PAN and the PRI have complained of voter fraud in Mexico City, where approximately 1700 PRI polling booth representatives clandestinely worked for Cárdenas. Porfirio Muñoz Ledo, formerly the head of the PRI and Cárdenas's master tactician, is fully acquainted with the levers necessary to manipulate the electoral system.

Although internally divided, the PAN may recover and halt Mexico's strides toward a two party system dominated by the PRI and Cárdenas. The PAN would, at minimum, hope to slow Cárdenas's momentum with a PRI-50%, PAN-25%, Cárdenas-25% balance. However, the PAN optimally aspires to a two party, PRI-PAN system. Little-publicized polls taken in advance of the 1988 election suggested a rough 40-30-30 split of voter preferences, while Gallup suggested that the PRI retained a commanding lead.[2] Post-election polls undertaken within the PRI, the PAN, and the PMS suggest similar configurations revolving around 40-30-30 distributions in the three largest cities of Mexico: Mexico City, Guadalajara, and Monterrey. The PRI appears to be regaining force in the aftermath of the election, Cárdenas subsiding, and the PAN drawing near to and surpassing Cárdenas. In the short term, any development in which the PAN increases strength at the expense of Cárdenas would be reassuring to a Mexican business community that views a Mexico dominated by two left-of-center parties with trepidation.

The 1991 midterm elections may break Cárdenas and assist the PAN. The PAN's strength is in the northern states and the early phase of Mexico's electoral calendar is weighted toward the north. The PAN may repeat its former successes in elections scheduled in northern cities such as Chihuahua, Jalisco, Hermosillo, and Ciudad Juárez. Many early gubernatorial races occur in states where the PAN is strong. The PAN wins may restore greater ideological balance to the party system. However, they may also divide the nation into an

---

2 *Bendixen & Law*, June 1988; *El Norte*, June 1988; *ECO/Gallup*, June 1988.

unstable partisan configuration in which no single party can muster a solid plurality.

Worst Case Scenarios

Electoral reform is likely to raise the hackles of conservative, hardline forces within the PRI. The so-called "dinosaurs" may be ill disposed to change of any sort and may be able to prevail over Salinas. Even the internal reforms of the PRI necessary to the successful restoration of dominance by the PRI have been stubbornly resisted by the party's sectoral apparatus. The very notion that the PRI must become electorally competitive is revolutionary in some quarters. A stalemate between the PRI hardliners and Salinas reformers resulting in a closure of the electoral system is conceivable. As one reformer on the front lines of the battle mused, there is a danger that the vested interests within the party may fatefully line up one side of the great political divide, while mass consensus turns against the PRI. Thus, muddling malaise or hardened repressive rule by the PRI is not a remote scenario. In such scenarios, creeping praetorianism, labor indiscipline, and electorally-related protest would result in the increasing ungovernability of Mexico.

If electoral scenarios seem fraught with the dangers of division and populism, failure in the electoral arena could lead to more dangerous expressions of social frustration. A closure of legal, electoral avenues of political action could lead to the radicalization of protest. *Cardenismo* unites radical fringe groups, the old Mexican Communist Party, peasants, the lumpenproletariat, and the street gangs of Mexico City. Less restrained elements within the Cárdenas clique may be tempted to flirt with social and political destabilization. Impatient radicals could be mobilized to pressure the PRI with urban protests, rural insurgency, and urban terrorism. Such scenarios inevitably raise the specter of repression and wholesale destabilization.

One component of a disintegrating political situation could include a chaotic situation in the political capital, Mexico City. The PRI lost the two senatorial seats of México to Cárdenas forces, which are concentrated in the capital. The total PRI vote in the forty districts of Mexico City barely reached 27% of the vote. Massive opposition demonstrations indicated that the 20 million inhabitants of the traditionally quiescent capital had awakened. Plagued by increasing crime on the streets, an unreliable police force, and numbing pollution, Mexico City has been catapulted to priority status. The cabinet designation of trusted Salinas advisor, Manuel Camacho, to the mayoral post of Mexico City is an indication of the importance that the PRI assigns to rewinning Mexico City. It is not inconceivable that opposition resentments and popular frustration with difficult living conditions could make the strategic capital city a nightmare for the PRI.

The strength of Cárdenas in rural states such as Guerrero brings back memories of the protracted rural violence and military counterinsurgency of the late 1960s and early 1970s. The flow of arms from the United States and other sources into Mexico, although largely drug related, could assume a more ominous political dimension and exacerbate Mexico's chronic rural violence. The political sympathies of the Mexican military become a crucial variable should worst case scenarios of rural insurgency or urban terrorism come to pass. The Mexican army has traditionally been a loyal pillar of the PRI and is believed widely to hold conservative political views. However, *Cardenistas* insist that the Mexican army is divided with a significant portion sympathizing with or remaining neutral toward Cárdenas.

Institutions and the Operational Norms of Democracy

Mexico's party system is not the only institution undergoing alteration. The disruption of President de la Madrid's last State of the Nation address was a symbolic culmination of attacks on the mystique and prerogatives of Mexico's imperial presidency. President de la Madrid assumed an office tarnished and burdened by the sins of his predecessors.

The strong showing of opposition parties in the Chamber of Deputies reinforced the shift in the distribution of power away from the presidency and toward the Congress. President de la Madrid had encouraged the development of a stronger legislative branch, hoping that congressional checks and balances would institutionalize accountability. However, the Salinas administration will be the first PRI government to face real restrictions on the exercise of executive power. Because the PRI possesses a slim majority, the Salinas administration will have to engage in legislative coalition building. The passage of constitutional reform, which requires a two thirds majority, can no longer be accomplished by presidential fiat. Opposition parties may further narrow the PRI's majority control in the 1991 congressional elections.

The Mexican Congress could provide a classroom for the development of much needed democratic skills in the arts of negotiation, consensus building, and compromise. In the process of negotiation, opposition parties may learn the value of tolerance as they share the burdens of responsibility. To the extent that the tantrum-prone Mexican opposition adopts a degree of legislative pragmatism, this will be a healthy development. At the same time, Mexico's executive branch will learn the limitations of power.

The institutional structure of the Mexican legislature is sure to experience modifications and evolution in the next six years. For example, greater attention to the development of committee systems and to congressional staffing are likely. Some consideration may also be given to waiving Mexico's prohibition on reelection for Congress. Another target of reform may be the 200 proportional seats in the lower chamber, created as a political crutch to assist weak opposition parties. These seats eventually may be phased out as Mexican opposition parties gain strength in single member districts. The gradual shift toward plurality elections would encourage the building of party infrastructure, promote ideological moderation, and consolidate the party system as smaller parties are eliminated by winner-take-all races.

Institutional change must be accompanied by basic changes in the norms and operational code of Mexican partisan competition. Mexico lacks the concept of a loyal opposition. Within the Mexican opposition, many seek nothing less than the annihilation of the PRI -- all or nothing. The PRI, with its years of intransigence, shares responsibility for this state of affairs. The PRI has yet to make the leap toward the concept of an alternation of powers. Transitions to political democracy are made possible by the existence of an implicit understanding of respect for the vote and mutual nonaggression with guarantees of political survival in the event of a loss (Rubio, 1988).

Ideological moderation and consensus building skills among party leadership are prerequisites of a stable transition to democracy. The parameters of the Mexican ideological spectrum always have been exceedingly wide, accommodating everything from Trotskyite to Sinarquist political parties. However, ideological fanaticism was the luxury of a political opposition that was essentially irrelevant and utterly without responsibility. If Mexico's opposition parties truly aspire to the responsibilities of leadership, they must adopt positions grounded in practical realism that will not polarize Mexican society.

Finally, patience is the key to Mexico's democratic experiment. It would be all too easy to destroy, in a righteous frenzy of democratic zeal, the fragile institutions of political order. Since the early 1980s, Mexico has been sprouting messiahs -- charismatic, impulsive opposition leaders eager to cleanse the political world of its sins. They can be found in the *Panista* barrios of Chihuahua and in the *Cardenista* barrios of Mexico City. They see, often with great clarity, the failings of the PRI-state. When compared to the over-intellectualized technocrats and cynical apparatchiks of the PRI, these opposition leaders are compelling and attractive.

Less precise, however, is their vision of a future political order. A responsible party system is not built in one day. An effective legislature cannot be crafted in one year. Optimally, Mexico would develop these institutions by expanding political opening at the municipal, gubernatorial, and congressional level. The PRI no longer may be capable of inspiring. Nonetheless, the responsibility of the PRI lies in recapturing the patience of Mexico's inspired dreamers, convincing them that the PRI can be trusted to manage wisely the transition in the interest of all Mexico.

190

References

Bendixen & Law, June 1988.

El Norte, June 1988.

ECO/Gallup, June 1988.

Grayson, George. 1989. *The Mexican Labor Movement*. Washington, D.C.: Center for Strategic and International Studies, Significant Issue Series.

Monsiváis, Carlos. 1987. *Entrada libre: crónicas de la sociedad que se organiza*. Mexico: Era.

Rubio, Luis. 1988. "Hacia el ethos democrático." *Vuelta* 144 (November): 56.

Wiarda, Howard J. 1989. "The Unraveling of a Corporatist Regime," in *Friendly Tyrants: A. U.S. Policy Conundrum*. Adam Garfinkle and Daniel Pipes (eds.). Washington, D.C.: Foreign Policy Institute.

12

The Transfer of Power
in Mexico

By José Carreño Carlón[1]

Synopsis: The Call for Democracy

In the July 1987 issue (No. 115) of the journal *Nexos*, I wrote an article on the signs of the exhaustion of not only the method of *transferring* presidential power, but also the larger topic of which it forms part: The erosion accumulated over various six-year terms by the methods of *exercising* presidential power itself.

At that time there were signs indicating the end of a long and efficient political cycle, that of absolute presidential power in Mexico, which began to take shape with the fall of the *caudillo* system in Mexico when the last *caudillo*, Alvaro Obregón, was assassinated in 1928. The process was consolidated when Mexico's last "strongman," Plutarco Elías Calles, was exiled to La Jolla in 1936. This paved the way for the concentration in the president of the Republic, beginning with Lázaro Cárdenas, of virtually all the nation's positions of command, as well as control of essential political, economic, social, and military decisions. The concentration of presidential power virtually has been limited only by a time factor, since the term lasts for six years. But a prerogative has transcended even that limit: The presidential choice of a successor. This prerogative arises from the president's control of all basic political forces through the ruling Institutional Revolutionary Party (PRI) from explicit and implicit agreement on the part of the real factors of power, and from his power to act as arbiter of all the social interests that confer his status as a symbol of national unity.

Among other important benefits that encouraged national development, the presidentialist stage of Mexico's history enabled the post-revolutionary state to attend to two social demands that had existed but had not been satisfied from the time of independence to the 1930s. The first was to prevent rulers from remaining perpetually in power, and the second to prevent military *coups d'etat*

---

1 José Carreño Carlón is *Secretario de Divulgación Ideológica del CEN del PRI*.

or civil war as recourse in the struggle for power and as a means of transferring political command.

The Mexico of that period, however, gave rise to its own contradictions and to new social demands, which were reduced to a single demand in the 1980s: The demand for democracy. This demand came about because the wide-ranging agreement between the political forces in the governing party, within which they settled their differences and interests, left little room for the development of other parties. Consequently, the lack of development of other parties kept electoral competition very weak. In turn, weak electoral competition led to the backwardness or underdevelopment of the Mexican electoral system.

Furthermore, the system of factions within the governing party, which acted to the detriment of its internal life and its capacity to satisfy the interests of its militants and organizations at all times, began to spark off intermittent restlessness among some members, who, during different periods -- most frequently at the local level -- abandoned the party to lead the election campaigns of opposition parties. This has been a key factor on different occasions, both at the national and the regional levels, in increasing the electoral strength of certain opposition parties, improving their competitiveness, and pointing up the deficiencies of the electoral system by denouncing its real distortions and defects.

Those defects frequently have been exaggerated by some parties and blamed unilaterally on their opponent, with the aim of justifying their own defeat and of preserving and increasing their citizen support by keeping post-election protests alive; exerting pressures, either to obtain concessions of electoral posts that have not been clearly won through the ballot; or for different reasons that range from a desire to erode, weaken or topple the regime under the ideological assumption that all evils are concentrated in the so-called Mexican political system, to the venting of individual differences by those who have been left aside, or, in their judgement, have not been duly appreciated by successive groups in power.

Aside from these or other more or less fragile motives, a serious analysis of the anachronisms and distortions of the Mexican political system, even in the impassioned atmosphere of hotly disputed elections, is undoubtedly called for to press forward with the corrections and urgent changes demanded by the electorate in Mexico, and echoed by international public opinion.

The 1988 Agenda

In regard to the current process for the transfer of powers in Mexico, it seems essential to try to put some order into the discussion. I propose that the following points in this discussion be dealt with in the chronological order in which they have arisen as critical topics:

1. From August 1986 to October 1987, the method of selecting the Institutional Revolutionary Party's presidential candidate.

2. In July 1988, the underdevelopment of the Mexican electoral system.

3. From July to September 1988, credibility and results of electoral procedures.

4. The transition between the end of one cycle and the beginning of a new Mexican political era.

The Method of Selecting the PRI's Presidential Candidate

In August 1986 around twenty PRI members took the initiative to form an internal movement, initially called the *democratizing*, or *critical current*, as one group member preferred to call it. In fact, it was a critical attitude that dominated the initiative, although the criticism stemmed from different causes, including (A) concern regarding the social and political effects of the economic adjustment policies, since the effects were harmful to the party; (B) deterioration in international prestige of the regime after the elections in Chihuahua; (C) subordination of the party to the executive branch; and (D) the traditional method of selecting the presidential candidate.

The last two points, regarding the party's relations with the president in power and his decisive role in the selection of the presidential candidate, were the ones that were to cause the rupture. Neither of these points could be modified in the narrow margin of one year that remained before the nomination, because in one year the party could not build and develop the structures, forums, methods, and political culture that it had not built or developed in sixty years. The main proponents of the critical movement were aware of this situation and knew that the task would require much more time to come to fruition. But others, who from the cradle had enjoyed and later played a leading role in and benefited from the post-revolution system's methods of exercising and transferring power, insisted on haste. There was no democratizing innocence in the demand, but rather pressure in terms of political realism, initially in order to regain a share of influence for the group or its individuals in the traditional process of presidential succession, and to capitalize by gaining power in the subsequent administration, since their term of office in the administration in power was coming to an end and their prospects for continuity and promotion were not clear. Later on, once the internal pressure had been disregarded, the Movement, called *Democratic*, upon breaking away from the PRI, sought and obtained the presidential nomination of the Authentic Party of the Mexican Revolution (PARM) for the most outstanding former PRI member of that group, Cuauhtémoc Cárdenas. Only a few months earlier he had finished his term as governor of Michoacán, the birthplace of his illustrious father, Lázaro Cárdenas, a national figure able to attract broad groups to the causes linked to his name and to his descendants.

But the zeal for internal democracy in the PRI was only a means of exerting pressure to seek a share of influence and power, as was demonstrated by the vertical manner in which the presidential candidate, Cuauhtémoc Cárdenas, was chosen both by the PARM and by the People's Socialist Party (PPS), replacing the candidate it had already announced. The Socialist Workers' Party, which changed its name to the Party of the Cardenista Front for National Reconstruction, and a collection of groups -- some formed on the spot and others self-proclaimed parties -- formed the National Democratic Front (FDN), which the Mexican Socialist Party (PMS) joined at the last minute after forcing its presidential candidate, Heberto Castillo, to step down, even though he had been nominated in much-publicized preliminary elections designed to highlight the democratic calling of the leftist core, the successor of the old Communist Party.

Above and beyond the implications of this party mixture in the distortions of party interplay -- which will be reviewed further on -- it should be stressed that the objective sought and achieved beyond all expectations was the electoral effectiveness of the *Cardenista* candidate.

In addition to the wisdom of nominating Cuauhtémoc Cárdenas because of the left, but basically, for purpose of this analysis, among the broad base of the PRI supporters -- the former PRI leaders' fine intuition allowed them to perceive the electorate's broad discontent with the social costs of the crisis and with the adjustment policies, and provided them with the opportunity to exploit this discontent with a candidate who was the son of a figure deeply ingrained in the collective memory of Mexicans, and especially in the memory of the numerous traditional supporters of the government party.

The electoral consequences were not long in coming. And they were good for all the partners in this operation: For Cárdenas, for the other former members of the PRI who took refuge in his father's shadow, for the other parties that served as launching platforms, and even for a collection of personalities from the different factions of the left going far back in time and from all spheres -- universities, labor unions, *campesinos* and urban groups, now included or resuscitated to form a political presence without precedent in the past fifty years.

The Underdevelopment of the Mexican Electoral System

Two unequivocal signs of underdevelopment are lack of precision and lack of punctuality. Both signs reached a critical level of expression in the performance of the Mexican electoral system in 1988. In these expressions and in the system itself one must include, together with public agencies, the political parties -- all of them -- that took part in the war of imprecisions, delays, undue haste, and premature announcement of results.

Implanted in an overwhelmingly dominant party situation, containing very little social leeway for alternative options, the Mexican electoral system was neither designed nor prepared for stiff electoral competition. It has no precision instruments, and no tradition for adhering scrupulously to accuracy in handling numbers has developed among the parties. On the contrary, all parties -- for varying motives and interests -- joined in the establishment and general acceptance of rules and conventional practices containing a high degree of discretion in presenting election returns.

There are many examples. Before political reforms that span the period from the system of party deputies established in 1964 to the 1986 Electoral Code, which broadened the system of proportional representation, opportunities for opposition parties to obtain seats in the Chamber of Deputies by majority vote in a district were minimal and sporadic, and continued to be so until 1988. Such opportunities came about when some dissatisfied local leader of the PRI broke away to another party, taking his supporters with him, or when some strong local figure arose, often representing the rightist National Action Party (PAN) in some locality, or when the high degree of discretion of the electoral system came into play and a candidate of the opposition was granted a victory not validated at the polls. This offered advantages to all: In that way the PRI would punish one of its own candidates when he or his political group had become a political liability. The term "sacrifice" was coined for this procedure. These "sacrifices" helped improve the image of the system by giving the stamp of real competition to some local elections, or by providing a scenario of minimal plurality in the Congress and encouraging the opposition party so favored, at times, in return for soft-pedalling their claims in another disputed electoral contest. At the same time the parties that received such favors would obtain positions that they had not expected to obtain.

Since 1964, reforms were aimed at putting an end to this anachronistic system of "compensations" and were intended to bring a quota of opposition party candidates to the Chamber of Deputies, even though they had not won in their districts, provided their parties had obtained a minimal percentage of votes nationally. These deputies were designated in accordance with the order of the highest number of votes obtained by the opposition candidates in their districts. But from the start of the system of party deputies it was necessary once again to make use of the discretional margins in interpreting the results. First, the Popular Socialist Party did not obtain the minimum number of votes that were legally required to be eligible for a quota of representatives in Congress. Thus it was necessary to interpret the law in the broadest possible manner so as to make room for them. Second, their traditional leader, Vicente Lombardo Toledano, did not appear on the list of aspirants of his party with the largest number of votes in order to have the right to a seat in the Chamber of Deputies. Thus it was necessary to have recourse to the discretional margins to make him a deputy. Finally, although the PAN did obtain the necessary percentage to be eligible for seats not won by majority vote in its districts, its national chairman, Adolfo Christlieb Ibarrola, was not among those with the highest number of votes in his party, so again it was necessary to use this traditional, flexible and imprecise method to award him a seat in the Chamber of Deputies.

For the election of 1979, a new political reform widened the opportunities for the parties to obtain seats in the Chamber of Deputies even without having won a single one of the 300 electoral districts by majority vote. To that end, in addition to the 300 deputies elected on the principle of majority vote, another 100 seats were added on the principle of proportional representation, also known as *plurinominal* seats. These seats were distributed among the parties according to the percentage of national votes they obtained, and to the regional lists of candidates of each party, in the order chosen by the parties themselves. In the final year that this reform and the Law of Political and Electoral Organizations and Processes (LOPPE) was in force, in the 1985 parliamentary elections, the flexible imprecision of the Mexican electoral system opened the door of the Chamber of Deputies -- with well-grounded doubts about its percentage or the overall vote -- to the Trotskyist Revolutionary Workers' Party (PRT). The Chamber also was reopened to the PARM, a party that had lost its registration three years before in the 1982 presidential elections owing to its meager election result of 242,187 votes, or 1.05% of the national total. The PARM vote rose to 2.27% three years later, with no satisfactory explanation for this phenomenon, bearing in mind that these were intermediate elections in which voter turnout is historically lower.

Perhaps a parallel can be drawn with miracles such as the ones made by the former Mayor of Chicago, Richard Daley, among other electoral wizards or local bosses at an international level, but with a number of Mexican peculiarities. Whereas in the United States electoral manipulation scandals are not used against the prestige or even the myths of the country's democracy, in Mexico the political parties themselves have propagated a culture of electoral skepticism, despite the fact that deviations or discretional margins have frequently occurred through agreements between the parties involved, and despite steps taken in periodic reforms to encourage plurality and provide opportunities to opposition parties in the context of the historically determined reality of a party with a broad majority, precisely because of the breadth of its original alliances and coalitions.

The 1964-1986 reforms ended with the new Electoral Code of 1986, which underscored the critical extremes of the Mexican electoral system. On the one hand, emphasis was placed on government -- directed electoral bodies and processes, which irritated the opposition. On the other, a further step was taken toward what has been described as excessive paternalism or protectionism for the opposition parties, by increasing to 200 the number of deputies elected by proportional representation, in addition to the 300 elected by district majority, which provoked apprehension in a number of the PRI groups. It is true that for the first time the PRI would have a right to complete its quota of majority seats with additional access to *plurinominal* seats. However, it is also true that the new reform annulled all differences between the effort and value of obtaining a seat in the Chamber after winning a district by majority and the fact of being awarded a parliamentary seat by appearing on a list drawn up by the party leadership, often without the slightest personal identification with the voters. Through a series of elaborate operations, the same result is always reached: Independent of the number of seats won by majority in the districts, each party has a percentage of seats in the Chamber equal to the percentage of its national vote. This step has not been taken in the most advanced multiparty systems, in which, even though a certain number of deputies is elected according to the principle of proportional representation -- frequently decided on by the party leadership, as is the tradition in continental Europe -- preference is given always to the numerical weight of the seats won by majority vote in the districts. Thus preference is shown to the value of votes obtained through candidates' identification with their parties, which is more in keeping with the Mexican tradition and similar to the traditions in Britain and the United States.

In its first test, the 1988 elections, both the traditionalist faction of government -- directed electoral processes -- and the reformist or protectionist faction that advocated the encouragement and promotion of opposition parties entered a crisis. They were faced with an electorate that had opted for a broadly competitive style of election for which neither the electoral bodies, nor the parties, and neither the conventional practices nor the experience of political, government, PRI, or opposition operators were prepared. On July 6 the government and the PRI were blamed for all the harmful aspects of the electoral system, which were the result of the system's underdevelopment and which affected all the political protagonists whether in favor of *apertura* or of protectionism in terms of the disadvantages of paternalism.

The inaccuracies, confusion, delays, or premature announcement of election returns, of which all parties were guilty, were blamed exclusively on the government and the PRI. However, the governing party suffered and accepted the most adverse electoral results in its history. It had a net loss, without an even remote precedent, of 66 of the 300 majority-vote districts, and a drop of over ten percentage points in the total votes for deputies -- from 62% to 52% -- which, in keeping with the new aperture policy in 1986, reduced its proportion of seats in the Chamber of Deputies by the same percentage.

To give a comparison of this situation, the Conservative Party in Great Britain, which has a simple relative majority electoral system, has maintained a comfortable majority in the House of Commons even with only slightly more than 30 percent of the total votes.

Under legislation prior to 1986, but with the same 1988 poll results, the PRI would have kept 234 seats out of 400 in the Chamber of Deputies -- 59%. This number would have been sufficient to ward off expectations of constitutional crisis in the electoral certification processes of the Chamber itself and of the presidential election, arising from the precariousness of the majority, in conditions of inexperience and tension, unknown to all participants and to several generations of Mexican politicians.

Irregularities, defects, and biases that are inherent to an underdeveloped electoral system could, in any case, have benefited both the PRI and the opposition proportionally. This may have been true, particularly in the case of the *neocardenista* candidate, to judge by repeated accusations by the PAN members, based on numbers and on an important fact: There may have been a shift of a good number of local bosses from the PRI to the FDN at the voting booths, particularly in Michoacán, Guerrero, Morelos, and the Federal District, where the PRI did not even have representatives in more than 1,700 of the 7,000 booths.

While the PRI only had representatives in 71% of the voting booths during the presidential election, at least a representative of an opposition party was present in 72% of the booths. If we only count the official voting booth results in report sheets signed by an opposition party, that is, if we disregard the voting booths in which the opposition had no representative, the PRI's presidential candidate still obtained a majority of the votes.

Other calculations were made to dispel the doubts sown in public opinion by the opposition parties. For example, votes in the booths where the PRI candidate obtained more than 80% of the votes were disregarded and the results still indicated that Salinas de Gortari obtained a majority of votes. To give some idea of the changes that occurred on July 6, whether in the electoral hegemony of the PRI or, if you wish, in the dominion over the election process and the culture of the party that wins all of the votes, seven years ago, Cuauhtémoc Cárdenas, as the PRI candidate, obtained 100% of the votes in one fourth of the booths when he ran for governor in state elections in Michoacán. During the presidential elections this was the case in only four percent of the voting booths.

In another calculation, votes were disregarded in the booths where abstention was under 30% and a calculation also was made in which rural votes were eliminated and only those in cities were counted. In both cases, the majority vote was still obtained by the man who became president -- Carlos Salinas de Gortari. Another cause of mistrust set forth by the opposition was that the PRI candidate had more votes than the PRI candidates for Congress, about 400,000 more. They did not, however, draw attention to the fact that Cuauhtémoc Cárdenas obtained 700,000 votes more than the candidates of his parties to the legislative branch.

There is another calculation not previously made but which is worth making here. Apart from the probable biases caused by the underdeveloped electoral system, the number of voters who abandoned the PRI to join the *neocardenista* front can be detected from the official results. The PRI votes in 1988 in relation to the presidential elections in 1982 dropped from 71.63% to 50.74%, that is, 20.89 points. The drop results in a nearly 23% increase over previous votes for the *Cardenista* parties, which benefited from the shift away from the past PRI vote: The present party of the *Cardenista* Front for National Reconstruction increased from 1.52% in 1982 to 10.51% in 1988; the People's Socialist Party rose from 1.6% to 8.93% and the Authentic Party of the Mexican Revolution went from 1.05% to 5.22%.

The National Action Party (PAN) only increased from 16.42% to 17.07%, an important fact for binational reflections between Mexicans and North Americans. Apart from unique domestic factors that gave rise to the turn of events in the 1988 elections, a parallel could be drawn between what has happened now and what happened in the 1952 elections.

In the mid 1940s, at the start of the Cold War and in the framework of the Truman Doctrine, the United States repeatedly pressured the Mexican government to "democratize" its political system along the lines of setting up a competitive two-party electoral system, with the PRI alternating in power with the PAN. Similar campaigns were conducted by the United States government during President Reagan's first term and part of his second. Ambassador John Gavin's regular meetings with leaders of the PAN and other conservative groups increased PAN's contacts with the most conservative sector of Washington and encouraged the prospect of strengthening the rightist option, with a view to defeating or breaking the Mexican system in the 1988 election through a supposed "democratization," as happened in the Philippines. This was advocated openly by the PAN presidential candidate. Perhaps it is coincidental, but forty years ago, Truman's intention of promoting the PRI-PAN two-party system was followed by the integration in 1948 of a party of the left, the former *Partido Popular* (People's Party) and the shift, also to the left, of a major contingent of the PRI leaders who went over to the side of the dissident candidate General Miguel Henríquez Guzmán, who headed a coalition of center-left parties and organizations for the 1952 election. This is similar to what followed the tactic of the Reagan years of promoting the progress of the new PAN in 1988. Today, just as in 1952, the presidential candidacies of the right faded in the face of the heavy vote in favor of the left.

In summary, within the crisis of underdevelopment, the Mexican electoral system registered a real change from past results. A major shift occured in the correlation of forces, not only of the electorate as a whole but also in representation in the Chamber of Deputies, where there was almost a tie between the number of the PRI votes and the votes of the opposition forces of the left and right combined.

Credibility in the Operation
of the Electoral System and Its Results

With the left and the right united in their campaigns to denounce alleged preparations for a fraudulent election; with the credibility provided their allegation by the cumulative erosion caused by an anachronistic electoral system; and with popular discontent stemming from the economic crisis expressed in the balloting, when, on the evening of July 6, unmistakable signs of underdevelopment appeared -- imprecision and unpunctuality -- the circle of the crisis of credibility in the operation and results of the electoral system was closed.

With no proof or basis in fact, since voting still was going on in many polling places, the presidential candidates of the PAN, the FDN, and the PRT appeared in person at the Federal Electoral Commission and made allegations of fraud. In response, that highest official electoral organ promised to issue preliminary results that night. But those results had not appeared by dawn of the following day.

On the same evening of the elections, the PAN presidential candidate claimed victory with the same lack of accuracy as a spokesman for the FDN presidential candidate when he informed the international press of his victory. After midnight, in the absence of official figures, on the basis of its own information and in view of the premature, contradictory announcement of victory on the part of the opposition candidates, the PRI also announced the victory of its presidential candidate.

As of July 7, taking advantage of the lack of official results, a war of information broke out in the form of battles over figures. Consequently, more doubts arose as to the election results, which served to increase confusion. Once district vote counts had been completed (on July 10) and as official figures were released by the Federal Electoral Commission (CFE), the opposition changed its strategy and embarked on a phase of a general questioning of figures and accusations of generalized irregularities. A week later, once the official district vote counts had been announced, the PRI presidential candidate recognized the enormous rise in votes for the opposition, the end of the virtual single party era and the beginning of stiffer electoral competition.

In the days that followed, the PAN candidate changed from vindicating his victory to pressing for an annulment of the elections, and the FDN candidate began to insist on "cleaning" the results. It was in this atmosphere that the sessions of the Federal Electoral Commission began to issue proof of majority victories in electoral districts and appoint deputies through the principle of proportional representation.

The values at stake were clear to the parties involved. The PRI devoted all its efforts to maintaining its precarious majority, which the opposition sought to diminish further and eventually eliminate. The terms of debate, however, were confused by the moralistic sensationalism of those who sought to disqualify the battle of the majority to retain its majority. The social climate propagated the success of those battling to disqualify the results, as did some foreign correspondents who, taking advantage of the worldwide loss of prestige of the Mexican electoral system, seemed to act as if they were on a mystical crusade by openly siding with the claims of the opposition.

A similar situation developed during the sessions of the Electoral College for certification of the elections for deputies by the Chamber itself. When the opposition realized that no provisional seats of the PRI would be turned over to the opposition, the latter initially tried to prevent the College from being installed by physically assaulting the tribune of the Chamber. The issue was settled through negotiation. As a result, the opposition was given an equal number of votes in the certification committees and even gained a majority vote in one of the committees.

In the course of the College's deliberations, entire days were taken up by the opposition's delaying tactics and the recesses requested by majority leaders to seek agreements that would normalize the installation of the Chamber within the period provided for by the Constitution. And in this regard, the issue was settled with a regressive arrangement whereby the opposition, in the old style of "sacrifices" prior to the reformist-protectionist era, gained majority victories which were legally unfounded and invalidated by figures.

When the certification of the election for deputies was about to be resolved and measures were being taken to normalize the procedure for installing Congress, the course of Congress's opening session, in which the final report of the president in power is heard, and the subsequent certification of the presidential election, the PRI called for a national agreement in which, among other points, it proved that it was willing to reach an agreement with the opposition in an effort to "fully clarify" the "general results" of the election "based on the voting records and in strict compliance with the procedures and proof established by the Law." The PRI mentioned "a serious effort to settle well-founded differences and to submit, in detail, the resolution of the Electoral College to public opinion."

But the climate of confrontation continued. Previous agreements were not fulfilled by the opposition groups, as demonstrated by the commotion they created and their walking out of the session of the General Congress at which the president read his State of the Nation Report. A hopeless climate of distrust was produced, which blocked any procedural or substantive agreement, and the majority decided not to delay the certification of the presidential election any further. The opposition once again assaulted the podium to prevent the reading of the decision, which, for its followers in the national and international press, became a defeat for democracy. The majority did the same, to protect and guarantee the reading of the decision; the press interpreted the majority's move as an attack on democracy.

As occurs with the exercise of political rights throughout the world (even more so when these rights suffer from a number of anachronisms) and that interpretation, which is always subject to opinion, and discussion, and the correlation of party forces, contentious issues are decided by the majority without settling the controversy. Hence effort was made to discredit the majority by calling it everything from self-established, self-appointed, mechanical, deaf and blind, to antidemocratic.

Rhetorical excesses even have compared the terms of a hard-fought and controversial election, clouded by the underdeveloped electoral system and political culture of those involved with alleged breaking of the law, lack of legitimacy, the imminence or consummation of a "technical *coup d'etat*," the approach of "emergency powers" or of a "dictatorship" when the most belligerent legislative branch in 50 years is in session, the most hostile press of the century is circulating with full guarantees and ample support and there is a climate of unprecedented tolerance for demonstrations of public dissent, which provide evidence of the equally unprecedented, effective observance of the Constitution and respect for individual and group rights.

But the credibility crisis in the electoral system is a factor that has real and decisive political force. The new Mexican society, the new citizenry, expressed its decision to change from an invincible party system that did not require much accuracy in substantiating its victories, to a system of hard-fought competition, which calls for simplifying and updating standards, as well as precision in the election processes, figures, and vote counting.

The Development of a New Mexican Political Era

By the middle of September and the beginning of October, the presidential candidate of the PAN showed a willingness to calm things down. And the FDN candidate's call for the president-elect to resign so as to make way for a new election seemed increasingly merely a catchphrase intended to keep his party's ranks united.

But the 1988 election was not only traumatic for the PRI because of the losses and reverses it suffered and which have led to internal discussions regarding its decision-making methods and its need to modernize. Even more traumatic seems to be the debate among the parties of the FDN after their electoral gains. These now are involved in a crisis of misunderstandings about the merit of their election results and about the permanent nature of their coalition ties. Meanwhile, things are going no better for the PAN, owing to the disputes between those adhering to the traditional PAN ideology and the so-called new PAN ideology as espoused by the party's presidential candidate in the recent election.

A fundamental aspect of the electoral system's underdevelopment, however, is to be found in the underdevelopment of the political parties themselves, in their recurrent organic crises, and in the fact that they are not active in all parts of the country.

If, as now seems predictable, the political activity of the opposition during the final months of 1988 was directed toward consolidating what it gained in the election and to building party organizations on a more permanent basis with a view to future successes, then the process of transition can flow along the lines of major national agreements with the PRI. Then the new administration can deal with the urgent matter of developing the electoral system as well as other basic issues, such as reactivation of the economy, the debt, public safety, and the war against poverty, in terms that approximate those that were set forth by the president-elect to his former opponents.

If the death of the last *caudillo* in 1928 marked the end of the period of *caudillos* in Mexican history and the beginning of the period of complete dominance by the presidency in Mexico, the 1988 election marks the end of the latter cycle and the beginning of a new era of national accords. This will lead to an openly competitive electoral system in Mexico, a balance of power between the Executive and Congress and decision-making through open public debate or in concert with comparable political forces.

But the cycle that is coming to an end is showing the enormous extent of its achievements in its final stages. It began with a gunshot, yet is ending with the elections. This fact is bound to transcend the temporary controversies of the present transition.

Reference

Nexos. 1987. (No. 115) July.

13

The Political Future as Viewed by the PAN

By José Antonio Gándara Terrazas[1]

Presidential succession in Mexico, its electoral antecedents and its consequences for both Mexico and the United States, is a theme that offers many points for analysis, among which the most important are the composition of political forces before and after the election; Mexico's social and economic circumstances; the rivalry for power among the different currents within the official party; the use and abuse of presidential power; the current socio-economic conformation of the Mexican people; the position of the Catholic Church; the views of the Mexican military; the position of the United States government; the legal framework in which the elections developed; and the civic-political aspirations of the Mexican citizenry. While each one of the above topics deserves its own analysis, the object of this chapter is to present the National Action Party's (PAN) point of view about the presidential succession and its possible consequences.

Some say Mexico is a country where "nothing happens." By this they mean that the events that take place in Mexico would, in any other country, provoke armed uprisings, riots, military takeovers, *coups d'etat*, revolutions, and the overthrow of the government. But in Mexico, nothing happens. It is important to note that the Mexican people have not opted for violence to solve the grave problems that party dictatorship and hereditary presidentialism have provoked.

It is fitting to recall that only sixty years ago, during the revolution, the country was still fighting for power with arms; the specter of violence is not absent from the Mexican political panorama; and the presidential election of July 6, 1988, could have set it loose. In spite of what the Institutional Revolutionary Party (PRI) says, it is not true that social peace has been preserved in Mexico thanks to the PRI government. The truth is, social peace has been preserved in spite of the Mexican government's talent for repression: Political and social leaders have not wanted to cause large sectors of the population to suffer injury

---

1 José Antonio Gándara Terrazas is a representative of the National Action Party (PAN) and a Federal Deputy.

though insurrection, even though the motives and auspicious moments for such insurrection have been numerous. Indeed, the PAN believes that the path of violence only brings death, destruction, and retrogression. No country can move forward through any process in which its sons kill each other. Unlike any other election in the post-revolutionary era, that of July 6th signified for Mexicans a great, emotional burden and took place in explosive circumstances.

The country is immersed in a grave economic crisis of political origin that has been developing for eighteen years and has caused unemployment; a lowering in the standards of living; a loss of buying power; the collapse of the economy; social tension; an overwhelming foreign debt, the great part of which has been contracted by the PRI governments behind the backs of the people and without legal authorization of the legislature; serious problems caused by corruption, inefficiency and wasteful extravagance of the coterie in power, which have carried the Mexican people's patience to its limit; and excessive public spending by a government (not only the "guardian" but also the business manager of the economy) that has demonstrated innumerable times its lack of business ability and its corruption and waste. This has caused the people to mistrust the government for having lied and falsified reality so many times and for its refusal to acknowledge local triumphs of the opposition, thus obstructing democracy and provoking major resentment among the population.

It was in the midst of this state of affairs, this brewing cauldron, that the presidential election of July 6, 1988 took place. During the campaign, two activists from the opposition were assassinated by the police in Oaxaca. In Ciudad Juárez, Chihuahua, a fifteen-year-old girl sympathetic to the PAN died after being stoned by mobs contracted by the PRI. In Mexico City, two assistants near one of the opposition candidates were assassinated three days before the election. The election occurred after eight months of campaigning on the part of six different candidates: Three from the left; one from the extreme right; one from the PRI, which includes members from the extreme right; and one from the PAN. If anything was clear during the campaign it was that the majority of the Mexican people did not accept the candidate from the official party.

The legal framework in which the electoral process was developed was the Federal Elections Code, which the opposition had criticized as a partial and cleverly fixed law that did not guarantee, as in fact became the case, clean elections. In three years' time, the PAN has found 115 standard procedures that the government and official party have used for electoral fraud. On this occasion, the government and the PRI created many more. Some of the irregularities and electoral fraud committed during the last election are outlined below.

1. The Federal Elections Code was designed to favor the party in power and to leave the opposition in a defenseless position.

2. Electoral organizations, totally controlled by the system, had absolute control over the preparation, development, and supervision of elections.

3. Voter lists were created on which appeared names of people who did not live at the indicated addresses, were registered more than once, had died, or who supposedly lived at nonexistent addresses.

4. Up to twenty-five percent of the voters, those whom the PRI supporters had detected through their polls as opponents, were eliminated from the voter lists and could not vote.

5. The deadline for voter registration was December 31, 1987, yet three years earlier registration had lasted until March 31 of the election year.

6. Of those who did manage to register, it is estimated that around three million people did not receive their registration cards, without which they could not vote. These cards were used throughout the country by fake voters who favored the PRI.

7. During the entire campaign, the government abused its control over unionized peasants and farmworkers, first obliging them to attend the PRI ceremonies and later to vote for official candidates.

8. The excessively expensive PRI campaign was paid for with public funds and employed personnel, equipment, and vehicles of all governmental departments and state businesses, including the military.

9. The methods to promote the official candidate, as directed by the Secretary of the Interior, were used to such an over-saturating degree that they provoked citizens' rejection.

10. The government refused to number ballots progressively, to print registration cards with a photograph for infallible voter identification, or to use truly indelible ink for the voter's thumbprint. It turned out that the ink used was removed simply with water.

11. Throughout the nation's 300 electoral districts, 54,646 polling booths were installed for the election of president, senators, and federal deputies. This means 163,938 individual results. In 27% of those 54,646 booths, that is, 14,754 booths, there were no representatives from opposition parties. The PRI fixed thousands of the booths in order to obtain 100% to 667% of the votes from the list of registered voters. The lack of representatives does not justify the fraud. It was in the poorest and most isolated states, in the steepest mountains, among Indians of the different regions that PRI says electors voted hugely in its favor. Most assuredly, full of civic fervor, the people of these places voted for the party that has sunk them in misery.

12. In the northern states of Mexico, where the opposition is very strong and identifies with PAN, the government applied the pedagogy of fraud to teach citizens that it would be useless to vote because, in any case, the federal election would be falsified. This was because the federal elections of 1982 and 1985 and the intermediate, local elections of the past six years were fraudulent. In

other places, PRI organized military movements in the days before the election which so intimidated the citizens that they did not vote.

13. Out of three-hundred electoral districts, 15% did not have enough ballots. In 20%, the presence of opposition representatives was not allowed. In 10%, ballot boxes were stuffed before the election. In 19%, representatives of the opposition were expelled. In 9%, ballot boxes were robbed before votes were counted. In 10%, bags of votes were introduced during the election. In 30%, voters were permitted to vote without their registration cards, and in 26%, it was discovered that the same groups of voters controlled by the PRI voted several times.

In spite of the fraud described above, the people of Mexico voted against the PRI and the government. That vote was so large that the government was not prepared. The Secretary of the Interior publicly had offered to announce the results that very July 6th. The results were so unfavorable for the government that it had to face the ridicule of announcing that the computer system was "down." The government took almost one week to cover up the results and to proclaim its victory with 50.36% of the total vote.

In light of this monstrous electoral fraud, the PAN took the position that no one could know who had won and that this fact would annul the elections. Cárdenas declared that he had won. Some time later, as everyone waited for him to defend the triumph he claimed, he took the PAN's position and asked for annulment of the elections.

I am a federal deputy. I am part of the current legislature in the Chamber of Deputies and so I was part of the Electoral College that ratified the election of the deputies and the president of the Republic. What happened in the Electoral College is a disgrace to the government. We were furnished with information from only 29,999 voting booths for the presidential election. We were denied access to information from the other 24,647 booths, and the government never has revealed it.

The 54,646 boxes of votes for the deputies, and the 54,646 boxes of votes for the president were found stored under military guard in the cellar of the congressional building. The law says that these votes must be made available for analysis. We were neither allowed access to them nor permitted to bring them to the Chamber, not even to the adjudicating commission. For twenty-one days, the Electoral College was the narrow funnel through which all national electoral fraud passed.

All opposition parties verified the fraud. Of the 233 deputies that made up the PRI's majority, not even 160 won cleanly. Even then, the PRI needed more falsified votes so its vote by district would be congruous with that which was fixed for the candidate of the official party. With complete cynicism and in the face of the most dramatic proofs of electoral fraud, the PRI obtained for itself 260 deputies, 27 of which were elected through proportional representation, in order to keep a representation of 260 deputies as opposed to the opposition's 240. This includes having removed a deputy who had renounced the PRI and gone over to another party on the left in order to replace the deputy with one from the PRI.

The PRI obtained the ratification of the presidential election by buying the vote of three deputies from the left. This is why the candidate from the official party was elected president by 263 out of 500 deputies, and not by the majority of the Mexican people. The PAN voted against the ratification while the other opposition parties abandoned the assembly before the voting.

It is said that the PAN has gone from being the second to the third political force in Mexico. However, I would like this point of view to be analyzed in light of the following facts: As an individual party, the PAN occupies second place in the Chamber with 101 deputies; the party in third place has 38. Of those 101 PAN deputies, 38 are from the majority. The party that follows has eight, without taking into consideration those candidates that were held in common.

It is only by linking the four opposition parties together that they have more deputies than the PAN, with 139 to 101. But this coalition now shows grave signs of weakening as a consequence of ideological incompatibility, degrees of radicalism, and the struggle for leadership. The new president no longer will be able to change the Mexican Constitution with only the constituent deputies of the parliamentary PRI group, now that the PRI has only 260 deputies out of a required 334. He will have to agree with the opposition upon a direction for the country.

The PAN does not give any credence to the figures for the official vote. The electoral fraud was gigantic. Therefore, as an attempt to deduce trends, the use of these figures can be an interesting exercise, but in no way do they reflect the Mexican electoral reality.

The issues described above are now facts whose usefulness is rooted in the attempt to derive implications for two countries. The premature congratulations of the president of the United States -- the election had not even been ratified -- to the official party's candidate caused bad feelings in many sectors of Mexico. This leads us to assume that the next regime will receive from the United States support at least equal to that which the current regime has been furnished. Because of electoral fraud and the new president's image of illegitimacy, many Mexicans of all political persuasions will find it worrisome and disillusioning that the United States should continue to support what is considered a party dictatorship.

It is well-known that the Mexican government continues to find it worthwhile to present the left as a threat to stability. Yet the growth of that left fundamentally came from a splitting away from the official party. The real growth is smaller than supposed when measured by determining the percentage of votes that are only an expression of protest and those that are derived from conviction.

Mexico's relations with the United States will be defined once it is clarified which faction of the PRI will prevail over the rest. It will be defined if the new government understands the message of the vote and decides to carry out a true democratization of the country, permitting the emergence of a solid and subsidiary society which consists of more society and less state and which promotes unity among Mexicans.

If the prevailing faction is made up of the dinosaurs -- those members of the PRI who seek power for the sake of power itself, who oppose democratization and wish to keep the country as their personal hunting ground -- then the United States ought to prepare itself to live with a neighbor with potential problems of domestic violence, major economic problems, an abundance of undocumented people, and the danger of regional destabilization.

If, on the other hand, the new government becomes a populist government with the intention of waving the banner of *Cardenismo*, and regaining the lost sectors of the population, then Mexico will debate again demagogy, populism, the standstill in production, capital flight, the attack on private property, the economic debacle, and the grave risk that revolution will break out.

Which trend will Mexico follow? For the good of all, including the United States, one hopes it will be that of democratization. Nevertheless, this path will be slow, difficult, and risky as long as the United States insists upon supporting a government whose legitimacy is doubted by its own people.

14

The Presidential Succession: A Commentary

By Ricardo Pascoe Pierce[1]

With platitudes, we affirm that the destinies of Mexico and the United States are closely linked. Although at times, through repetition, such platitudes lose all meaning, at others, through certain events, they acquire a new significance. This is what has happened because of the Mexican presidential succession. The federal elections of July 6, 1988 drastically and brutally have changed the political physiognomy of Mexico. This is going to have a far-reaching effect upon relations between the United States and Mexico. Thus, a quick look at what is happening in Mexico is both useful and makes sense. Not simply an exercise in politics, economics, and sociology, it attempts to review the fundamental factors that initiated the transformation in Mexico.

Platitudes are concerned with obvious facts. The two countries share not only a long border, but also problems of migration, trade, drugs, transportation, and energy, not to mention each nation's strategic interests. These all are unseverable interests and links. Any reflection upon the situation in Mexico and the requirements of the United States necessarily has to start from an acknowledgement of the countries' ties. Therefore, the change of power in Mexico -- which also occurred in the United States in November 1988 -- necessarily concerns the relationship between the two countries.

The first fact to be verified is that Mexico changed as of July 6, 1988. This too becomes a platitude. All analysts, be they students of politics or simply citizens, who reflect upon this question will consider that Mexico changed on July 6th. By virtue of the fact that every person's mind is a separate universe, perhaps it would be interesting to give form and substance to this affirmation. In order to define the elements in transformation, it is necessary to consider a few fundamental points. One is the change in attitude among the Mexican people. The transformation of July 6th was, among other things, a change of mental state. The Mexican people discovered that it is possible to defeat the Institutional Revolutionary Party (PRI). This is of utmost importance and sig-

---

1 Ricardo Pascoe Pierce is a representative of the National Democratic Front (FDN).

nificance. First, it is a well-known fact that the PRI did not want the people to become aware of its vulnerability. But second, the PRI mobilized all forces possible to reinforce the myth of its invincibility in the eyes of the Mexican people. So effective was its labor of concealment that national and international political opinion polls, along with other measures, assumed change would be impossible. This indeed proved to be a big myth. The change that took place after July 6th definitely occurred in the psychology of the people.

In a political regime such as Mexico, a change in mass thinking is of major importance. But other elements of national politics also changed. The PRI discovered that it could lose elections. This was because we consider it an unquestionable fact that the PRI lost. Obviously, it denies having lost, as happens in every regime with a state party. The rigid character inherent to the current government impedes a smooth transition to an open political system. Nevertheless, it is a fundamental change that the citizens, including those who belong to the PRI, have realized; that is that the PRI is able to lose elections. Therefore, it is seen as a highly vulnerable political instrument.

On the other hand, the certain possibility of the PRI's electoral defeat demands the formulation of a proposal for another government. The political/electoral mobilization was not in vain, in that it expressed and channeled the demand for change in the government's institutional/political charter. The option of creating new arenas for influencing policy and orienting governmental decisions will be the most important result that can arise from the debris of the new political regime. Behind these elements illustrating the extent of change in Mexico there lies a substantive problem. Traditionally, electoral fraud in Mexico has served as an instrument not so much to win elections as to *legitimize* the government it brings to power. Seen this way, fraud has not served to defeat opposition but to offer the image of a popular government in a happy country where the population recognizes in the government and its leaders a legitimacy and consensus beyond all doubt and questioning. The political difficulties with governing that have confronted Miguel de la Madrid during the last six years have come about not so much from questions as to whether he won or not, but from the impression that his election lacked full legitimacy. In the case of Carlos Salinas de Gortari not only did the conviction spread that he (just as his immediate predecessor) did not win the election legitimately, but also the version that he simply lost the election. For that reason, the government officially chosen by the election of 1988 not only lacks legitimacy but also legality.

The fight for installing a legitimate government in Mexico has let loose a profound dispute not only over the control of public power, but also over the definition of policies to be followed in the next few years. In essence, the political quarrel revolves around the creation of a regime characterized by flexibility, change, and the tolerance of contrary views, or the eventuality of a regime with politically rigid institutions and intolerant of listening to or debating the opposition. This dispute occurs in factions of society that try to choose between the democratic option or the authoritarian temptation. This dilemma is damaging, and arises from the domination of a state party government, the outstanding feature of Mexican society.

This state party government, whose central trait is corporative control of citizens and social organizations, has fallen into the most profound crisis. The official party was not born within society, in order later to take power *from the outside*, but is an instrument that was born *within* the state and responds to the propositions and interests of the heads of official institutions. This explains why there is no partisan militancy in the PRI, but bureaucracy. Owing to the nature of the state party, whose structures both control and organize the fundamental productive sectors of society, its corporative character has dragged society into the dilemma of authoritarian institutionalization or democracy. It is a regime in which the official party controls the fundamental sectors of society, seeking to convert them to its own logic and to satisfy the needs of the state. It is a party formed under the logic of state power, which explains why it has not been able to act as would a party that had taken power in a political demonstration of legitimacy and force (be it electoral force or another), such as occurs in societies with the option of leadership alternatives. The state party government defines and establishes the parameters, in essence, of what happens in the country. It is a regime that is heading society into a crisis of incalculable consequences. The sixth of July staged the majority of Mexicans' vote of repudiation of the state party's government. Nevertheless, July seventh witnessed the return to work, to school, to the *ejido*, to the office or market. It confirmed that the corporative structures of the state party have not been fundamentally disturbed, at least for the present. The regime has suffered a mortal blow to its legitimacy and legality, but it has lost very little of its capacity to exercise state control upon society. This places society within a grave crisis and before a dangerous dilemma. It is a central problem of power that Mexican society will have to resolve quickly.

The above puts forth doubts as to the possibility of Mexico's becoming a society republican in its government and contentious in its elections. The conclusion, to which one would have to arrive by using absolutely formal logic based on this election, is that official inclination to transform the elections into a contentious arena does not exist. If corporatism were eliminated as the heart and center of the state party's government, it would be feasible to democratize Mexican society without taking the path of suffering and violence. In that regard, the attitude and willingness of the very forces linked to the PRI and the state will be decisive. Nevertheless, it remains to be seen up to what point the PRI will permit a free, contentious, electoral expression on the part of the citizenry. Recent state elections have demonstrated the obstinacy of the system. For this reason, the new party that emerged from the political/electoral process developed during Cuauhtémoc Cárdenas's campaign faces a fundamental task: The radical transformation of the state party's government toward a republican system of government. It will confront the challenge not only of building a great electoral force, but also of giving a true and mortal blow to the state party's government. In this way, the doors will open for change toward a republican and democratic regime. Thus, we will be able to leave behind the authoritarian threat that in these times definitely faces the country.

The electoral results that the National Democratic Front (FDN) succeeded in obtaining show convincingly that Cuauhtémoc Cárdenas Solórzano won the elections. This is not an ideological allegation void of foundation. It is the product of improved availability of information. The opposition forces were able to integrate sufficient information to know what were the true election results. Records from more than 50% of the polling places were reported to counting centers established by the opposition and which offered an important perspective on the final results. This is a new political phenomenon in the country because the control of electoral information always had been in the hands of the government. It is interesting to note that the opposition had, in its entirety and at the national level, more representatives at each polling place than did the PRI. In the Federal District, the opposition covered all the polling places while the PRI failed to cover one thousand of these. The phenomenon of veracious and efficient electoral information is an example of the energy and organizing ability of the Mexican opposition forces. This leads to the view that, in the short run, the government no longer will have the option of distorting election results. In turn, this will oblige the state to accept its conversion into a fully democratic regime, able to accept its electoral defeats. Otherwise, it will have to begin an authoritarian project to halt the advance of contentious electoral forces in the country. This is the dilemma that faces the people of Mexico today.

15

The Mexican Presidential Election in the Mass Media of the United States

By Leonardo Ffrench Iduarte[1]

Introduction

From a Mexican viewpoint, the coverage of the July 6, 1988, Mexican presidential elections by the United States print and electronic news media was, to say the least, abundant. However, in terms of quality it cannot be said that the coverage was as altogether balanced, thorough, or made within the proper historical context, as would have been desirable.

Quantitative Assessment

The above assertions are based on daily readings, starting in January 1985, of eight newspapers and four weekly magazines which either have national circulation or are considered especially influential in the United States;[2] and also on regular monitoring of the major television networks and radio stations. The conclusion drawn is that the Mexican issues receiving the most intensive coverage -- including reports, editorials, columns, op-ed pieces, and comments -- were the earthquakes that struck Mexico in September 1985. However, the election may have resulted in a larger number of reports, considering the much longer attention given by the United States media to this subject.

---

1 Leonardo Ffrench Iduarte was Minister for Press and Public Affairs, Embassy of Mexico, Washington, D.C. Currently he is Deputy Secretary for the Foreign Press at the Office of the Presidency of Mexico.

2 The *New York Times,* the *Washington Post*, the *Washington Times*, the *Wall Street Journal*, the *Journal of Commerce*, the *Los Angeles Times*, *USA Today*, and the *Christian Science Monitor*, as well as the magazines *Newsweek, U.S. News and World Report, Time*, and *BusinessWeek*. These publications have been listed in decreasing order by their amount of coverage in July 1988 of the Mexican elections.

References to the Mexican electoral process began to appear early in 1987, when a group of important members of the Institutional Revolutionary Party (PRI) decided to foster the development of a "democratizing current" within the party. The media coverage of this event intensified when the democratizing group made a definite break from the PRI and subsequently joined various center-left parties to propose the candidacy of Cuauhtémoc Cárdenas for the Mexican presidency. Another development which was given special attention took place in August 1987, when for the first time in its history the PRI officially announced that "six distinguished members[3] of the party were being considered as the possible PRI nominees to succeed President Miguel de la Madrid; and that these candidates must make publicly known the policies and programs they would adopt if nominated." Another widely reported news story was the announcement made in Mexico on October 4, 1987, that three PRI sectors[4] simultaneously decided to present the candidacy of Carlos Salinas de Gortari for the presidency. However, the highest coverage of the Mexican electoral process took place in July 1988, immediately after the election, and, to this date, comments on the Mexican electoral process continue to be published, although sporadically.

Beginning in 1987, and concluding in October, 1988, the above twelve major newspapers and magazines had published a total of over 250 editorial notes, articles and columns averaging 750 words. In July, 1988 alone there were 124 news items published about the Mexican presidential election.

The attention given by the electronic media was no less, although it was basically limited to the month of July, 1988, and in particular to July 5th through the 17th. The coverage stopped once the preliminary official results of the vote-count were announced and the massive demonstrations, called by the contending parties to show their strength and unity, began to dwindle. In the 13 days from July 5th to the 17th, the major United States national television networks[5] devoted more than 200 minutes in total to the Mexican elections. The greatest coverage was provided by UNIVISION, probably because 60% of the network's Spanish-speaking audience is of Mexican origin. UNIVISION spent a total of over 100 minutes reporting the Mexican electoral process in each of its two daily national newscasts. Following this network in decreasing order of coverage were CNN, PBS, ABC, CBS, and NBC.

---

3 By alphabetical order Ramón Aguirre, Head of the Federal District Department; Manuel Bartlett, Secretary of Internal Affairs; Alfredo Del Mazo, Secretary of Energy; Sergio García Ramírez, Attorney General; Miguel González Avelar, Secretary of Education; and Carlos Salinas de Gortari, Secretary of Budget and Planning.

4 The Mexican Confederation of Workers (CTM), The National Confederation of Peasants (CNC), and The National Confederation of Popular Organizations (CNOP).

5 ABC, CBS, CNN, NBC, PBS, and UNIVISION (formerly Spanish International Network S.I.N.).

With regard to the major radio stations, coverage was very similar to that of TV, since most of them have permanent correspondents in Mexico or in neighboring Central America, and some sent special envoys to cover the elections.

To the amount of coverage by the national news media in the United States must be added the possibly even greater attention, both in English and Spanish, that the Mexican elections received at the local and regional levels in areas near the Mexico-United States border and cities and regions in other parts of the United States with a high population density of Mexicans and/or United States citizens of Mexican descent.

In-depth analyses also were published by scholarly journals such as *Foreign Affairs,* a publication of the Council on Foreign Relations; *Foreign Policy,* of the Carnegie Endowment for International Peace; and *Washington Quarterly,* published by the Center for Strategic and International Studies, among others. These articles were written by experts on foreign affairs in general, or Mexican affairs in particular, like Henry Kissinger, Cyrus Vance, William Rogers and Delal Baer; and they essentially referred to the political climate in Mexico following the July 1988 elections. Apart from reflecting the personal ideologies and interests of the writers, as well as their perspectives on Mexican reality, the articles also suggested foreign policies and actions to be followed by the United States Administration and Congress in order to strengthen the cooperation of the United States with Mexico.

Informative bulletins and newsletters on Mexico also were issued by a mushrooming number of councils, committees, consortia, institutes and study centers specializing in Mexico or United States - Mexican relations. Some of these institutions have been founded by experts and reliable scholars on international matters, who have shown a serious interest in improving reciprocal knowledge and understanding between Mexico and the United States; but others, unfortunately, seem to have been established by "experts in fundraising activities" who seek only personal benefit.

The special interest in Mexico seems to date from the onset of the current Mexican economic crisis, an event which made many people in the United States "discover" the existence and relevance of Mexico. However, these analyses are sometimes so far from describing actual conditions that the writers seem to be "inventing" rather than "discovering" Mexico.

If we compare the attention given by the United States media to the electoral processes that took place about the same time in other countries of interest and importance for the United States, the coverage of the Mexican elections is so much greater that it would seem unjustified or unusual if it were not for the reasons that motivated it. To give some examples, the press in the United States referred to the French elections only one week before and after they were held. The elections in Ecuador received but a couple of days' coverage before and after. And even the Chilean plebiscite received less attention than the Mexican elections, although it was an event of great historical significance for the United States because of its direct involvement in the 1973 *coup d'etat* by Gen. Pinochet.

The main reasons motivating the extensive coverage of the Mexican electoral process seem to be, among others, the almost paranoid fear among some in the United States that the economic crisis which Mexico has been facing since the beginning of the 1980s could lead the country to the loss of political stability and social peace; and the foreseeable effects that such a situation would have for security in the United States and its relations with its neighbor to the south. Another reason is clearly the memory of the hotly contested elections held in the United States bordering Mexican states of Sonora and Nuevo León, in 1985, and in Chihuahua, in 1986; as well as the supposedly growing number of sympathizers and followers being gained by the conservative and pro free-enterprise National Action Party (PAN) -- then Mexico's second major party. Another factor to be taken into account seems to be the widespread Hollywood cliché of Mexicans as violent people in general.

Quality of Coverage

A global assessment of the quality of the hundreds of reports and comments produced about the 1988 Mexican presidential elections by the major United States media shows that around 41% were fairly balanced; 38% varied from unfavorable to very unfavorable; and the remaining 21% were either favorable or, in a much smaller percentage, very favorable. This assessment points out the general tendency towards objectivity of most of the United States media, which is to be praised.

In this section, however, it seems important to emphasize some of the various misconceptions and stereotypes that have resulted from the coverage of the Mexican elections by the media in the United States, since several of them have made similar inaccurate comments and identical major omissions. Here we must consider how important such news items are to achieving an understanding of the Mexican political system as a whole, and that such understanding requires making the readers aware of the historical context in which the events reported are taking place.

For example, countless reports refer to the elections as "tainted by accusations of massive fraud," to Carlos Salinas de Gortari as the "Harvard-trained economist," to Cuauhtémoc Cárdenas as "the son of the most revered Mexican president," and to Manuel Clouthier as "the successful farmer and private investor." The National Action Party (PAN) is described "as the party in favor of free-enterprise," while the PRI is referred to as "the party which has been in power since its foundation almost sixty years ago."

Furthermore, the media in the United States seem to take pleasure in stressing the accusations of "massive electoral fraud" made by the defeated parties and candidates, without taking into account the possibility that they may be basically an excuse to justify defeat, as well as an effective, although not very elegant, way of gaining supporters and sympathizers among not very well informed people.

But even more important than the often misleading clichés created by the media is the omission of data which would allow the public in the United States to understand better the Mexican political system and its historical development.

To offset such an omission of information, it would be desirable for the media to include, at least once in a while, in their reports and comments a summary of the gradual but constant evolution of democratic conditions in Mexico. This evolution has gone hand in hand with growing levels of education and economic development, and has been shaped by the cultural traditions of the Mexican people, some of which date from pre-Hispanic times and are still firmly rooted.

Thus, it seems very important to point out that, in less than a century, Mexico has evolved from an eminently rural nation under a feudal system with a population of less than 10 million people -- whose life expectancy was an average of 35 years -- to a mostly urban society of over 80 million people, half of whom are under 20 years old and can expect to live to nearly 70. And that, following a bloody social revolution which decimated the population and was the first of its kind in the 20th century, Mexico, a nation with 90% illiteracy and a patriarchal dictatorship, became a corporate state where free enterprise and education flourished. Mexico reached an average annual economic growth of 6% of GNP during 40 years, beginning in the 1940s. Today Mexico has a less than a 10% rate of illiteracy, contains a large diversity of foreign and domestic information media, and the individual freedoms embodied in the Mexican Constitution are zealously respected and enjoyed by its people.

To further provide a frame of reference for the recent presidential election in Mexico, it seems necessary that the United States media refer at least in passing to Mexico's advances in representative democracy during the last fifty years. These advances include the following: In 1954 Mexico recognized women's right to vote and be elected. In 1963 seats were reserved in the Mexican Congress for minority party representatives, thus ensuring these parties' ability to participate and express their opinions in the nation's Congress. In 1970 the age for enjoying citizenship rights was lowered from 21 to 18. In 1973 the minimum age required to be elected as representative and senator went down from 25 to 21 and from 35 to 30, respectively. Also in 1973, the national political spectrum was enlarged as the number of officially registered political parties increased from four to seven. In 1977 Mexican electoral law was amended to expand even more the proportional representation in Congress of all parties participating in the elections. In 1986 amendments to the Constitution and electoral laws raised the number of seats in the Chamber of Deputies from 400 to 500, and it was established that, of the 200 seats reserved for proportional representation of the contending parties according to their voting percentage, at least 150 (30% of the total) are to be exclusively assigned to minority parties.

To allay the apparent anxiety created in some public opinion sectors in the United States by the official announcements of the split within the PRI and the candidacy of Cuauhtémoc Cárdenas[6] to the Mexican presidency, it would have been useful if the major United States media had commented on the fact that such division within the PRI was neither the first nor the only one in the party's history, as some media assumed and mistakenly reported.

Allowing for different historical conditions and circumstances, similar situations occurred in 1929, when José Vasconcelos, a former Secretary of Education, opposed the nomination by the National Revolutionary Party (PNR) -- one of the PRI predecessors -- of Pascual Ortiz-Rubio as its presidential candidate. Moreover, Vasconcelos presented his own candidacy and received the support of Mexican intellectuals and a large part of the middle class. A similar case occured in 1940 when Gen. Juan Andrew-Almazán, a former Secretary of Communications, left the Party of the Mexican Revolution (PRM) -- immediate predecessor of the PRI -- to oppose the official candidacy of Gen. Manuel Avila-Camacho. In 1964 Ezequiel Padilla, then Secretary of Foreign Relations, expressed his disagreement with the nomination of Miguel Alemán by leaving the nascent PRI and presenting his own candidacy to the presidency. In 1952 Gen. Miguel Henríquez Guzmán -- former official at the Department of the Federal District, did the same by opposing the candidacy of Adolfo Ruiz-Cortines. And, to conclude, in 1982 Manuel Moreno Sánchez, leader of the Mexican Senate from 1958 to 1964, left the PRI to compete with Miguel de la Madrid for the presidency.

The United States media also generally have failed to provide information on basic aspects of the Mexican electoral process and legislation, which are essential to understanding the difficulties for a "massive electoral fraud" to occur. I am referring to information on the guarantees and provisions established by the Mexican Political Constitution and Electoral Laws. Other omissions by most media in the United States were the facts that the elections were supervised in 98% of the 54,461 polling stations[7] and that there were a total of almost two million persons, representing all political parties, who directly participated in the different levels and steps of the electoral process, many of them with the specific task of preventing irregularities, acting as poll-watchers. Some of those guarantees are the following:

---

6 Former Under Secretary for Forestry and Wildlife, as well as senator and governor of the State of Michoacán.

7 *New York Times* article by Larry Rohter, published on page A2 of the July 7, 1988 issue, under the title of "As Mexicans Vote, Fraud Is Alleged."

A.- In order to prevent manipulation of election results by a single party, representatives of all parties and candidates are requested to be present at each and every one of the polling stations. Before the election takes place, representatives of the parties to the District Committees may, if they wish, sign the back of the ballots to be used in that district's polling stations. And the same may be done for the ballots of a particular polling station by representatives of all parties and candidates who supervise it. If this is the case, when the ballot boxes are opened at the end of the election day, any ballot that does not bear the appropriate signatures can be cancelled (Art. 246 of the FEC, an agreement unanimously approved by the Federal Electoral Commission on June 30, 1988).

B.- All persons wishing to vote must show their voter's card and one other I.D. with a photograph. When a person casts a vote, his/her voter card is punched in the corresponding space and that person's right thumb is stained with indelible ink, thus preventing anyone from voting more than once. The voter's name is checked against the electoral rolls, to make sure that each person votes in the appropriate polling station and district (Arts. 274 and 261 of the FEC). If a person has a voter card for a particular polling station but his/her name does not appear in the station's electoral roll, he/she can vote as long as the total number of persons in the same situation does not exceed 10% of the votes cast in the station.

C.- To avoid the possibility of ballot stuffing before the elections, the representatives of the parties and candidates must make sure that the ballot boxes are empty before the election, and certify this fact in the station records. The voters present at the polling stations when the election starts are also shown the empty ballot boxes (Art. 252 of the FEC).

D.- In reference to the allegation that some people could not vote because their polling stations did not open on time or were closed early, it should be indicated that no polling station can be closed before 6:00 p.m., and that they must remain open as long as there are persons waiting in line to cast their ballots (Art. 266 of the FEC).

E.- At the end of election day, ballot boxes are opened in the presence of representatives of the parties and candidates, and vote counters start the tally one vote at a time, verifying the legality of each ballot. When the vote count ends, the ballots are returned to the boxes, which are sealed also in the presence of representatives of the parties and candidates, as well as of the electoral authorities supervising the polling station (Art. 275 of the FEC). The number of votes cast is checked against the actual number of persons voting in each station.

F.- Representatives of the parties and candidates present at each polling station sign all certificates recording the station's activities, and receive copies of each of them. These certificates include information such as opening and closing times, vote-count results, complaints, number of ballots cast, and so on.

Representatives of the parties and candidates keep the copies of the station's certificates for their own records, and as a means to check the figures and results of their station against those released by the electoral authorities (Art. 183, 265, 270, 274 and 276 of the FEC).

G.- Once ballot boxes are sealed and bear the signatures of the representatives of the parties and candidates supervising the polling station, they are taken to the District Committee by the electoral authorities and by any party or candidate representative who desires to accompany them. The boxes are received by District officials and by other representatives of the parties and candidates (Art. 277 of the FEC).

H.- To avoid alterations in the actual number of votes received by a party or candidate, upon completing the vote scrutiny, each station's record must also show the total number of unused or annulled ballots.

I.- Upon completing the vote scrutiny, a poster-size sign with the electoral results is displayed outside the polling station for everyone to see. This sign also bears the signature of all electoral officials and representatives of the parties and candidates supervising the particular station (Art. 282 of the FEC). The same is done at the Office of the District Committees, where results of the polling stations are displayed.

J.- With regard to complaints about changing the location of the polling stations, such a change can be decided by electoral officials, so as to ensure the voter's right to secrecy and to provide the best possible facilities. However, if a change of address is to take place, the electoral authorities and representatives of the parties and candidates must display a notice at the door of the originally announced location, with directions to the new station (Art. 255 of the FEC).

K.- Elections can be annulled in a particular district when irregularities are substantiated for 20% or more of the district's polling stations (Art. 337 of the FEC).

L.- In order to prevent the inclusion in the electoral rolls of non-existent or dead people, all parties receive a copy of the rolls several months before the elections take place, so that checks and corrections may be made. Every party and all political organizations have a responsibility and obligation to help in this task. Likewise, government offices recording citizenship changes and deaths of Mexican citizens over 18 years old, have a responsibility to convey this information to the National Electoral Roll Desk, so as to update continually the electoral rolls (Arts. 132 to 157 of the FEC).

In addition, any complaint made by the contending parties in the election must be submitted with the corresponding substantiating evidence to the Federal Electoral Tribunal. The Tribunal consists of nine persons, proposed by all parties and approved by Congress, who have never been candidates of any party to an elective post, and who have a national reputation for their honesty and in-depth knowledge of Mexican law.

Even though it is understandable that in such hotly contested elections people would like to know the results as quickly as possible, the Federal Electoral Commission is allowed up to one week to render its preliminary official conclusions and results. Pursuant to this provision, in the 1988 presidential elections the Commission released the election results on Wednesday July 13, 1988 -- that is, exactly one week after the ballots were cast (Arts. 296, 303 and 305 of the FEC). Subsequently, the Commission's results were qualified and made official by the new Chamber of Deputies, acting as the Electoral College.

Despite these and other guarantees and provisions, Mexicans are, of course, the first to admit that Mexico's democracy is not perfect, as there are no perfect democracies anywhere in the world. Also, Mexicans are aware that the electoral proceedings and legislation have to be constantly improved and updated.

In this regard, Mr. Carlos Salinas de Gortari, Mexico's president, has stated clearly that there are four immediate-action programs he intends to implement as soon as he takes the office of Constitutional President of Mexico. These programs enjoy the support of the immense majority of Mexicans and involve finding solutions to the foreign debt problem, reducing the extreme poverty of some sectors of Mexican society, improving public security, and modernizing and simplifying the Mexican electoral legislation and processes to make them more in accordance with the country's current reality and expectations. This position of the then next Mexican president was not widely reported by the United States media.

Mr. Carlos Salinas de Gortari has also said, and I quote, that "the modernization that Mexico demands and [to which he is fully committed] requires that we be open-minded so as to see the need for changes and to encourage those changes; but it also requires reflection, so as to take firm and careful steps at all times, since there is no point in changing for the sake of changing, or to accept change as an inevitable misfortune. We Mexicans want a popular and nationalistic modernization which will result in social justice and more vigorous democratic conditions. Such is our call, and it should also be our resolve and our commitment."

Some Conclusions

The coverage of the Mexican presidential elections by the media in the United States was a very important vehicle for making the United States and the world aware that, although the system is imperfect, Mexico enjoys an increasingly strong and active democracy.

It is also important to acknowledge in this brief analysis that the Mexican political system, in comparison with that prevailing in the United States, is not as easily accessible, and that it issues information mostly through post-facto press releases. Representatives of the United States media, in contrast, are used to having daily briefings from spokespersons of several government agencies, and often can obtain additional information from other sources simply by a telephone call. The only way of overcoming these differences in the future seems to be for nationals of both countries to accept and partially adapt to each other's ways, if there is a mutual desire to improve communication and reciprocal understanding.

Also, observers in the United States should not lose sight of the fact that, despite our nations' geographical proximity, Mexico and the United States are still culturally "distant neighbors;" and that, in order to improve their knowledge of each other and their bilateral relationship, the two nations must develop their shared interests, while building upon their points of agreement and respecting their differences.

And last but not least, it would be useful for the United States media to become aware that Mexico is emerging as a new country with a strong democracy; this birth should be credited to Mexicans and only to Mexicans. In the same manner, the healthy development of the system will be the sole responsibility of Mexicans, and primarily of those who will have it in their power to lead the country towards a better future.

Finally, the United States public and its leaders should be aware that if the economic crisis in Mexico continues in the coming years and the standard of living of most Mexicans is reduced even more, it will not be at all unexpected for the electorate to hand the political power to the opposition. Conversely, if living conditions improve, democracy continues to be strengthened in Mexico, and decentralization takes place during the next few years, it shouldn't come as a surprise for the party in power to win the next elections by an even higher margin than it did this past July 1988.

16

Consequences of the Political Transition in Mexico on Its Relationship with the United States

By Edgar W. Butler[1]

José Luis Reyna[2]

Societal Tensions in Mexico

Currently, there are substantial societal tensions in Mexico. From one point of view, these tensions were engendered by the economic crisis (Report, 1989:35ff), while others believe that the tensions are a result of other social forces in Mexico but have been intensified by the economic crisis. One fallout of the economic crisis may have been the conflict that emerged during the 1988 Mexican presidential election. In past Mexican presidential elections there have been reports of fraud and manipulation of the vote, but in the 1988 election there also was a charge that an opposition candidate actually won the election. While the presidential election took place on July 6, 1988, agitation concerning the outcome has continued. Tensions developed over the election, which may only be symptomatic of multiple other concerns, possibly will continue during the entire presidential term, until 1994. Societal stresses, strains,

1 Edgar W. Butler is former chair and currently professor of sociology at the University of California, Riverside. He is co-director of the UCR Database Project which is computerizing population and economic development data on the Mexican states and *municipios* for statistical analysis and geographic base mapping. He has co-authored a series of articles on fertility, migration, and various other aspects of Mexico and is co-author of the *Atlas of Mexico* (Westview Press).

2 José Luis Reyna is former director of *Facultad Latinoamericana de Ciencias Sociales* (FLACSO); and currently is the secretary-general of *El Colegio de México* in Mexico City. He has published extensively on various aspects of economic development, political mobilization, and democracy in Mexico. He is also a member of the governing board of the *Universidad Nacional Autónoma de México* (UNAM).

and major cleavages within Mexico which previously were latent, or are now emerging, have important implications for Mexico and for relations with the United States.

Contemporary Organization of the
Mexican State and Political System

Up until the 1988 Mexican presidential election, the state and the Institutional Revolutionary Party (PRI) were literally one and the same. However, the major cleavages in Mexico at the moment revolve around the dominant political party and the two opposition parties, the National Action Party (PAN) and the National Democratic Front (FDN). While the PAN and the FDN ideologically are at opposite ends of the spectrum, apparently they are collaborating with each other in contesting the PRI's governing of the country. In addition, there are tensions within the PRI involving what some call the "*técnicos*" or the "blackboard boys" (Fuentes, 1988), and the "dinosaurs" or the old guard (Muñoz, 1988a; Fuentes, 1988). In fact, some FDN major actors were former members of the PRI who, for various reasons, helped form the FDN. Now attempting a political comeback in Mexico also is the Catholic Church (Hanratty, 1988). The Church has by law been excluded from Mexican politics for over fifty years.

To illuminate our discussion and to demonstrate the importance of these cleavages for bilateral relations, a discussion of several different perspectives on decision making is presented as they possibly may be related to contemporary Mexico. Up until the 1988 presidential election, Mexico had been viewed as a monolithic state; that is, the nation was dominated by the PRI party as an organization and by the president as an individual who invariably was a member of the PRI (Reyna and Butler, forthcoming). The general consensus was that Mexico was an authoritarian state. In bilateral relations, the president represented all of Mexico.

As a result of the 1988 presidential election, Mexico now must be considered as a nation in political transition (see Reyna and Butler, forthcoming). One possible future alternative is for Mexico to become a repressive state and to crush the opposition. Generally, such a possibility has been rejected by virtually everyone in Mexico, including the current president. However, several other possibilities exist: (A) The establishment of countervailing elites, (B) the development of an amorphous political structure, or (C) the creation of a pluralistic society.

Countervailing Elites. There is little likelihood that countervailing elites will emerge in Mexico. Countervailing elites have veto capability but do not have the power to carry out governing (Galbraith, 1956). The emergence of countervailing elites in Mexico is considered highly unlikely primarily because of the evolution of a three-tiered party structure in the 1988 election of the PRI, the PAN, and the FDN[3]. Further, given ideological differences among these parties, it is considered highly unlikely that any two of them will join together to form a coalition strong enough to countervail the remaining party. In other words, the PAN and the FDN are at the opposite ends of the political spectrum with the PRI occupying what in Mexico has been defined as the middle. Thus, any coalition would appear to require the joining of either the PAN or the FDN with the PRI. Given the current political climate in Mexico this possibility appears to be beyond the realm of immediate possibility.

Amorphous. A very real alternative for Mexico is the development of an amorphous political structure. An amorphous structure consists of a variety of groups, none of which has enough power to accomplish its goals or objectives, but each of which has veto power. The current situation in Mexico could develop into an amorphous structure by a split between the *"técnicos"* and "dinosaurs" in the PRI, a strengthened PAN, and the coalition making up the FDN splitting up into its component parts. Another possibility is for the emergence of the PAN as primarily a northern urban party with urban pockets scattered throughout Mexico, the PRI as a southern rural party, the FDN as a Federal District and middle-Mexico party, with various leftist splinter parties having strength in distinct political districts.

Such developments could result in a plethora of competing groups, none of which would be strong enough to obtain its goals and objectives. In such a development, the PAN probably would emerge as the strongest party. However, undoubtedly it would have to contend with fluctuating veto blocks, depending upon the issue at hand.

Pluralistic Structure. The development of a pluralistic political structure appears to be the forecast of most commentators. A pluralistic system, or the so-called democratic system, generally is defined as a political system with shared decision-making by a variety of groups and interests. For the development of a democratic, pluralistic system, there must be an allegiance to the idea of shared decision-making. In Mexico there remains serious concern about whether or not the "losers" in the 1988 presidential election share the view that they lost the election. Further, there is ample evidence that the PAN and the FDN are not necessarily going to assist in governing the country. Whether or not a pluralistic power structure will emerge in Mexico in the near future remains questionable in at least three different ways. First, is the PRI willing to share in decision-making? Then, are opposition parties willing to concede the election to the PRI and assist in making the important decisions that impact the country? Finally, are all political parties willing to compete in subsequent elections and then abide by the results? That is, undoubtedly the winners will

3 Parts of the FDN have now evolved into the Party of the Democratic Revolution (PRD).

be good winners, but will the losers be good losers and contribute to governing the country while attempting to attain power in subsequent elections?

Generally, Mexico was viewed until 1988 as having a relatively closed organization of the state with a monolithic political system, but with some vestiges of pluralism. Over the past several years the government-sponsored opposition political parties mandated political reforms that at least required some minority parties be represented in one of the legislative bodies, and presumably was easing restrictions on the mass media (see Ffrench, 1990). Previous to the 1988 election, despite some appearances of openness in the society, only periodically was real political opposition generated, and even then only in localized areas. Seldom did political opposition threaten either the PRI or the government. On the rare occasions when it appeared that the threat might become a real one, repressive measures were taken by the government.

The question now, of course, is what about the future? Did the Mexican presidential election of 1988 alter the organization of the state and turn Mexico into a society with a more pluralistic political system? If, even as some already are suggesting, the FDN should fade away or become impotent, the impact of the 1988 election on bilateral relations needs to be examined. Basically, it is assumed that the old way of doing things in Mexico is in process of dramatic change, and to a more pluralistic political system which will impact the organization of the state. That is, it appears that the president of Mexico does not have the same power as in previous years.

It is likely, then, that the Mexico of the future will be somewhat different from that of the past. Of the several possible scenarios that may emerge in the future, from our view, two realistic options exist. We have labeled these two options the *Pluralistic Scenario* (PS) and the *Authoritarian or Repressive Scenario* (RS).

The pluralistic scenario, to be sure an optimistic one, assumes a liberalization and/or democratization of Mexican society will take place which will be incorporated into the organization of the state. This optimistic view has two necessary conditions. First, the debt problem must be solved in a manner that will allow Mexico once again to sustain economic growth. Second, various contending political forces in Mexico must exhibit "good faith" with each other and with the government. Both of these requirements are necessary conditions for Mexico to move into a more pluralistic mode and open government; neither is sufficient, both are necessary.

A pessimistic view of Mexico in the future sees a repressive state with a monolithic political system and closed state organization. Given the increased political awareness of the Mexican population, if Mexico becomes a more authoritarian state, extremely repressive measures will have to be undertaken, perhaps requiring the military and police to become actively engaged in forceful repression (Muñoz, 1988b).

These two possible directions of Mexican society have important implications for relations between Mexico and the United States The old Mexico and/or authoritarian regime meant that the United States could deal with one interlocutor. However, if a pluralistic structure emerges in Mexico, there may be various forces in Mexico which view issues and the relationship with the United States in widely divergent ways. Thus, the emergence of a pluralistic structure in Mexico does not necessarily bode for easier bilateral relations. In fact, just the opposite may be true (see Molinar, 1990).

Regardless of an authoritarian or pluralistic structure in Mexico, undoubtedly Mexicans will continue to evaluate and rate problems in a different manner than the United States. Most people in Mexico view the debt as being the most important agenda item in any bilateral meeting, whereas the United States would counter that the drug problem is the most important agenda item for discussion. Further, there is a difference of opinion in Mexico regarding the importance of undocumented migration. These areas of concern, of course, are not isolated from other problems. In Mexico the debt problem is related to the economic crisis, economic stagnation, capital flight, etc. Similarly, in Mexico the drug problem is less one of usage but more of how to combat production of a lucrative product in an otherwise stagnated economy.

The debt problem in the United States is of less importance to the government but increasingly will become part of the government's concern if Mexico is unable or is unwilling to service its current debt and/or needs to expand its debt. While undocumented migration from Mexico to the United States generally is not connected to the influx of drugs from Mexico, they both have a common element in that they pose security questions to the United States. That is, they both are related to the loss of control of the border and thus impact the security of the nation.

One of the basic problems that will be facing the new Mexican government is that of coming to grips with conflicting internal and external political forces. For example, there is substantial internal pressure to declare the debt null and void, or certainly to renegotiate the debt by having at least part of the payments going to reduce the principal. On the other hand, there may be such extreme economic pressure in the future that Mexico may need to go further into debt.

If Mexico indeed becomes a more open and pluralistic society, there will be dialogue among contending groups as to what should be done about the debt, drugs, and undocumented migration, among many other problems. Thus, decisions made in Mexico as a result of contending forces may be substantially different than those expected by the United States. For example, there is substantial sentiment in Mexico to ask complete "forgiveness" for the debt; other important views range from having payments partially go to reducing the principal and part to interest, to those few who view total repayment as being necessary. Since there are extreme differences in Mexico regarding various policy alternatives related to the debt, there undoubtedly will be negotiation in Mexico both within the PRI and with opposition parties about what should be done about the debt. *Internally* the new rules of negotiating within Mexico certainly have implications for Mexico - United States relations. While the United States may continue to deal with the president of Mexico regarding the debt, the drug problem, and undocumented migration, among other issues, the president now has to accommodate various political forces in Mexico regarding what agreements can be made with the United States.

The discussion presented below focuses on four bilateral concerns: The debt, drugs, undocumented migration, and tourism. Three of these topics have varying degrees of salience on one side of the border as opposed to the other, while the fourth concern is used as an illustration of an important area of exchange between Mexico and the United States which has not generated much discussion in either country.

A Multifaceted Perspective on Bilateral Relations between Mexico and the United States

One assumption consistently made about bilateral relations between Mexico and the United States is that if the countries get together they can solve the major joint problems facing them (Report, 1989). Neglected in this approach, although often recognized, is that Mexico and the United States "differ sharply in history, culture, political outlook, social organization, and economic development" (Report, 1989:viii). That the countries do differ sharply in a variety of ways has substantial implications for bilateral relations. Thus it is not just a matter of the two countries getting together to solve their major joint problems. Rather the internal contradictions of attitudes and beliefs in each of the countries must be taken into consideration before bilateral issues can be resolved in a mutually satisfactory manner.

Any bilateral attempts at solving joint issues will be doomed to failure unless it is recognized from the very beginning that there are *three different arenas of contention*. First, there is the internal dynamics of decision making in Mexico which has changed substantially within the past year. While the United States may still deal with one interlocutor -- the president -- the president now has to consider the various contending forces in his own party, the opposition parties, and public opinion. Thus, what may be viewed as a satisfactory outcome internally in Mexico may be considered undesirable by the United States. The conflict between what can be negotiated in Mexico among the various contending groups, e.g., within the PRI between the *técnicos* and *políticos*, and between the PRI and the emerging political forces represented by the PAN and the FDN, influences bilateral relations by determining what areas of contention can even be considered as being negotiable and by setting boundaries in any such agreements.   Thus as we pointed out earlier, societal stresses, strains, and major cleavages within Mexico which previously were latent, are now emerging, *internally*.   These new rules of negotiation within Mexico certainly have implications for Mexico - United States relations.

Then, there is a lack of consensus in the United States regarding most issues that impact Mexico and the United States.   As an example, there is a continuing sharp disagreement between the executive and legislative branches over the "certification" or "decertification" of Mexico with respect to its drug control efforts.

Also, in each country there are varying degrees of importance attached to various issues interfacing between Mexico and the United States.   Further, bilateral relations are impacted by differential evaluation of various issues in each of the countries.   So, in reality, bilateral relations between Mexico and the United States are substantially impacted by the internal decision-making processes in Mexico and the United States.

In addition to these general concerns, there are several rather pervasive attitudinal factors that need to be taken into account in any bilateral discussion involving Mexico and the United States.   Generally, in the United States it is assumed that Mexico has the same ordering of concerns and priorities that the United States has.   Of course, this is patently false.   In addition, the extent of Mexican nationalism has largely been ignored in the United States.   Any leader in Mexico who appears to be overly conciliatory to the United States would soon lose all respect of the Mexican population.   While people in the United States do not know, have forgotten, or ignore that Mexico has lost over half of its territory over the years to the United States, all Mexicans are well aware of this fact and it colors their perception of the United States and of what kinds of accommodations can be made to the United States on any given issue.

The paradigm that guides the rest of this discussion focuses on four areas of bilateral relations listed earlier: The debt, drugs, undocumented migration, and tourism.   Each of these issues is examined with regard to its importance in Mexico and the United States and then in respect to its importance in bilateral relations.   The degree of tension within Mexico and the United States and in bilateral relations is systematically examined.

The general conclusion is that there is differential evaluation of each of these concerns in Mexico and the United States which in turn presents particular problems in their resolution at the bilateral level.

The Mexican Perspective

There are now several contending forces in Mexico that may make it particularly difficult to develop a consensus regarding each of these areas of concern, except possibly for tourism.   If Mexico is now a more pluralistic state with a president that must negotiate within his own party and with the legislature in order to make important decisions, an evaluation of who these contending forces are and how they view the resolution of each of these issues is important. If consensus cannot be reached in Mexico, of course, it will be difficult for the government to present a unified position in any bilateral discussions and agreements to be made with the United States. Table 16-1 presents in much simplified form various issues, the contending forces, and a preliminary examination of the views that contending groups hold regarding each issue. In Mexico, for these concerns, it is fairly safe to assume that there is no consensus, and that the importance of each is differentially important to various groups in Mexico. Generally, the government/PRI holds different views than that of the FDN and the PAN; however, the FDN and the PAN obviously also are not in agreement on all issues. This, of course, might be expected since the FDN is generally assumed to represent the left in Mexico and the PAN the right.

The Debt. There is substantial disagreement in Mexico about what to do about the debt. The range of opinion is from voiding the debt entirely, or at least establishing a moratorium (FDN) to paying the debt in full (PAN ideology). The PRI appears to be in the middle, recognizing that the debt is stifling economic development but also knowing full-well that there are negative consequences of voiding or even establishing a moratorium on debt payment. The debt, among all other issues, is of paramount interest to all political parties and influences all other issues in contemporary Mexico. In addition, it is the primary issue separating parties from each other.

Drugs. In Mexico, there is substantial agreement that the drug problem is primarily a United States problem that only peripherally involves Mexico. That is, virtually everyone in Mexico views the drug problem from the demand perspective. If there was not a demand for drugs in the United States, Mexico would not have the problem. Mexico has drug-related problems only because of pressure from the United States to stop the flow of drugs through Mexico and to eradicate drug-oriented crops.

Undocumented Migration. In Mexico, the range of opinion about undocumented migration of Mexican citizens to the United States is relatively narrow. Virtually all parties and public opinion support the necessity of such migration, especially because of the relief of labor force pressures in Mexico and the monetary resources sent back to Mexico by workers in the United States. Undoubtedly, the *Cardenistas* would prefer that such dependency upon the United States eventually would be overcome by economic development in Mexico.

Tourism. Tourism is one of the leading economic activities in Mexico. Public opinion is generally favorable toward its development with most focus on its income producing aspects. There has been virtually no analysis of its possible negative consequences in respect to dependency on other nations. Currently, tourism and its increasing development is not a critical issue in Mexico.

The United States

In the United States there is a lack of consensus regarding Mexico's debt and undocumented migration. While there may be more substantial internal agreement in the United States than Mexico on what should be done about drugs, in the United States this generally means that Mexico should do something about the supply rather than the United States eliminating the demand. Each of these issues is indicated on Table 16-2, with the contending forces highlighted and their views presented.

The Debt. So far in the United States the Mexican debt has been of general concern only insofar as it impacts other relationships. However, in the future there probably will be more reliance on government initiatives. Recently the United States government has been involved in developing at least one mechanism -- the Baker plan -- that potentially could have resolved the debt, but that solution has been acknowledged as a failure by its architect. The United States also must recognize that any action taken related to the Mexican debt may establish a precedent (Purcell, 1988:181). Generally, the Mexican debt is of much less concern in the United States, however, than the drug problem.

Drugs. A word of explanation may be necessary here regarding United States views about drugs. While the United States Congress has been unwilling to certify that Mexico is doing all it can do to eradicate drugs flowing from Mexico to the United States, former President Reagan signed an Executive Order accepting the Mexican position that they were doing all that they could to stem the flow of drugs . Of course, within the Congress there was substantial sentiment to accept the Mexican attempts in good faith. In any case, the point here is that a major decision had to be made in the United States regarding Mexico and that there was substantial disagreement as to what that decision should be.

Undocumented Migration. The United States position on both legal and illegal migration from Mexico to the United States has been inconsistent, and at times even contradictory. Simcox (1988: 211) has noted that in the United States migration policy has been oriented for interest groups needing low cost laborers. The Simpson-Rodino blueprint regarding undocumented migration into the United States, primarily from Mexico, was passed by the Congress and signed into law. However, there is ample evidence that in the United States there is considerable range of opinion about the law. There continues to be utilization of undocumented workers in the United States by agribusiness, some industries, and in private households. The government is utilizing considerable resources in dealing with the undocumented, albeit in an unsystematic and inefficient effort that appears almost by design to subvert the law. Portions of the labor movement clearly would like to see the flow of undocumented workers reduced. Generally, the degree of consensus in the United States over undocumented migrants is less than that over the control of drugs. The contending forces over undocumented migration are not the same as those which are concerned with the debt.

Tourism. The flow of tourists from the United States to Mexico is not an issue in the United States.

Mexico-United States Bilateral Relations

The foregoing discussion had as its goal demonstrating that various issues are examined differentially in Mexico and the United States. Further, it is apparent that there are various groups in each of these countries that have different views of these concerns, that they differ in what degree they are considered to be problem, and what are the appropriate actions that could or should be taken in regard to them. These simple points are exactly those that are severely neglected in most discussions of bilateral relations between Mexico and the United States, and sometimes deliberately so (Report, 1989).

The obvious point, one that is often conveniently overlooked, is that when consensus is lacking in Mexico or the United States as to what is considered a problem, the degree of importance of the problem, and what should be done about it -- if anything -- bilateral agreements are influenced. This lack of internal consistency, especially in the extent to which each of the countries differentially evaluates the problem, becomes a potential point of conflict between the two countries. As Table 16-3 illustrates, differential internal evaluations of issues made in Mexico and the United States have implications for bilateral relations.

The Mexican debt is a problem illustrating quite clearly how the internal evaluation of a concern impacts bilateral relations. For Mexico the societal tension developed over the debt reduces all other issues into insignificance. The debt is of the utmost importance to Mexico because without its obliteration, drugs, undocumented migration, and other major internal problems of Mexico cannot be resolved. Why this is so is rather easy to demonstrate. The debt is related to drugs in that drugs are a lucrative product both in production in Mexico and as an employer of persons to help move the drugs. Drugs are much more lucrative than other agricultural production. But even leaving aside this aspect of the drug problem, currently a substantial portion of the Attorney General's budget in Mexico is being used for drug eradication (some estimates are as high as 60% of the budget).

Undocumented migration is substantially related to the debt and may become increasingly more so during the next decade. If the United States severely reduced the flow of undocumented workers to the United States, there would be a twofold impact upon Mexico. First, the flow of money from the United States to Mexican workers would be halted. Second, the extent of surplus laborers in Mexico could become an unmanageable burden. While these two implications are immediate, over the long term there is even greater potential impact upon Mexico and United States bilateral relations by virtue of the demographic fact that between 800,000 and one million new working-age persons per year for the next decade will be entering the labor force in Mexico (Simcox, 1988).

Mexico needs to expand its economic development substantially to be able to utilize this large scale emerging labor force. Thus, currently there is an interrelationship between the debt and undocumented migration, and the future may result in an even stronger relationship depending upon Mexico's ability to expand its economy.

In the United States, the drug problem is considered the major bilateral problem with most of the blame for the problem being placed on Mexico rather than users in the United States. The drug traffic generates income for Mexico but currently the Mexican government is spending substantial amounts of its resources on drug eradication. This expenditure is primarily at the instigation of the United States since the general view in Mexico is that the drug problem in fact is really a United States problem (del Villar, 1988). Thus in bilateral terms, the drug problem in the United States is of paramount concern whereas in Mexico it is only important because of pressure by the United States. The degree of tension between Mexico and the United States over the debt is evaluated as being at an intermediate level while the tension level regarding drugs is extremely high because of the asymmetric power of the United States compared to Mexico.

Undocumented migration is of importance in the United States while it is of relatively little concern in Mexico. Undocumented migration could become an area of high bilateral tension if the United States seriously carried out the Simpson-Rodino law. Undocumented migration and the safety valve effect of relieving the labor surplus problem in Mexico and of bringing monetary resources into the country are of extreme importance to contemporary Mexico. As noted earlier, this impact may become even more significant in the future with the great expansion of the Mexican labor force age population. The bilateral relationship between Mexico and the United States currently appears to be fairly stable but the future offers opportunity for great conflict.

Finally, the bilateral aspects of tourism are included here only to demonstrate that generally there is consensus in Mexico that the tourist trade is a valuable source of income. Little attention has been paid to potential negative impacts (Butler et al, 1989). Similarly, little attention is paid in the United States by the media, government, or others to any unduly negative aspects of tourism on the United States. Clearly, then, the degree of conflict and tension involving tourism in bilateral relations is virtually nonexistent.

Conclusions

Without serious evaluation of the *internal* political dynamics of Mexico and the United States as they impact bilateral relations, the atmosphere of tension between Mexico and the United States over various bilateral issues can be intensified in the future. This increased tension and conflict is highly probable given the difficulty in each country of developing consensus regarding major bilateral issues. Thus, the political realities in the United States and Mexico cannot be ignored as implied by the Bilateral Commission (Report, 1989). In fact, just the opposite is the case; the political reality in each of the countries determines what can or cannot be accomplished in regards to important bilateral issues.

A glossing over of the political realities within Mexico and the United States and how they shape bilateral relations must be recognized or bilateral problems will remain unresolved and become increasingly a source of greater tension between the two countries.

Acknowledging that consensus does not exist in either Mexico or the United States may be the first step in resolving mutual problems. To ignore these differences stimulates some of the acrimony that now exists and would undoubtedly perpetuate it in the future. Neither country can afford such ignorance if the United States is to maintain its internal security and Mexico is to retain its sovereignty.

Clearly there are more than enough Mexico - United States bilateral issues to be resolved. The problems are especially acute considering that there are great economic disparities between the two countries. These economic disparities must be overcome if bilateral relations are to be mutually advantageous and non-exploitative. This means that the Mexican debt must be solved and/or that the United States must contribute financial resources to resolve bilateral problems. The economic interdependency of the two nations requires now that development be examined in a bi-national perspective.

Without recognizing the crucial dimension of the rapidly expanding Mexican population, especially the labor force component, no bilateral problems will be resolved. Both the economic interdependency and population factors impact the legal and undocumented migration from Mexico to the United States. No bilateral problem will be resolved without a thorough knowledge and understanding of the changing political climate in Mexico and of the lack of consensus regarding Mexico in the United States. Political change in Mexico is such that no guidelines exist to aid in the solution to bilateral problems. In the United States, there is a sharp division about the importance of Mexico and how much economic assistance should be given to Mexico. Further, there is no consensus between the two nations as to what are the major bilateral issues. The asymmetrical power relationship that exists must be overcome if bilateral problems are to be resolved.

In the future, Mexico - United States relations can become extremely cordial, or they may become intractable over an impasse in solving political, social, and economic problems. Our conclusion is that the problems will continue unless there is recognition that political dynamics in each country influence what can and cannot be done in regards to each of the various issues.

On the Mexican side it must be recognized that many of the critical issues discussed in this paper involve what many people in the United States perceive as a "security" problem; this is especially true of the drug and immigration issues. It is to the benefit of the United States that Mexico be a stable society and that these issues be resolved in a satisfactory manner for both countries (see Calif. Task Force . . . 1987).

On the other hand, it must be clearly understood in the United States that while most Mexicans admire many things about the United States, they also have a deep mistrust of the United States' intentions. Mexicans are both aware and wary of the cleavage that exists in the United States regarding Mexico and its importance. On both sides, perceptions and misperceptions influence behavior towards the other country. To ignore them is to indeed ensure that none of the bilateral problems will be resolved. Indeed, "Trying to get Mexicans to be like us is foolish." Similarly, people in the United States do not have to be like Mexicans. However, we both can recognize that the differences need not handicap solving bilateral problems.

Table 16-1
Mexico: Issues and Contending Forces

Issue	Contending Forces	View
DEBT	PRI/Govt.	Negotiate reduction
	FDN/Congress	Void/Moratorium
	Congress	Void
	PAN/Congress	Void
	PAN Idealogy	Pay in full
	Public Opinion	Void
DRUGS	PRI/Govt./PAN	Eradicate in Mexico, accommodating U.S., but drugs are primarily a U.S. problem
	FDN	A U.S. problem only
	Public Opinion	A U.S. problem only
UNDOCUMENTED MIGRATION	PRI/Govt.	Positive – a safety valve for surplus labor in Mexico and brings earnings in valuable dollars to Mexico
	PAN	As above – willing to cooperate with the U.S. to control the problem
	FDN	Does not want to depend upon the U.S., but presumably all right until Mexican economic development absorbs labor surplus
	Public Opinion	A necessity

Table 16-1 (continued)
Mexico: Issues and Contending Forces

Issue	Contending Forces	View
TOURISM	PRI/Govt./PAN	OK; brings in dollars and strengthens relationship with U.S.; continue large-scale development
	FDN	Creates dependence on U.S.; no or at least less development and reliance upon tourism
	Public Opinion	Brings in capital

Table 16-2
United States: Issues and Contending Forces

Issue	Contending Forces	View
DEBT	Executive & Congress	Only a problem if it impacts other relationships
	Banks, IMF, & World Bank	Want repayment, but willing to negotiate
	Public Opinion	Mexico should pay
DRUGS	Executive	Willing to accept limitations of Mexico's ability to control
	Congress	Less willing to accept Mexico's ability to control
	A Few (powerless)	Legalize as solution
	Public Opinion	Blames Mexico, not U.S. suppliers and users
UNDOCUMENTED MIGRATION	Most Government/ Labor	Reduce flow
	Agribusiness and Some Corporations	Need cheap labor
	Public Opinion	Mixed
TOURISM	None	All right as is

Table 16-3
The Degree of Tension in Mexico
and the United States by Various Issues

Issue	Degree of Tension in Mexico	Degree of Tension in Bilateral Relations	Degree of Tension in the United States
Debt	High	Medium	Low
Drugs	Medium	High	High
Undoc. Mig.	Low	Medium	Medium
Tourism	Low	Low	Low

References

Butler, Edgar W., Hiroshi Fukurai, and James B. Pick. 1989. "Tourism and the Economies of Mexican States," in *Dynamics of Business in Latin America*, Hooshang Kuklan and Robert Vichas (eds.). North Carolina Central University, pp. 165-171.

California State Task Force on California-Mexico Relations. 1987. *Strengthening California-Mexico Relations*. Sacramento, California.

del Villar, Samuel I. 1988. "U.S. Anti-Drug Policy: Mexico Should Cut the Gordian Knot," *UC MEXUS News*, 23 (Fall):2-4.

Ffrench, Leonardo. 1990. See chapter 15 of this volume.

Fuentes, Carlos. 1988. "The New Mexico: A Multi-Party State Emerges from Ashes of Sanctified Rule," *Los Angeles Times*, October 11.

Galbraith, John. 1956. *American Capitalism: The Concept of Countervailing Power* (rev. ed.). Boston: Houghton Mifflin.

Hanratty, Dennis M. 1988. "The Church," in *Prospects for Mexico*. Washington, D.C.: Foreign Service Institute, U.S. Department of State, pp.113-122.

Molinar Horcasitas, Juan. 1990. See chapter 8 of this volume.

Muñoz, Sergio. 1988a. "A Political Face Lift for Mexico," *Los Angeles Times*, May 10.

Muñoz, Sergio. 1988b. "What Mexico Needs is Conciliation," *Los Angeles Times*, July 16.

Purcell, John. F.H. 1988. "Mexico's Debt: A Banker's Perspective," in *Prospects for Mexico*. Washington, D.C.: Foreign Service Institute, U.S. Department of State, pp. 179-201.

Report of the Bilateral Commission on the Future of United States-Mexican Relations. 1989. *The Challenge of Interdependence*. New York: Lanham.

Reyna, José Luis and Edgar W. Butler. Forthcoming. "The Political Transition in Mexico: Its Impact upon Mexico-United States Relations," in *Neighbors in Crisis*, Daniel G. Aldrich Jr., and Lorenzo Meyer (eds.). Boulder, Colorado: Westview Press.

Simcox, David. 1988. "Demography, Development, and Migration," in *Prospects for Mexico*. Washington, D.C.: Foreign Service Institute, U.S. Department of State, pp. 205-217.

17

The 1988 Mexican Presidential Election and the Future

Edgar W. Butler[1]
Jorge A. Bustamante[2]

Democracy in Mexico

A view propagated by many is that democracy is a cure-all for what ails Mexico and for Mexico-United States relations. Little explored, however, is that the emergence of pluralism in Mexico in fact may make it more difficult to render decisions and to act upon them promptly. Despite some contrary views (Baer, 1988b), electoral democracy may, in fact, not stabilize Mexico but render it indecisive. Another clear danger exists for Mexico as indicated in the frequent disappointments at what democracy accomplishes (Converse, 1988/89). Democracy is not a cure-all. In addition, "voters around the world are more pleased with the blessings of democracy when their own party is in power than when it is in opposition" (Converse, 1988/89). Further, there are different versions of democracy, including populism which focuses upon the popular will as opposed to a less demanding view in which leaders are chosen by ballot and voters hope for the best until the next election.

---

1 Edgar W. Butler is former chair and currently professor of sociology at the University of California, Riverside. He is co-director of the UCR Mexico Database Project which is computerizing population and economic development data on the Mexican states and *municipios* for statistical analysis and geographic computer mapping. He has co-authored a series of articles on fertility, migration, and various other population aspects of Mexico and is co-author of the *Atlas of Mexico* (Westview Press).

2 Jorge A. Bustamante is president of *El Colegio de la Frontera Norte* (COLEF), professor of sociology at *El Colegio de México*, and adjunct professor of sociology at the University of California, Riverside. He is an advisor at the highest levels of the Mexican government and his editorial writings about Mexico-United States relations have been published widely in the popular press of both countries. Among his research interests are the economic crisis along Mexico's northern border and Mexico-United States migration.

Also, democracy is not an all-or-nothing matter (Bollen and Jackman, 1989:612). If democracy can be considered as a continuum, the question then becomes the degree to which Mexico has moved along the road to "democracy" rather than if Mexico is democratic, which assumes that there are only democratic and non-democratic societies. Thus, democracy may have to be seen in Mexico as a matter of degree, viewed in an evolutionary perspective that involves changing criteria and definitions of democracy itself.

Among some of the criteria that might be used to determine the degree of democracy in Mexico are the following: "(1) The executive must be elected or be responsible to an elected assembly in (2) at least two consecutive and free and fair competitive elections in which (3) at least approximately a majority of the population has the right to vote, and during which (4) the rights of speech and assembly are respected" (Muller, 1988:54).

Also, a consideration might be made as to whether or not each vote is equally counted. Finally, a criterion measure might emphasize the extent to which various groups who were previously excluded are acquiring political power; political power in this sense meaning that they have to be considered in making decisions (Bollen and Jackman, 1989:618). Obviously other criteria might be used to measure the degree of democracy in Mexico (see Bollen, 1980; Bollen and Grandjean, 1981).

Democracy in Mexico may result in multiparties and not a two party system like the United States. The multiple Mexican parties most likely will evolve along ideological lines (Muñoz, 1988a), e.g., the National Action Party (PAN) on the right, the Institutional Revolutionary Party (PRI) in the center, and the National Democratic Front/Party of the Democratic Revolution (FDN/PRD) on the left. Note that the PRI has been considered by some as a rightist party (Reding, 1988b). Further, an assumption shared by many in Mexico and the United States is that the FDN represented the emergence of a "viable" left in Mexico. However, there are several other possibilities that could explain the emergence of the FDN. First, there is a distinct possibility that economic problems faced by Mexico engendered the FDN. This perspective clearly insinuates that economic woes are the primary cause for the emergence of opposition centered in the FDN. Another argument is that the FDN is a temporary alignment of parties and groups that exists only because of Cárdenas and that the coalition will disappear when he is no longer a viable candidate. Finally, there is the prospect that alignment of the so-called left parties is a matter of temporary convenience since there was a candidate available who appealed to them and who could focus their dissatisfaction with the government and its policies. If either of the latter two assumptions is correct, the left will splinter if the personality withdraws from the scene or is no longer considered a viable candidate. Again, which of these alternatives will become manifest will only be confirmed by future events. Our conclusion is that any coalition centered around one person eventually will disintegrate. As an example, in the 1988 presidential election, three parties founded and funded by the PRI broke ranks and supported Cárdenas; however, two of these parties by 1989 had already left the FDN/PRD.

An additional question about democratization in Mexico might be asked about the selection of candidates *by the various parties*. That is, within the parties was the candidate selection carried out democratically ? Most argue that in 1988 the PRI followed substantially the same rules as previously but with some token competition. On the other hand, did the FDN select Cárdenas democratically? Similarly, will the PRD have competition within the party to select its next presidential candidate, or is the result already ordained? The PAN, of course, argues that they did follow democratic canons in selecting their candidate in 1988. A similar question is appropriate for the minor parties.

Democratization of Mexico

Conditions for the emergence of democracy in Mexico have been reported as follows:

(1) The development of a political party system that engages in constituency building (Baer, 1988b).

(2) The political parties must articulate clear programmatic and ideological positions (Baer, 1988b).

(3) The political parties will have to develop rules of the political game and then follow them, win or lose. This involves developing mutual trust among parties (Baer, 1988b).

(4) Opposition forces that formed the FDN/PRD alliance must be able to consolidate their constituency into a major political party; it cannot rely only upon discontent with the PRI for its votes (Fuentes, 1988).

(5) The electoral system needs to be made more modern and agile (Fuentes, 1988).

(6) Finally, a yet to be accomplished condition is that opposition parties, if they win, have to demonstrate that they can lead once they obtain power (Fox, 1989:42).

Middlebrook (1986:103-104) argues that it is up to the opposition parties to develop coordinated strategies that advance alternative programs and to increase their electoral support. Opposition parties must expand their mass organizational bases if they are to have effective national impact. In addition they must establish national and local political alliances if they are to be successful over the long term. All of these efforts involve work and slow progress with frequent reverses.

Evolution or Revolution?

Mexico may have undergone a revolution (Baer, 1988b) as a result of the 1988 Mexican presidential election or the revolution may be more of an illusion than reality (Fox, 1989). Only time will tell which is the correct assessment but in any case the 1988 election was extraordinary for Mexico (Fuentes, 1988). While change has always occurred in Mexico, the pace of transformation has increased (Muñoz, 1988). In the 1988 election there was increased competition for votes; this rivalry may further escalate in the future. The modifications occurring in Mexico may be irreversible; Salinas has been quoted as saying "whoever does not understand the new reality of the country will be dragged down by it" (Muñoz, 1988b). The metamorphosis taking place in Mexico may mean the demise of the PRI and the political system as it currently exists.

What has transpired in Mexico is that Congress has more power, the president less; the executive is now subject to checks and balances with the legislature ceasing to be a rubber stamp (Fuentes, 1988). On the other hand, with opposition emerging, benefits may not only accrue to Mexico but also the president since he no longer will be responsible for every decision.

Future alterations may come from the PRI and government itself, or they may come from the thousands of citizens who became politically aware during the 1988 presidential election; from beneath the change may be accommodated by the PRI and government, or the possibility of a popular, "uncontrolled revolution" exists (Cornelius and Craig, 1988). Thus some argue that the real turning point in Mexico's political transition was due to the hundreds of thousands of citizens who actively participated in electoral politics for the first time (Fox, 1989:40).

A viable democracy requires a substantial, high quality, intelligent, informed public if it is to exist without deteriorating into anarchy. Converse (1988/89) has observed that democracy may involve the election of centrists since the masses have relatively little information and want to avoid extremism. The safe place is a middling position. On the other hand, informed voters are more likely to have centrist-avoidance. For the near-term future in Mexico this implies that the electorate will be centrist oriented and that the PRD and PAN will remain minority parties unless they avoid extreme positions. That is, while they may win a few elections here and there this will be the exception rather than the rule.

The Choice between Democracy and Authoritarianism

Mexico has entered an era fraught with risks and opportunities for change (Baer, 1988a:77). One of the risks is that Mexico must choose between evolution and revolution. Thus, Mexico may face a choice between expansive democracy or authoritarianism (Fox, 1989). At least one scenario implies that violent repression is possible in Mexico (Muñoz, 1988b). Fox (1989) declared that one of the major challenges facing the *Cardenistas* is building on his mass appeal without provoking repression. Repression, undoubtedly, would result in violence. If large-scale violence broke out in Mexico, there would be only one real loser -- *the nation itself*.

Political Realignment

Some argue that the "corporate state in Mexico" is in a state of demise. Others imply that Mexico is in a transitional phase (Baer, 1988b:1); however, Cárdenas (see Reding interview with Cárdenas, 1988a) apparently would only alter the corporatist state being oriented from the PRI to his party.

One implication of the 1988 presidential election is that *caciques*[3] have lost control of the electorate. However, since there were substantial urban-rural differences in the electoral outcome (see chapter 2), this loss of control by *caciques* may be centered among labor and professionals and not among peasant organizations. The PAN is strongest in exactly those regions undergoing *modernization*, e.g., urban and industrialized with higher level education and incomes, in contrast to the PRI that garners support from rural agricultural areas. The question remains as to whether the PAN or the FDN/PRD will emerge as the primary opposition party.

Mexico-United States Relations

There is a great deal of ambivalence in the United States regarding democracy in Mexico. Why? Is it because the United States has been able to control Mexico up until now and the United States does not want change? If there is too much comment or evaluation in the United States this may be perceived as being meddling. For the United States, it is necessary to consider that a politically weakened Mexico poses a great challenge (Baer, 1988a:78), notwithstanding the United States' moral preference for a democratic Mexico. Mexican stability is not only essential to the domestic security of the United States; it is the precondition that makes possible commitments in Europe and elsewhere around the globe (Baer, 1988a:86). Thus, in the United States policymakers hope that the PRI regime will prove resilient enough to enable

---

3 *Caciques* are political bosses.

the United States to avoid the difficult choice between supporting a weakened authoritarian government as opposed to an experimental democracy.

Irregularities and Fraud

As usual in Mexican elections, there were numerous reports of irregularities in the 1988 presidential election. Part of the post-election surveys carried out by the PAN (1988) were compared to official election results for the border states in chapter 3 and some questions were raised about the comparability of results. However, the PAN comparisons were flawed because they did not clearly specify in which areas or parts of districts the surveys were carried out. The FDN (Barberán, et al., 1988) also evaluated official election results by several different statistical techniques (see chapter 3 for details). Because of methodological flaws, neither of these efforts conclusively demonstrated fraud. This is not to deny there may have been irregularities, but only to indicate that the evidence remains inconclusive. The post-election delays in conveying election results may have been a result of Salinas's low margin, thus the "alchemists" were brought in to adjust the figures; possibly Salinas had to intervene to prevent overzealous *Priístas* from padding the vote; the distinct possibility exists that some *Priístas* were disguised *Cardenistas*, i.e., working within the party to sabotage the Salinas vote; finally it is clearly within reason that the election results were fairly accurate (Baer, 1988b).

For all concerned in Mexico, the question of how reliable and valid election results can be established in subsequent elections is an extremely important one since there is constant agitation in Mexico regarding election results and real or imagined fraud. Legitimacy is a crucial issue that needs to be resolved decisively.

The Future

Appreciation of what the future holds for Mexico can only be a result of gross speculation. Democracy may not be a cure-all for the problems that now face Mexico. There will have to be more heed paid in Mexico to what is meant by "democracy" and "liberalization" and to what is expected of the system in those regards. Closer attention will have to be paid to the electoral process so that no fraud and/or manipulation is carried out by any of the parties and/or groups or individuals. The changing power base of the political parties, public opinion, and evolving ideologies will impact the future of Mexico. It remains to be seen whether or not the PRD will remain as a viable political party or if it will splinter into its multifarious factions.

Dialogue undoubtedly will take place within the PRI; these discussions will shape the goals and objectives of the party and its success in subsequent gubernatorial and presidential elections. Particular attention will have to be given to building alternative party structures or the opposition parties will fall to the wayside. Opposition parties, when they obtain political office, will have to demonstrate that they can lead once they obtain power.

So far Mexico has undergone an evolutionary process in the political sphere; it remains a question as to how much aversion the opposition and opposition political parties have to violence. Further examination will have to be made before it can be concluded that the degree of dissatisfaction that existed in 1988 will continue and to what degree the opposition was only related to the economic problems facing Mexico and thus did not represent a shift in ideology, i.e., to the right or to the left. It can be anticipated that in the future, opposition will continue to be exerted more strongly in some states than others.

The impact that the changing political climate in Mexico will have on Mexico - United States relations remains to be seen. However, it is clear that the president of Mexico no longer can speak as representing all of Mexico since there are opposing viewpoints being expressed by the PAN and the PRD.

Perhaps one of the major problems facing Mexico will be how to establish the legitimacy of election results to the satisfaction of all those involved. Mexico will not long survive if there continues to be conflict and charges of fraud over electoral results. In the 1988 Mexican presidential election, all three candidates claimed to have won the election; obviously any democracy to survive requires that the losers acquiesce to the results and begin preparing for the next election. In other words, to be a mature democracy, the winners have to be allowed to lead -- at least until the next election -- while the losers are preparing a better campaign so that they can win the next election.

For better or worse, as a result of modernization and liberalization, future political campaigns in Mexico can expect more "polling" and more "marketing" (Muñoz, 1988a).

Finally, researchers in the arena need to recognize the difference between expressed individual preferences that somehow do not seem to be connected with electoral outcomes whereas at the larger, aggregated level there is substantial stability (Converse, 1988/89:7).

References

Baer, M. Delal. 1988a. "Mexican Democracy between Evolution and Devolution," *Washington Quarterly*, 11 (Summer):77-89.

Baer, M. Delal. 1988b. "The Mexican Presidential Elections: Post-election Analysis," Report No. 2. Washington, D.C.: Center for Strategic & International Studies, August 15.

Barberán José, Cuauhtémoc Cárdenas, Adriana López Monjardín, and Jorge Zavala. 1988. *Radiografía del fraude*. Mexico: Colección: Los Grandes Problemas Nacionales.

Bollen, Kenneth A. and Burke Grandjean. 1981. "The Dimension(s) of Democracy: Further Issues in the Measurement and Effects of Political Democracy," *American Sociological Review*, 46: 651-659.

Bollen, Kenneth A. 1980. "Issues in the Comparative Measurement of Political Democracy," *American Sociological Review*, 45: 370-390.

Bollen, Kenneth A. and Robert W. Jackman. 1989. "Democracy, Stability, and Dichotomies," *American Sociological Review*, 54 (August):612-621.

Converse, Philip E. 1988/89. "Perspectives on the Democratic Process," *IRS Newsletter*, (No. 2):4-10.

Cornelius, Wayne A. and Ann L. Craig. 1988. *Politics in Mexico: An Introduction and Overview*. San Diego: Center for U.S.-Mexican Studies, University of California.

Fox, Jonathan. 1989. "Towards Democracy in Mexico?" *Hemisphere*, Winter: 40-43.

Fuentes, Carlos. 1988. "The New Mexico: A Multi-Party State Emerges from Ashes of Sanctified Rule," *Los Angeles Times*, September 9.

Middlebrook, Kevin J. 1986. "Political Liberalization in an Authoritarian Regime: The Case of Mexico," in *Elections and Democratization in Latin America, 1980-1985*. Paul W. Drake and Eduardo Silva (eds.). San Diego: Center for U.S. - Mexican Studies, University of California.

Muller, Edward N. 1988. "Democracy, Economic Development, and Income Inequality," *American Sociological Review*, 53: 50-68.

Muñoz, Sergio. 1988a. "A Political Face Lift for Mexico," *Los Angeles Times*, May 10.

Muñoz, Sergio. 1988b. "What Mexico Needs Now Is Conciliation," *Los Angeles Times*, July 16.

PAN. 1988. *Mitos y verdades de las elecciones presidenciales de 1988 y comentarios al proceso electoral federal de México de 1988*. Mexico: PAN.

Reding, Andrew. 1988a. "The Democratic Current: A New Era in Mexican Politics, Interviews by Andrew Reding," *World Policy Journal*, 5.

Reding, Andrew. 1988b. "Mexico at a Crossroads: The 1988 Election and Beyond." *World Policy Journal*, 5.

Salinas, de Gortari. 1988. *Excélsior*. July 8.

Story, Dale. "The PAN, the Private Sector, and the Future of the Mexican Opposition." In *Mexican Politics in Transition*, Judith Gentleman (ed.). Boulder: Westview.

Unomásuno. 1987. June 11.

Unomásuno. 1988. May 29.

Voices of Mexico. 1988. March-May, p. 25.

Index

260